T0273910

Sleep & Sorcery

Enchanting Bedtime Stories, Rituals, and Spells

ABOUT THE AUTHOR

Laurel Hostak Jones (she/her) is a writer, audio producer, and Witch based in Philadelphia, Pennsylvania. She has a background in theatre and a lifelong devotion to studying mythology, folklore, and literature—with a particular interest in high and late medieval texts connected with the Arthurian Legend. Her podcast Sleep & Sorcery weaves universal themes into original, magical sleep stories and meditations. Sleep & Sorcery has been helping listeners sleep meaningfully since 2021, and in 2023 the podcast reached over 2 million downloads. Laurel is a member of the Order of Bards, Ovates & Druids, a nature-lover, and mother to Arthur.

Laurel Hostak Jones

Sleep & Sorcery

Enchanting Bedtime Stories, Rituals, and Spells

Chicago, Illinois

Sleep & Sorcery: Enchanting Bedtime Stories, Rituals, and Spells copyright ©2024 by Laurel Hostak Jones. All rights reserved. No part of this book may be reproduced in any manner whatsoever without written permission from Crossed Crow Books, except in the case of brief quotations embodied in critical articles and reviews.

First Printing. 2024.

Paperback ISBN: 978-1-959883-33-3
Hardcover ISBN: 978-1-959883-74-6
Library of Congress Control Number on file.

Cover design by Wycke Malliway.
Edited by Becca Fleming.
Typesetting by Gianna Rini.
Illustrations by Gianna Rini.

Disclaimer: Crossed Crow Books, LLC does not participate in, endorse, or have any authority or responsibility concerning private business transactions between our authors and the public. Any internet references contained in this work were found to be valid during the time of publication, however, the publisher cannot guarantee that a specific reference will continue to be maintained. This book's material is not intended to diagnose, treat, cure, or prevent any disease, disorder, ailment, or any physical or psychological condition. The author, publisher, and its associates shall not be held liable for the reader's choices when approaching this book's material. The views and opinions expressed within this book are those of the author alone and do not necessarily reflect the views and opinions of the publisher.

Published by:
Crossed Crow Books, LLC
6934 N Glenwood Ave, Suite C
Chicago, IL 60626
www.crossedcrowbooks.com

Printed in the United States of America.

For Arthur & Derek, my loves

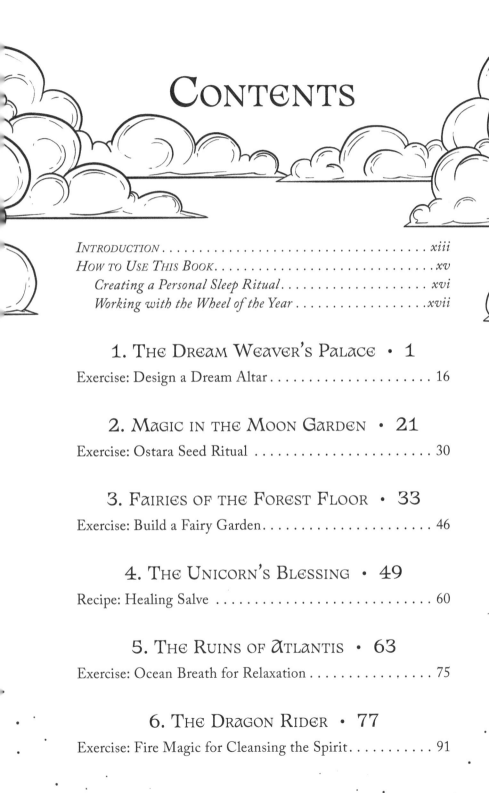

CONTENTS

INTRODUCTION . . . . *xiii*
HOW TO USE THIS BOOK . . . . *xv*
  Creating a Personal Sleep Ritual . . . . *xvi*
  Working with the Wheel of the Year . . . .*xvii*

1. THE DREAM WEAVER'S PALACE • 1
Exercise: Design a Dream Altar 16

2. MAGIC IN THE MOON GARDEN • 21
Exercise: Ostara Seed Ritual 30

3. FAIRIES OF THE FOREST FLOOR • 33
Exercise: Build a Fairy Garden 46

4. THE UNICORN'S BLESSING • 49
Recipe: Healing Salve 60

5. THE RUINS OF ATLANTIS • 63
Exercise: Ocean Breath for Relaxation 75

6. THE DRAGON RIDER • 77
Exercise: Fire Magic for Cleansing the Spirit 91

7. THE HOLLY KING & THE OAK KING • 93

Exercise: Ritual Walk for Summer Solstice. 103

8. DREAMS OF THE BLUE LOTUS • 105

Recipe: Lavender & Mugwort Dream Tincture 117

9. TALES BY THE TAVERN FIRE • 119

Exercise: Journal Practice for Lucid Dreaming. 129

10. CAULDRON OF CERRIDWEN • 133

Exercise: Automatic Writing for Inspiration. 144

11. THE MIDNIGHT CARNIVAL • 147

Exercise: Sleep Spell Sachet. 159

12. SECRET OF THE SELKIE • 161

Exercise: Ritual Bath to Shed the Skin. 175

13. THE GREEN KNIGHT'S GAME • 177

Exercise: Invocation for the New Year 190

14. THE SONG OF PERSEPHONE • 193

I. Demeter 193
II. Persephone 197
Exercise: Maiden, Mother, Crone Meditation 202

ENDNOTES 207

INTRODUCTION

When my son Arthur was born in January 2021, everything changed. I made the seismic transition from independent woman to mother during the pre-vaccine height of the COVID-19 pandemic, in a time of real fear and uncertainty. I was isolated from my village, navigating postpartum depression and anxiety, and utterly sleepless. When I think of those early months of motherhood now, I can't believe I made it through the loneliness and exhaustion. The hardest part of all was feeling suddenly severed from myself—my identity, my passions, my independence. I worried I would never find myself again.

I spent the first year of Arthur's life (and the first year of my new life) slowly crawling back to myself. Or, more accurately, crawling forward—toward a new version of me. A me with a differently shaped body and a mind re-wired to protect the precious little life I'd made in Arthur. This process of moving back into myself (through hard work and lots of therapy) brought me to *Sleep & Sorcery*.

All I've ever wanted to do is write. Language, in my estimation, is magic. It's alchemy. The selection and arrangement of words can create the most potent emotional response, the purest transformation of experience, and the transcendency of the soul. My return to creative writing was a portal—during the time I felt most disconnected from my identity—to my innermost self.

Sleep & Sorcery began as a podcast. I had experience in the audio sphere from years of producing *The Midnight Myth* with my husband Derek. The notion of crafting stories intended to induce sleep meant there was space to experiment with sound and meaning, exploring concepts and spaces that felt rich to me without the need for extensive conflict or perfect structure. And I could make something of value from the sustained sleep deprivation of a new parent. The notebook and keyboard became my altar, a powerful tool in a ritual writing practice. I strove to create welcoming, safe worlds inspired by the stories and themes I love most—folklore, fantasy, mythology, Witchcraft, and Druidry. Realms woven together through poetry and voice that could become cozy dreamscapes. I write my stories in the second-person perspective, so listeners can, in a sense, choose their own adventure, infusing the world with their own identities and histories. Every story is a little bit of sorcery, meant to cast a spell and create an energy shift within you.

The book you hold in your hand now is a collection of these stories, brought forth from an intuitive and ritual writing process. They are intended for relaxation, meditation, and, ultimately, inducing sleep. One story, "Song of Persephone," is exclusive to readers of this volume. Each story invites you, the reader, into an experience of the magical or otherworldly. Paired with each story is a suggested ritual, meditation, or spell to deepen your connection to the natural world and support meaningful rest. Know that these are invitations only—methods I've learned or used to support my own practice. The ingredients, spaces, or tools associated with the exercises are just that: tools. They may support you or augment your relationship to the exercise, but you don't *need* them. All you need, in any case, is already within you.

Remember, too, that the stories are spells in themselves. They gather their power by virtue of the relationship you create with them—with the archetypes and possibilities therein. Language is magic. Lose yourself in the stories. Use them as a portal to your wildest dreams.

Blessed be,
Laurel

How to Use This Book

What is "meaningful rest?" In a culture that encourages—and often demands—that we burn the candle at both ends, sacrificing our wellbeing for the pursuit of greater and greater productivity, rest is both an essential and transformative act. For those of us who practice magic, rest and sleep can become as integral a part of our craft as anything we do in our waking lives. Sleep can be medicine. Dreams can aid us in divination. A peaceful night of restorative sleep—or a power-nap to pull you through a strenuous day—can recharge our body, mind, and spirit. Meanwhile, waking activities that ground us in the present moment, strengthen our connection to the rhythms of the natural world, or simply allow us a break from exhausting cycles, are, in their own way, *restful*.

I hope the stories, exercises, and spells in this book—this bedside companion—can support your journey to more meaningful rest. You'll find stories and activities in this book designed to induce sleep or deepen relaxation, but you'll also find creative exercises, ritual walks, and other active engagements that aim to create restful rhythms.

CREATING A PERSONAL SLEEP RITUAL

The most important spell you can cast is one you create for yourself. I encourage you to take some time to devise a nightly sleep ritual that's personal to you. It can change and adapt over time, just as you do. It can be as simple or as multi-layered as you want it to be; the most important thing is to see your nightly ritual as meaningful and mindful. Consider adding or augmenting some of the exercises in this book if they support your nightly routine.

My nightly ritual looks something like this:

I am a parent, so it all begins with my child's bedtime routine. When it's time to tuck in, we reset our space (clean up the toys sprawled across the floor!), and head upstairs as a family. After a bath, he gets into PJs, we read a few stories, and sing a song together. It's the same song every night, "In My Life" by the Beatles. Now that he's a little bigger, he sings along or even leads us.

After lights out for my son, I head back downstairs for a cup of tea or a nightcap with my partner. If it's a nice night, we spend some time sitting together on the front porch. We water and admire our flowers in season. We observe the moon and stars. I love to burn a stick of incense on the porch to encourage relaxation. Almost every night, we naturally voice our gratitude for our home, our neighbors, our friends, and our family. This time outside acts as a threshold between the busy day of work and parenting on one side, and the slow, contemplative time of rest and recharging on the other.

At our bedtime, we do the basics: brushing our teeth, getting into pajamas, setting the temperature just right...I usually break out some lavender lotion or body oil. We listen to audiobooks or podcasts as we fall asleep to help calm our thoughts. Sometimes, I'll practice progressive muscle relaxation or a self-guided visualization exercise as I lie in bed, waiting for sleep.

It's simple—but all these cues come together to induce a state of peace. My nightly routine is a spell I cast, an accumulation of energy and intention. With every repetition or recitation of the ritual, it embeds itself deeper in my unconscious. I approach sleep with the same care and investment as my career, my craft, and my family: because rest is essential. Quality sleep, or lack thereof, can change us.

Think about what you already do each night, the habits you've formed, and the impact they have on your ability to turn off and rest. What can you add or change to give yourself a greater sense of serenity and wellbeing? How can you turn those simple actions or routines into ritual and ceremony? If you take a nightly bath or shower, how can you embrace the magic of cleansing your body and mind? If you have pets who share the bed with you, how can you show gratitude for their presence and protection? If you read or journal before going to sleep, how can you make that practice even more intentional?

I hope this book becomes part of your sleep ritual, whether you read a few pages of your favorite story or incorporate any of the accompanying exercises. The stories herein build upon connected themes, but they are designed to be read in any order. The threshold of sleep is a place of magic: furnish it with meaning.

Working with the Wheel of the Year

The stories and exercises herein are loosely organized around the Wheel of the Year, the cycle of seasonal festivals and sabbats observed by most earth-centered spiritual traditions. The solar festivals (solstices and equinoxes) are bridged by seasonal celebrations that correspond with the changing characteristics of the natural world and the harvests. While you may read or perform the exercises in this book at any time they call to you, you might find increased connection or potency by seeking correspondences with the rhythms of nature. Because this framework is presented as a wheel, there is, naturally, no beginning or end.

Below are the proposed correspondences between the stories/ rituals and their seasonal celebrations—but remember, there is no wrong way to engage with the material.

IMBOLC: Observed on or around February 1, halfway between the winter solstice and spring equinox. Though Imbolc occurs during the coldest time of the year for most countries in the Northern

Hemisphere, it is seen as the gateway to spring. Snowdrops are among the first flowers to appear. Shortly thereafter, the earth begins to soften and flower again.

* *The Dream Weaver's Palace: Design a Dream Altar*

Ostara: Observed in accordance with the vernal (or spring) equinox. Ostara frequently coincides with the Christian celebration of Easter, and both share symbolism of eggs, rebirth, and rabbits.

* *Magic in the Moon Garden: Ostara Seed Ritual*
* *Fairies of the Forest Floor: Build a Fairy Garden*

Beltane: Observed on or around May 1 or when the hawthorn (May) tree begins to bloom with abundant mayflowers. Beltane welcomes the transition from spring to summer. Situated opposite to Samhain on the Wheel of the Year, it is a time when the veil between worlds is thin.

* The Unicorn's Blessing: Healing Salve Recipe
* The Ruins of Atlantis: Ocean Breath for Relaxation

Litha: Observed at or near the summer solstice (June 21 in the Northern Hemisphere, or December 21 in the Southern Hemisphere). This sacred fire festival, sometimes recognized as Midsummer, marks the longest day of the year. At this time of peak sun, the Earth prepares to turn toward darkness.

* *The Dragon Rider: Candle Magic for Grounding*
* *The Holly King & the Oak King: Summer Solstice Ritual Walk*

Lughnasadh/Lammas: This seasonal festival, observed on or around August 1, marks the start of the harvest season with the grain harvest.

* *Dreams of the Blue Lotus: Lavender & Mugwort Dream Tincture*
* *Tales by the Tavern Fire: Journal Practice for Lucid Dreaming*

Mabon: Observed at the autumn equinox when the night and day occupy equal hours. Marking the second harvest festival, Mabon is a time for giving thanks at the height of autumn.

✱ *Cauldron of Cerridwen: Automatic Writing Exercise for Inspiration*

Samhain: Observed around November 1 and coinciding with secular Halloween festivities, Samhain is the final harvest festival. As the skies darken and leaves fall, it's a time to honor our loved ones who have passed beyond the veil.

✱ *The Midnight Carnival: Sleep Spell Sachet*

Yule: Observed at the time of the winter solstice (December 21 in the Northern Hemisphere, and June 21 in the Southern). On the shortest day of the year, the Oak King wins the battle against his brother the Holly King, and the Earth, emerging from darkness, moves once more toward light.

✱ *Secret of the Selkie: Ritual Bath for Shedding the Skin*
✱ *The Green Knight's Game: An Invocation for the New Year*

Imbolc/Ostara: The wheel turns on, and this collection of stories ends where it began, with the return of spring. The sleeping land awakens; may you be rested and ready to emerge.

✱ *The Song of Persephone: Maiden, Mother, Crone Meditation*

THE DREAM
WEAVER'S PALACE

At first, there's only fuzzy darkness, a blank space waiting to be filled in. You're quite certain you've just arrived, and yet you haven't the slightest idea how you came to be here—or where here is, for that matter. But surely, if you keep walking in this same direction, it will begin to look familiar soon and your purpose will come flooding back to you.

So you go forth, a lightness in your step that's refreshing. It's really not like you to get all turned around like this. The funny thing is, with each step, right where your foot hits the ground, a little pool of light blooms and illuminates your surroundings bit by bit. Around you, brought into relief by your footfalls, a landscape is materializing. Impeccably trimmed hedgerows, pebbled walkways, and flower beds rise to meet your gaze. It's nearly all visible now, coming to life all around you. A few more steps, a few more mesmerizing plumes of color and light paint the corners of your vision, till at last you can fully grasp the landscape. You wonder vaguely if this is the garden at Versailles or another of those perfectly manicured gardens that sprawl outward from European chateaus. There are rows of lemon trees, fields of garden pinks, voluptuous tulips, and hornbeams pruned in precise topiary. Spiral pathways through neatly groomed grass tempt you toward a lazy stroll.

You find yourself drawn toward a glimmer at the center of the garden, a dance of light that plays on the surface of water. As you move toward it, it reveals itself as a sparkling pool, very vast indeed for a garden feature. From a ways off, it seemed a perfectly natural ornament, but as you approach and stare from one edge of the pool across to the other, it feels as if you're gazing across a wide lake toward a very distant shore. You bend over the side to look at your reflection, and also because you're curious how many coins linger at the bottom of the pool—wishes underwater. A flicker of bright color catches your eye and attention though, as various vibrantly-hued fish dart across the pool. Such extraordinary colors they are: brilliant gold, deep crimson, and striking, electric blue. The pool is surprisingly deep; you find yourself straining your eyes to see its bottom, but the harder you look, the more it seems to sink away from you.

And rising from the center of the pool—it's a wonder you hardly noticed it till now—is a towering, sculptural fountain. Your gaze travels up the piece, taking in the many exquisite details: at the bottom, finned horses (these, you remember somehow, are called *hippocampi*, or Neptune's horses) emerge, heads in mid-toss, forelegs rearing. And on their backs are the most curious chimeras, which look like a hybrid of elephants and tigers. Atop them are a row of foxes, from whose hindquarters spring many tails instead of one. Resting on top of all the rows of strange and beautiful creatures is one great turtle. Water trickles and splashes over and through the pyramid of animals, and the sound is pleasantly musical to your ear.

What an unusual place, you think. Unusual and yet charming. The light is soft and lightly tinged with a honey-gold, bathing everything in sight, though you can't seem to locate the sun in the sky. No, it seems more like the light effuses in all directions so that nothing casts a shadow, but everything (yourself included) participates in the effort of illumination. You could easily lose an afternoon exploring all the wonders, nooks, and crannies of a place like this. But still, you're sure you came here for a reason—one more pressing than the pursuit of loveliness and leisure.

No sooner than this thought enters your mind, you become aware of a looming structure at the edge of the garden. A striking palace of Baroque design, with a cream-colored façade accentuated by scarlet trim, pilasters, lintels, and pediments. You make your way up the pebbled incline, moving toward the palace with a new sense of purpose. Whatever it is that brought you to this place surely lies within.

Leading up to the palace's lavish front doors is a divided imperial stair made of dark gray stone. Along each balustrade are sculpted gods and goddesses. Some you recognize from their implements, like Athena with her helm and spear, an owl perched on her shoulder. Others are less familiar. A figure with the body of a human woman but the long neck and head of a swan. Another, with four arms and bejeweled adornment, stands in the center of a lotus flower and holds two more in her hands. After a bit of pondering over whether to take the left or the right staircase, you make your choice and climb toward the entrance.

The towering doors are bronze-cast, with repeated relief patterns. The moon in many phases. Stars and constellations. You look for a knocker or a bell to ring, and in the absence of one, you decide to try the door yourself. To your surprise, it's not nearly as heavy as it appears. It pushes open with very little effort on your part. You step inside onto sleek marble floors.

Though the palace looked immense from the exterior, you can hardly believe your eyes beholding the cavernous space before you. It seems an entire metropolis could fit beneath the vaulted ceilings. Beyond the sparkling atrium, corridors appear to stretch indefinitely. There are extravagant frescoes on the walls, which only increase the sense of expansiveness about the place. Painted with trompe l'oeil, they create illusory gardens and courtyards that look only too easy to step into.

Concealed in the frescoes, and only betrayed by the barely visible cracks in the walls, you discover secret doors of all different sizes. Portals to hidden passageways, no doubt. What secrets must a place like this hold? You find one of these doors, a tiny one fit only for a small child, in a fresco illustrating the moss-covered ruins of a temple or castle. You crouch down, gently push it open, and poke your head inside to see what lies behind.

A gentle wind is present in the chamber behind the secret door, and a rustling sound that might either be rifled pages or feathered wings. As you take in the chamber by sight, you discover that it's both. The long and narrow chamber is an archive, or a library of sorts, in which a countless array of papers are presently being shuffled, organized, and filed. Though the doorway is small, as you strain your eyes to look upward, you count ten or more floors of activity within. And the archivists, busy with books and ledgers and scrolls, are squat, winged creatures with bright orbs for eyes. This archive is staffed, unmistakably, by owls. They push carts of paperwork along thin corridors, carry scrolls across aisles to other filing cabinets, and pore over documents at reading tables.

You notice that the cabinets and shelves are all meticulously labeled, though not using words. Instead, each is marked with a symbol or icon. You can see one marked with a crescent moon, another with a rudimentary house, one with a minimalistic wave pattern, and a very large row of stacks marked with a pair of wings. *What is it they're archiving?* you wonder.

Shimmying your shoulders into the little opening, you extend an arm toward a stack of paper within your reach and pull the top sheet down. The paper is covered in a string of small, arcane symbols, somewhat akin to runes. You can't make heads or tails of it. But the longer you stare, somehow, the more sense it begins to make. You start to understand it as a report, a log of some kind. There are repetitions and patterns among the symbols. You suspect you're very close to deciphering the meaning of the document when a rustle of feathers distracts you.

One of the owls, bespectacled and with tufted feathers on either side of his head, is coming toward you—walking, not flying—with a precarious assemblage of scrolls tucked under a wing. You surreptitiously slide the sheet of paper back onto the heap beside you. As he approaches, you can hear the feathered fellow muttering under his breath, some exasperated ramblings about discrepancies or efficiency or something or other. Then, he spots you, your head stuck through the tiny door, and meets you with an expression of only mild alarm.

"Excuse me," he says, casually.

Carefully, you remove your head and shoulders from the doorway, and the bird waddles out and past you, taking no further notice of you as he goes.

"Wait!" you call after him. The owl swivels his head round to look at you impatiently. There's a question on the tip of your tongue, which you sense he may be able to answer for you. *What was that question?* It's not "Where am I? How did I get here?" or anything so inane as that. You have to think for a moment, but then it comes to you like a bolt from the blue.

"Whose dreams are those?" you say, gesturing to the scrolls under the owl's wings. That's it—a little shiver of recognition runs over you—all those documents and books and ledgers are catalogues of dreams. The symbols make sense now: the wings refer to dreams of flight, the waves to dreams of oceans and beaches, and so on…The owls are archiving the records of people's dreams.

The owl narrows his eyes, as if for the first time recognizing that you are not one of his fellow recordkeepers. Nonetheless, he answers your question with a low degree of reservation.

"These are joint annotated records from two nights ago, across multiple dreamers in the Southern Hemisphere," he says, adjusting his spectacles. "But there's an error, you see, the same mistake in each of these, which must be corrected and stamped by processing before they return to recordkeeping."

"Oh," you say. "Of course. I'll let you go, then."

The owl begins to waddle on his way down the corridor, but a moment later, he stops in his tracks, swivels his head once more to look you up and down, then says, "Which department are you from, again?"

"Well, I'm not from any department, you see. I've only just arrived."

The owl's eyes widen.

"You're a dreamer!" he says with brimming fascination and concern. "But you really shouldn't be here at all…forget you saw me, actually. Off you pop, back to bed."

"But I'm really not sure of the way," you say. "Could you show me?"

With a shuffle and an almost-dropping of scrolls, the owl retrieves a pocket watch and checks it. He sighs.

"These reports will have to wait," he says, resigned. "Come with me, I'll take you to her."

You feel a spring in your step as the frazzled owl changes course, following him through the great atrium and down a columned corridor. You thank him for taking time to help you; he insists it's no trouble, though his hurried gait says otherwise.

"Can I ask your name?" you say.

The owl responds plainly, "Glaucus. Senior archivist." The edge of annoyance is softer now, and you have the distinct impression that he appreciates being asked his name instead of being seen only as one among a thousand recordkeepers.

"And if you don't mind," you add, "could you tell me who it is you're taking me to see?"

Glaucus hoists the slipping scrolls under his wing. "She's the one who makes the dreams," he says. "She'll know how to get you back where you belong."

What a wondrous thought, you reflect. You're going to see where dreams are made.

Glaucus leads you down the ever-lengthening hall. In between the ornate columns are enormous rococo vessels overflowing with floral arrangements. You recognize some of the flowers: poppy, delphinium, statice, and rose, but others are unfamiliar and indeed highly unusual. Exotic blooms with impossibly full petals, flowers with heads like bright-burning flames, and others that seem to be made from ice or crystal.

You pass, on your way down the never-ending corridor, a diminutive creature who appears to be spritzing one of the arrangements with water. Glaucus bids him a friendly greeting as you pass; up close, you notice that the little person has pointed ears, like an elf or a brownie, and the canister with which he spritzes the flowers is emitting not water, but a kind of sparkling vapor.

At last, the corridor is coming to an end; ahead, you observe a pair of tall, narrow doors of glass and delicate wrought iron. The iron dances in spirals and curls in a way that vaguely reminds you of the stunning metro stations in Paris. And the glass shimmers as you approach with a subtly changing tint: now pale green, now rich violet, now pink. How much of that color, you wonder, is coming from the material itself, and how much is generated by the activities within?

Glaucus halts in front of the doors and whispers to you that you should knock. You do so. Your gentle rapping comes across much louder than expected; you can hear its echo in the chamber beyond. After a moment of silent waiting, the doors swing inward, apparently of their own accord.

"This is where I leave you, Dreamer," says Glaucus, his tone now much gentler toward you. "Travel safe and rest well."

You watch as the kind owl hitches up the scrolls under his wing and waddles off again down the long corridor. You hope he's able to make up for the lost time. As for you, it's time to discover what awaits in the place where dreams are made.

As you pass through the iron and glass doors, you're not sure if you're entering a lush parlor, a greenhouse, or the laboratory of a mad scientist. First, your eyes are drawn upward toward the ceiling. Like the doors, it's made of decorative wrought iron and stained glass, reminiscent of a cathedral rose window. A diffuse light from above streams through the glass, bathing the whole chamber in a shifting interplay of the colors of the rainbow.

It's a glittering rotunda, and all round the curved walls are shelves of glass or crystal. These pick up the light from the stained glass even more, casting prisms across the room. There are curious objects lining the shelves, row after row, stacked all the way to the ceiling. Bell jars. You inspect the nearest, a curvilinear cloche, under which there is a little scene. A miniature diorama featuring dense birch trees and what appear to be tiny houses and buildings made of toadstools and beehives on the forest floor. Looking closely, you can see minuscule monarch butterflies floating about the diorama. *How charming and whimsical!* you think, getting lost in the tableau. But just as you're about to look at what's contained in the next bell jar, there comes a puff of pink, sparkling smoke, and the forest diorama has vanished. You release an involuntary gasp at the abruptness of the disappearance.

"Not to worry," comes a calm, musical voice from behind you. "That one's just been picked up by a dreamer." You whirl around to behold the speaker, whom you failed to notice in all the wondrous impressions of the chamber. In the center of the rotunda, there's a marvelous workstation complete with a drafting desk, a loom, a simmering cauldron, and an array of devices and contraptions you can't readily identify. Surrounding the workstation and spreading to the edge of the room till they rest against the shelves of bell jars are all manner of plants, herbs, and flowers in pots. You have to push aside a fern to reveal the face of the speaker who sits at the loom; all you can see now is the drapery of her dress, ivory silk trimmed with scarlet roses.

"It's all right," she says, beckoning you closer. Her back is to you, but you can see a cascade of auburn hair down her back and the suggestion of a diadem at her brow. She's busy working at the loom, evidently weaving a tapestry. The vibrant blues and greens of the threads blend into a lush, tropical palate; it soon becomes apparent that the weaving depicts a vibrant jungle.

Now the Weaver turns her head over her shoulder to look at you. You can see that the coronal on her brow is encrusted with rubies. Her own eyes shine like dark gemstones within a kindly face.

"Do me a favor, will you?" she asks. You nod, unsure if you have a voice to speak. "The fern beside you. Pull a frond from the plant."

You hesitate, not wanting to disturb such a beautifully flourishing fern. But the Weaver gives a subtle gesture of approval, and at last, you reach in and pluck one of the green fronds.

"Cast it into the cauldron," she says. You cross to the cauldron, toss the frond into the simmering liquid, and watch as it dissolves, turning the contents emerald green. A spiral of green steam rises from the surface, and the Weaver smiles. "Perfect," she says. "That's coming along nicely."

You are still drinking in the whole magical setting, tracing the rows and rows of bell jar scenes with your eyes. At last, you find your voice.

"So, each of these," you say, "is a dream?"

"Every one," smiles the Weaver. In the corner of your eye, another of the bell jars vanishes in a puff of purple smoke.

"And they disappear when someone dreams them?" you ask, turning the mechanics over in your mind.

"Plucked out of this space into the mind of the dreamer," she answers in a placid tone. "Sometimes the dreamer chooses the dream, and other times, the dream selects the dreamer."

The Weaver carefully removes the tapestry from the loom. *It's quite lovely*, you think—a jungle scene with leaves and vines, the faces of leopards and tamarins peeking from behind the ferns. As you're admiring the piece, however, the Weaver casts it irreverently into the cauldron. You stand there, mouth agape, watching it dissolve into the now-turquoise liquid within.

"Almost ready," she says, pondering. Then, as if struck by a sudden revelation, her face lights up and she quickly retrieves a phial of some electric blue powder from a rack behind the drafting desk. She uncorks the vessel, shakes the powder into the cauldron, and utters a sound of delight as the steam rising from the liquid takes the shape of a many-petaled flower. Then, without warning, she pushes up a sleeve and plunges her hand right into the liquid, up to the elbow. Presently, she begins to tug upward as though pulling something heavy from the depths.

The Weaver removes her hand in a gesture reminiscent of a chandler pulling a hand-dipped candle from the wax. She clasps a string, at the bottom of which is a small mass, dripping with the blue-green liquid. Once the final drippings fall away, however, you recognize it to be a lifelike—if tiny—rainforest, such as could fit in the palm of your hand. The Weaver places the tableau upon a pedestal, rubs her palms together, and—as if pulling glass out of thin air, conjures a rounded cloche to cover it. She bends slightly, squinting one eye to inspect the scene, then stands up straight, apparently satisfied.

"Would you kindly place this in the empty space over there?" she says to you. You jump to do her bidding, gingerly taking the glass bell jar over to the space where you first beheld the vanishing forest. You peer inside as you place it on the shelf, and you marvel at seeing little jungle creatures weaving in and out of the trees: toucans, jaguars, and tree frogs. Meanwhile, a few rows above, another dream disappears in crimson smoke.

You return to the Weaver, who reclines now at the desk, lazily folding and unfolding a small scrap of paper. It looks a bit like the practice of origami, but she folds such unusual shapes, frowns, unfolds, tries again, and repeats.

"What is your name, Dreamer?" she asks.

You actually have to think about it for a few moments. There's a name that floats to the forefront of your mind, the one you're fairly certain people call you in your waking life. But somehow, it doesn't feel like a name that has any meaning here. There's another name, though, that surfaces as you think: one that feels like a description of your deepest nature. This is the one you choose to say to the Weaver, and as it escapes your lips, you find it a very pleasing sound. You'll have to remember it when you return to your world.

"It's a pleasure to make your acquaintance," says the Weaver, tossing her final paper-folding creation into the cauldron, which gurgles and releases a curl of gray steam. "I must apologize," she continues, "I fear it's my fault you wound up here, all turned around as you are."

"How is that?" you ask, a spark of genuine curiosity rising. The specifics of this surreal palace intrigue you to no end, from the owl archivists to the Weaver's inscrutable methods.

"I work very hard," she sighs, "with little to no rest. For you see, there are always active dreamers at all hours." When she sees your look of concern, she adds, "Oh, there's no need for pity. I don't need the kind of things you mortals do. You could say I was made for this role. But sometimes..." her voice grows wistful here, "being so preoccupied with dreams and dreamers, my mind has a tendency to wander. What I think, feel, and dream can sometimes slip through into my creations. I think I must have been feeling lonely, or curious, or simply mischievous when I misplaced a door in one of my dreamscapes."

She sweeps a hand across her desk to pick up a small piece of white chalk. With intention and flourish, she proceeds to draw an arched doorway in the air before her. It's as though she carves lines of light into the atmosphere, which glimmer a bright white for several seconds, then fade and disappear.

Even as the illustrative door fades, you reach backward for the dissonant memory of entering the dream realm. Was there a doorway? Or a stairwell? You picture a free-standing door, stuck right in the middle of the fountain pool, surrounded by tulips and pinks in the palace gardens.

The Weaver stands as if possessed by sudden inspiration, crosses to a chamomile plant, and plucks one of its delicate white flowers. She gathers up a pinch of salt and casts both of these into the cauldron. The steam rises like the patterns on brocade.

The Weaver then reaches into the liquid again, pulling out another dreamscape. This one, at first, appears to be a simple china teacup, though with lovely hand-painted pink roses on the side and a gilded rim. But as you look closer, you realize that there is movement inside. You watch as a tiny tidal wave roars upward from inside the cup, cresting and falling in its enclosure.

"Come look," whispers the Weaver, beckoning you up close. You inch closer and squint to see the details of the waves. The spirals of white seafoam take the shape of galloping horses, and the crashing sound of the ocean becomes the cacophonous thunder of hooves. The Weaver places this one on the pedestal and then conjures its protective jar. This she hands to you, indicating another empty space for it to be placed upon.

You take your time in returning to the Weaver's side, stopping to peer into several of the cloches. The dreamscapes range from serene (a small fishing boat upon a lake surrounded by weeping willows) to whimsical (a chessboard with all different kinds of dogs for pieces) to entirely fantastical (a tiny medieval castle with a tiny, snoozing dragon curled round its spire). Here and there, one will vanish in another puff of colored smoke. You wonder lazily about the dreamers. Who reached in and plucked this dream or that? And what, of themselves, do they infuse the dream with?

When you do rejoin the Weaver, you ask about her process; how she creates such wondrous little dreams. Just in these few moments, you've observed her weaving at the loom, foraging for ingredients in her nursery, folding paper, and drawing in the air.

"Every dreamscape is different," she says. "Each one calls for its own tools, ingredients, and arts. My repertoire is always growing, as is my workspace."

"You mean," you say, "if you needed to use, say, a spinning wheel to create something…"

The words are hardly out of your mouth when you glimpse, in your periphery, an old-fashioned spinning wheel near the gardenias. You're certain it wasn't there before, not till you said it aloud. But can you be sure? The Weaver smirks.

"That is the general idea," she says. Then, with a kind of excited warmth, she says, "Say, would you like to help me make one? A dreamscape? One especially for you?"

Your heart flutters, and a "yes" is on your lips before you can think otherwise. In the moment, you can't think of anything you've wanted more than to design and create your own dream.

The Weaver introduces you to the many tools at her disposal: the drafting table, writing and drawing utensils, dried herbs, teas, and spices, threads and yarns for weaving, wool for spinning, and the live plants in the nursery. She describes the symbolic meanings and emotions associated with many of the flowers.

The butterfly milkweed, for releasing attachments and letting go.

The crocus, for youthful innocence and joy.

Witch-hazel, for enchantment.

Yarrow, for healing.

Gardenia, for love and good fortune.

Snapdragon, for strength.

She encourages you to pick a flower to serve as an emotional basis for your dream. How would you like your dream to make you feel? How do want to feel when you wake up? You ponder her explanations of the various meanings and finally select one, which you pluck carefully and drop into the simmering clear liquid of the cauldron. The liquid instantly takes on the hue of the flower. A good choice, the Weaver assures you.

Next, the Weaver says she always likes to fill every dreamscape with opportunities for adventure, which the dreamer can either explore or ignore. "It's like adding a little flavor," she says with a wink, then describes the different herbs, teas, spices, and crystals she likes to use.

Adding bay, for example, often yields dreams of success, glory, and athletic pursuits. Throw in a dash of this, and you might dream of competing in the Olympic games.

Rosemary, meanwhile, is associated with memory; add this, and you might reunite in your dreams with someone from your past or even venture into a past life of your own. Add black tourmaline, she says, and you'll create a pathway for releasing or reconciling those memories.

Add mint, cinnamon, or pyrite to dream of obtaining great wealth. Add chili or rose quartz to dream of romance. Blend as many as you like to pepper your dream with several potential adventures.

Lastly, into every dreamscape, the Weaver makes a creative offering. This is the spark that brings the dream to life, illuminates the world of the dream, and makes it feel real to the dreamer. Using any medium she likes, the Weaver crafts a work of art: a tapestry, a painting, a sculpture from clay, a line or two of poetry...whatever moves you. As long as it comes from a place of genuine curiosity and creativity, it will yield a dream world worthy of exploration.

You contemplate the many artistic forms available to you and consider into what kind of world you might like to dream. Maybe a distant planet where the plants and animals are all connected like some great psychic collective. Or a forgotten place of childhood bliss, like a woodland stream or a friend's backyard where you used to play. A sparkling city halfway across the world that you've always wanted to visit. The bottom of the ocean in the company of merfolk. The inside of a magic crystal, where everything appears in fractals and tessellations. There's no limit, it seems, to the dream worlds you can imagine.

At last, after pondering for some time, you have an image in your mind of the kind of wondrous, expansive world you'd like to see in your dream. You can already envision the choices your dream self could make within, leading to wild adventures or moments of tranquility and peace. You can imagine yourself waking from such a dream rejuvenated, surrounded by an aura of the emotion associated with your chosen flower.

The Weaver is patient. As you describe the world you envision for your dream, she nods and smiles. She asks how you'd like to craft the creative offering, which will help transform your ideas into a tangible dreamscape. Your eyes wander once more to the spinning wheel, which was either always there or sprung from your imagination only moments ago. There was something so magical about the vision of the Weaver seated at her loom when you first approached, something deep and mythic about the notion of threads woven together to form the backdrop of a dream. Your head is filled with floating imaginings: you can see the Three Fates, who alternately spin, measure, and cut the threads of human destiny. You can see the devious fairy tale imp, Rumpelstiltskin, spinning straw into gold to rescue the hero. A beautiful thought comes to your mind.

"If I spin the yarn," you venture, "would you weave the tapestry?" The Weaver's eyes light up at the idea of such a collaboration. She nods gently.

You take a seat at the spinning wheel. Somehow, your hands know what to do; you reach for the gauzy fiber in a basket at your feet, prepare the bobbin, and begin to feed the wool as you rhythmically press a foot into the treadle. The motion feels entirely natural, and before long, the spinning wheel begins to transform the white fiber into brightly colored yarn. Blue, magenta, forest green, and even metallic silver and gold spin onto the bobbin. It's as if the wool is responding to your thoughts to magically change its hue.

As the bobbin fills, the Weaver retrieves the spun yarn and sets about weaving. You continue to spin, all the while describing to her the vision you have for your dreamscape. It is both fantastic and familiar, cozy and eye-opening. As your hands and feet settle into the rhythm of spinning, your eyes trace the weft along the loom. Slowly but surely, your dreamscape is materializing in the tapestry. In and out, over and under she weaves. Up and down your foot treadles. The cauldron simmers. Every now and then, a dream disappears from the shelves—but there are countless more still waiting to be picked up by dreamers.

You're not sure how much time passes as you work. The quality of light through the stained-glass ceiling never changes to suggest nightfall or sunrise, and your fingers never tire from the work of spinning the yarn, but you feel as though days and nights have gone by. Months or years. *But that's how dreams are sometimes*, you think. All the time in the world rides by in the matter of a moment.

The Weaver's loom is filling finely. Slowly, you feed the last puffs of fiber through the spinning wheel and remove your foot from the treadle. You feel the ghost of the movement dance through your arms and legs, unready to come to stillness after long repetition.

"It's perfect," you say to the Weaver, beholding the tapestry on the loom. "Exactly what I envisioned."

"Well then," she responds. "Let us make your dream come true."

Carefully, you assist her in removing the tapestry from the loom. Just as before, you feel a twinge of sadness at the thought of casting such a beautiful work of art into the cauldron only to dissolve. But the Weaver assures you that it's not being destroyed—it's being transformed. It's an offering, a starting point for a whole, immersive world of your design. So together, you toss it into the bubbling liquid, which rapidly changes hue and releases a plume of decorative steam.

"It's ready," says the Weaver. "Reach in and pull it forth."

You roll up a sleeve, take a deep breath to brace yourself, and plunge your arm into the cauldron. *It's funny*, you think. You expected the simmering liquid to be scalding hot, but all you feel is a pleasant tickle. You move your hand under the surface, searching, until your fingers meet and clasp something like an upside-down fishhook. You've got it.

You tug upward, marveling at the substantial weight of the thing, until it breaks the surface. You and the Weaver watch as the liquid drips over the edges, revealing your personal dreamscape at the end of the string. You feel a gasp rise to your lips; the tiny scene, a whole world in itself, is more breathtaking and specific than you had imagined. The Weaver congratulates you on a beautiful achievement, extraordinary for your first try. You thank her for the guidance and collaboration.

She leads you to the pedestal where you place your tiny dreamscape. Here, it picks up the colored light streaming through the stained glass and sparkles. It moves, sways, breathes of its own accord. A living dream. Then the Weaver conjures a bell jar, pulling glass, like tissue paper, from the air, and encloses your dreamscape.

"I'm afraid this means it's time for you to be on your way," she says, repeating the name you gave her before. It still feels like a true name, but as it echoes in your head, your waking name rises to meet it. "When you leave here," she continues with a hint of sorrow in her voice, "you won't remember what passed within these walls or the gardens beyond. You were never meant to be here, Dreamer, but I've so enjoyed the company."

The thought of forgetting your time with the Weaver, your conversation with Glaucus the Owl, or the marvelous nooks and crannies of the palace weighs heavy on your heart. Without saying so, you make yourself a little promise: *I will remember. I will remember this dream when I wake. I will not forget.*

Then, the Weaver retrieves her piece of magic chalk, and she draws directly upon the bell jar, creating a tiny door in the glass. Its edges shine as though illuminated from behind.

"When you're ready," she says. Then she takes one of your hands in hers and plants a gentle kiss on your knuckles. It's a brief gesture, but it leaves you feeling cherished. With the same hand, you reach toward the tiny door, clasp its tiny doorknob, and pull it gingerly open. Though the door in the glass is only about the height of your pinky finger, as you bend yourself toward the bell jar, you can feel yourself shrinking, condensing, until you are small enough to crawl through on your hands and knees.

With wide eyes and a full heart, you enter the dreamscape you made. You turn around for one last look at the Weaver, but you find that the glass has vanished. The landscape of the dream has expanded to surround you in three dimensions. It is lifelike and marvelous, everything you could have hoped for. You set forth into the world of the dream, feeling emotion and excitement wrap you up.

Onward, to discover opportunities and adventures in this strange new place.

When you wake, safe in the comfort of bed, you hold still for some time. The dream lives in your body, in the corners, the fingertips, and the elbows. Between the bones and the fasciae. In the angle of an arm. In the pounding of your pulse in your ears. In the joints. If you can only hold still, all your angles and corners, you can hold it for a little longer. You can remember it all.

But alas, your stiff body feels a need to stretch, to reposition. An ache for comfort. So you move, and as you do, the dream falls away, slips through your fingertips like sand, rolls off of you like water, evaporates. You find a cozy, warm new position, your head and a hand resting on the soft pillow. Maybe it's the way just a trickle of moonlight shines through your blinds, or maybe some part of you is already half asleep again, but from here, it almost looks like there's a piece of string tied around one of your fingers. A shining slip of golden thread tied in a delicate bow. Shimmering. Like it's there to remind you of something you shouldn't forget.

It's still dark. Probably the middle of the night. So you close your eyes. And you go back to sleep.

Exercise: Design a Dream Altar

This creative ritual is designed to empower your dreaming self by infusing your subconscious with intention. Following the process set forth by the Dream Weaver in the preceding story, design your altar like a dreamscape. You can ritually "activate" the altar before bed as a means of winding down and easing your mind into a receptive state, or at any other time you're craving an escape.

If you work with deities, consider dedicating this practice to a deity you associate with creativity, liminality, sleep, and dreams. Hecate, Morpheus, Selene, Artemis, and Arianrhod may be appropriate stand-ins for "the Weaver."

SUGGESTED MATERIALS:

Fresh or dried flowers or plant material
Crystals or stones
Pen and paper
Tools of your preferred artistic medium, if applicable
Cauldron, bowl, or other vessel

* Before assembling your materials, consider the world you'd like to visit in your dreams. It can be as realistic, surreal, or improbable as you want. Think of the environment, the atmosphere, and the physical details of the dreamscape, but also consider how you'd like the dream to make you feel. How you would like to move through it. Is there an emotional or energy shift you're seeking in your waking life? How can your unconscious mind foster and support that shift? How can your altar reflect these energies?

* After you've spent some time thinking about this, consider symbolic or meaningful plants to include in your materials.

* Procure a live or dried flower, leaf, or other plant material that evokes the emotional landscape of your ideal dream.

* Procure stones or crystals that correspond to the content of your ideal dream. If you seek an epic, adventurous dream, choose energy-boosting crystals like aquamarine or red jasper. If you imagine a dream of coziness and tranquility, choose stones that support peace and relaxation, like selenite or amethyst. If you hope to dream of love, choose a stone associated with romance, companionship, and passion, like carnelian or rhodonite.

* Lastly, gather any materials you need to put forth a creative effort. This could be a few notes of song (in which case, you'll need either just your voice or a musical instrument), an illustration, a line of poetry, or any generative offering that speaks to you. You don't need to be a skilled artist to perform this ritual! This component is all about giving something of yourself to spark magic and change and doing so in a space that's safe and inviting.

ACTIVATE YOUR DREAM ALTAR

When you have all your materials assembled, arrange them on a clear surface, such as a desk or altar table, with the vessel or cauldron at the center. Designate your space as sacred in a way that's meaningful to you.

Take three deep, cleansing breaths.

Holding your flower or leaf, say the following incantation aloud, filling in the blanks:

I offer this [name of flower or leaf] to the Weaver,
to invite [desired emotion] into my dreams.

Place the flower or leaf into the vessel.

Holding your stone or crystal, say the following incantation aloud, filling in the blanks:

I offer this [stone] to the Weaver,
to invite [desired dream content] into my dreams.

Place the stone or crystal into the vessel.

Now take some time to generate a small creative offering with whatever instruments or materials you have. Say the following incantation aloud:

I offer this [song, poem, drawing, sculpture, etc.] to the Weaver,
to invite my heart, mind, and spirit into the dream world.

If you have a physical offering, place it within the vessel. If your offering is intangible or time-based, perform or release it now, directing your energy toward the contents of the cauldron.

Close your eyes and concentrate on the offerings you've made, the emotions and adventures you've imagined. Visualize your dreamscape coming to life all around you. Vivid and detailed. In your mind, explore the dreamscape, observe the details, and let it unfold before your mind's eye.

Spend as much time here as you like, weaving in and out of the paths your dreamscape makes available to you.

When you are ready, release the visualization and open your eyes.

Close your practice by offering gratitude to the Dream Weaver.

Arrange your materials meaningfully on an altar, desk, or table—preferably in a space you can see or visit each night before you go to bed. Acknowledge or practice in this space when you are preparing for sleep. Change, rearrange, or augment the materials on your altar whenever you like, or perform the activation ritual again to invite new spiritual connections in the dream realm.

Consider adding a meaningful interaction with your dream altar to the nightly ritual.

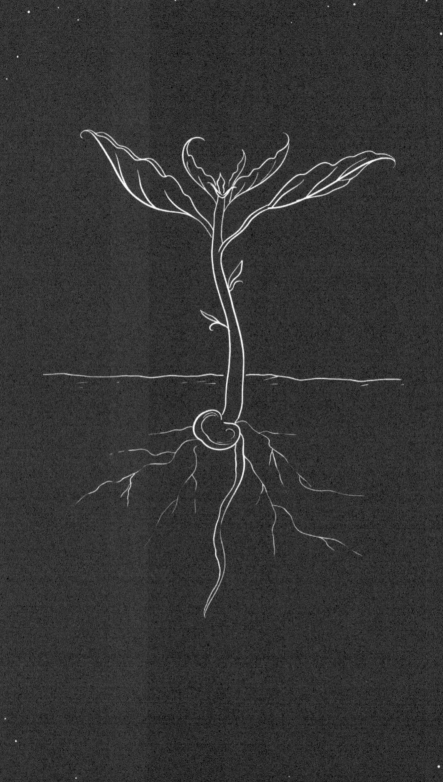

2

Magic in the Moon Garden

Tonight is the night, says a whispering voice, an incantation on the breeze. *Tonight is the night for flowers, tonight is the night for frolicking, tonight is the night to work in the light of the moon.* All down the day, in the lazy, lengthening sun, it echoes like a drumbeat in the mind. *Tonight is the night.* Like the buzzing of bees or the flutter of butterfly wings, which will soon return on the breath of spring. *Tonight. Tonight. In the light of the Alder Moon.*

For half a turn of the Earth, you've sheltered long inside, cocooning yourself in the warmth of the hearth. On crisp, light days, you've walked on crunching leaves, admiring spindly, bare-limbed trees, and even let your feet fall on powdery snow. But always, you've nestled back into the comfort of four walls, toasty by the fire and safe from wind and weather.

Now, as the earth softens, frost melting from the soil, you can feel yourself softening too. The buds are breaking open on the trees, seeds sprouting in the ground, and familiar bird songs returning to the skies. The robin and the myrtle warbler. The chatters and ticks of tree swallows. The gurgle of the red-winged blackbird. *Spring*, they sing. *Spring is come.*

The trouble is that you've grown used to winter, accustomed to the snug safety of the home like rabbits snug in their warrens, hidden away from the wilds. To welcome spring again is to step beyond the threshold, to open your heart once more to the wildness of the earth, and to shed layers that have become a second skin.

But under the thawing frost is that which you've missed most in this time of winter: your garden. A seed, a sprout, a bud—these are all potentialities. Like an egg unhatched, each seed contains immense possibility. Each sprout is only at the beginning of its journey, but it is imbued with the natural wisdom and magic of seasons past or of the elder plant that shed it. A chorus of questions come with spring: *What will bloom? What will return? What will languish in the ground, never growing to fruition?* It takes courage, you think, to be a plant. To break free of the seed shell and leave the warmth and safety of the soil. To coil upward toward the sun, to flower and to bear fruit, knowing you put yourself at risk of pelting rain and snow or dry weather and sustained heat. It takes courage to grow.

You brew a pot of tea, made from winter herbs harvested and dried: sage and mint whisper forth on spiraling steam, fresh and savory. You sip it slowly, blowing on the hot water to cool it, enjoying the end of your homemade winter tea mixture as you pass the time till dusk. It's your own personal tradition, a valued ritual, to welcome the spring by night: planting seeds in the silver of the full moon rather than by the golden light of day. And so close to the vernal equinox, when the day and night are equal measure, the full moon commands great magic. It is an auspicious time for sowing, for cultivation, and for rebirth.

The rest of the day is spent baking fresh bread—the scent of which conjures immediate coziness and feelings of abundance—sweeping the hearth to clear out the dust and stagnant energy, and reading a few pages from a book of poetry. The poems resonate with the voices of the natural world, singing of impossibly deep roots, of the irresistible call to migration, of the sublime majesty of mountains and lakes. You are ever conscious, these days, of the stretching daylight, the added minutes each day in which the sunlight lingers as though holding fast to the horizon, aching to see only a moment more of the earth's beauty. The quality of light is changing, too, every day. Stone gray melting to halcyon honey.

The moon is visible long before twilight, like a reflective disc over the trees; a blank space overhead that's perfectly round, imbibing the active light of the drooping sun. When dusk approaches, you notice the rustling of leaves and renewed activity in the shrubs around your cottage. You spot two little brown rabbits, almost spherical in shape, grazing near the green-stemmed forsythia, which is all abloom with delicate yellow flowers. When they become aware of your presence, the rabbits scurry out from beneath the bush and out of sight. You smile; it's good to see the return of these crepuscular creatures. Some gardeners might see rabbits and their kin as pests, but you can't help it: your heart melts to see their fluffy tails and twitching noses.

At last, the sun sets, leaving traces of violet and orange to linger in the sky before deep blue darkness takes over. You've had a little supper, accompanied by the still-warm bread, fresh from the oven. A bit of homemade elderflower syrup in your evening cup brings a wave of soft contentment over you, but heavy sleepiness remains at bay. *It's time*, whispers the little voice inside. *It's time to shed your skin.* You fill a basket with supplies: seeds and gardening tools. You carry a small lantern to light your way.

Stepping out the back door of the little house onto the stone walkway, which it seems was so recently blanketed and entirely obscured by snow, you make your way under the garden arch. It drips with evergreen clematis foliage, now sprouting buds of the white flowers that will soon open to the world. The hanging leaves tickle your face. Beyond the arch and surrounded by hedges of rich green holly is the moon garden. You feel an almost immediate sensation of opening or unfolding as you enter. You've passed from ordinary into sacred space, and your mind and body unfurl like the dew-dappled petals of a rose to greet it. Somewhere in a nearby tree, a mockingbird is trilling sweetly; he's singing a song to the moon, you think.

The moon tonight is surely one to illicit song; it climbs the horizon's ladder with pale and pearlescent brilliance, nearly as dazzling as the sun. Just now, you can only see it cresting over the hedges, a nightcap on their deep emerald, but its glow falls effortlessly upon the garden, reflecting on the silvery leaves of artemisia.

Since you last set foot in this soft and sublime place, untamed ivy has reclaimed the stone garden bench in a way that's rather picturesque. But the ivy and the wormwood are all that thrives tonight, so early in spring. There's much for you to do, in concert with the moon. You find yourself humming a little tune as you set about your work: a tune with no discernible melody and no repeated phrases, but a winding and wistful one that climbs the night air like unruly ivy from your lips to the moon.

With every seed you sow in the soil, you plant an intention, too. Every seed is a spell you cast in the earth, an offering to nature and her myriad spirits. Over your shoulder, the moon is rising high over the hedges. You don't even need to see it to feel its presence, for its light bathes you in cleansing coolness, falling on your shoulders and hair like a gentle mist. It feels good to have your hands in the earth again; it's cool and rich to the touch. Your fingers meet the soil with warmth and love. Moonlight dances across the ground and in the place between your fingers, nourishing the soil and the seeds therein. You feel a timid thrill as energy trickles from your fingertips like water, infusing the earth and blessing the seeds.

This is the very alchemy of spring, you think; the awakening of that which was dormant. The reenergizing of the earth and all her interconnected systems. And you, scatterer of seeds, mindful and deliberate gardener, are a catalyst of sorts. You can feel roots being put down and sprouts emerging, until, where moments ago there was only a tiny seed, now there is a blossoming crocus. Rippling petals of pale pink open to drink the mead of the moon. Your touch and your magic waken a whole flowering row of purple, white, and yellow crocuses with saffron threads that revel in the moonlight. It gives you a little burst of pride to see them spring to life before you; though you may not move mountains, you are grateful for the natural magic you possess. The blessed connection you have with plants and cycles of nature feels grand and important. If every seed is a spell, then a flowering garden of your sincere intentions must create meaningful change in the vibrations of the planet.

Oh, the moon, at this moment! How it hangs high and gleaming, so near, so magnified that it seems you could reach out and touch its cratered surface. The cascade of silver light sweetens all corners of the garden. It's no wonder, you think, that every culture tells such extraordinary stories about the moon; it's impossible to look upon such a wonder in the sky and not sense its magic.

The Greeks, for example, personified the moon as the goddess Selene. Like her brother Helios, the sun, she drove a chariot across the heavens each night to spread the sweetness of her light over the world. Casting her eyes and tender rays upon a field of sheep, she beheld for the first time the beautiful shepherd Endymion at rest beside his flock. And she was taken by a dizzying passion; how lovely he was in that peaceful state, with a dreamy smile curled across his lips. And how perfect, how pure he appeared when bathed in her light, reflecting back her own serene glow. Selene entreated Zeus for assistance: she would have the mortal shepherd be hers forever and always be so tranquil and beautiful. Zeus agreed, and he enchanted Endymion to eternally sleep, retaining his youth and beauty always. The charmed Endymion slept on through day and night and remained lovely as that first night. And all the while, he dreamt he held the moon in his arms.

So often, the moon has been associated with the feminine, for its softness in contrast with the harsher light of the sun. But the light of the moon is only a reflection of the sun, you remember. The moon's true power, though unseen, is in its closeness to the earth and its dominion over the tides. Drawn to and by the satellite, the oceans swell and surrender to its cycles.

As wielders of unseen but undeniable power, the Greeks identified two other goddesses with the moon. Artemis, of course, was goddess of the hunt. The eternal maiden who ran with deer and was wild as the woods. And then there was Hecate, the three-formed goddess who guarded thresholds and crossroads and walked with spirits beyond. She was a goddess of magic, a protector of Witches, and a teacher of herblore and poisonous plants.

The threefold lunar goddesses occupy your mind, standing at crossroads, tearing through wilderness, and driving chariots over slumbering landscapes. You hold them in your thoughts, distinct but interlaced, as you set yourself to the trellis on the garden's south border. You must tiptoe over the pale-yellow blooms of evening primrose, which must have crept into the garden through pollination in your absence, for you never planted them. You catch a whiff of candy-sweet perfume from them as you go.

It's the moonflower vine, wilting on the trellis, that you're drawn to. With tender hands and an open heart, you reach in and out of the gaps, retrieving and retraining the vine. Tying it to the scratchy wood with lengths of twine. Carefully handling the leaves. Under your nimble fingers, the shriveled blossoms seem to pick up their heads, encouraged. And, one by one, each with a little "pop" and a burst of lemon-edged musk, the buds spring open. The trumpet-like blooms seem to swoon toward the moon, each nearly as big as the palm of your hand, soft and white as fresh linen. The magic of the moonflower is its impermanence; these sweet blossoms, so like their namesake in shape, hue, and luminescence, open only for one night, closing again as soon as they're touched by morning dew.

Lost in admiration, your gaze tracing a spiral to the center of the flower, a rustle of movement sparks in your periphery. Very close to your feet, you catch only the faintest glimpse of another rabbit disappearing into the hedgerow.

It's fitting that the rabbits should make an appearance under the full moonlight. They are resurging just as the earth is in her spring-tide garment of green, but they have powerful connections to the moon, too. In Asian folklore, there are tales of the so-called Moon Rabbit, a companion of the lunar goddess Chang'e. You turn to the brilliance of the moon and squint to see if you can make out the patterns in its surface suggestive of the Moon Rabbit, mortar and pestle in hand, pounding the elixir of immortality.

The Cree people, too, saw a rabbit in the markings of the moon's surface, and they told stories of an ambitious rabbit who wished to ride the moon. The crane agreed to fly him there, the rabbit clinging to his legs as they went. That is why, they say, the crane has such long legs; carrying the rabbit to the moon stretched them.

With the moonflowers blooming brightly and in abundance, you work your way around the borders of the garden to tend to other shrubs and flowers. It's a mild night, with a dewy breeze just skimming over the hedges. You're struck by an urge to feel the grass between your toes; you remove your shoes and let your bare feet fall on the turf. How soft the earth is, and how comforting the cool grass. The snowdrops lining the garden path are already blossoming, like little white teardrops against the green. Each delicate one seems to exhale as you walk past.

The moon has risen to its zenith in the sky. Still, without the illusory magnification of the horizon, it appears dazzlingly large and close, as though you could stretch your arms straight upward and embrace it. You find you hardly need the lantern you brought. The silver veil of moonlight transforms every surface upon which it falls: every blade of grass, every bloom, every catkin. As the moon affects the tides, you can feel a tug within yourself, mind and body both succumbing to its call. As if the drops of water that make up your person are pulled, like magnets, toward the heart of it. You are in its sway.

You set about working with the hellebore, one of your garden favorites. Kneeling to the plot where their roots reside, you place a hand to the earth, feeling the subtle vibrations there. The hellebore, like you, can be reluctant to leave its chrysalis; it may need some convincing. Nature cannot be forced to obey your will, but it can be guided by the natural magic of the year. It takes courage to grow, you remind yourself. How can you make the space welcoming, safe, for the hellebore to join you? You sit beside the roots, hands in the soil, slowing your breath to align with the shiver of the earth. You send a message to the sprouted seeds and the deep roots through your intentions; a message not of expectation, but of unity. *We're in this together*, you aim to convey. *If I can soften, open, and stretch, perhaps you can too. It's safe, and I'm here beside you.*

In the soil, in the spaces between your fingers, and in the tremble of the deep earth, you sense resistance, hesitation. *It's okay*, you whisper. *Take your time. I took my time, too.* You sit with the roots for a while, letting go of expectation and acknowledgment of the passing minutes. Somewhere in the trees, the low, familiar call of a barred owl sounds. Moonlight penetrates the slipping sands between moments, infusing all with light and hidden music.

And then, something yields. At first, feeling a sensation of swaying forth, you think the earth is giving way. But the earth is solid as ever, supporting your hands and body. You realize, in a moment of clarity, that you are the one bending, swooning. The vestiges of resistance you felt in the earth and the hesitation you attributed to the hellebore was your own uncertainty. You hadn't realized you were still holding anything back, but as you finally let it go, you feel lighter, more open. As though your heart space unfolds like butterfly wings. You're able to take deeper, cleaner breaths, and your body feels more relaxed than before. You even feel a fluttering laugh travel from the depths of your belly to your lips. It feels so good to laugh in the garden.

As if responding to your easing, to your unbinding of emotion, the soil sparkles. Up from the ground twist spindly green stems, and from them sprout leaves and elegant flowers. Each petal drips from the stem till the blooms are full, cast downward and demure, as though the blossoms are afraid to behold the full moon. Ombres of green, pink, and white bleed to dappled patchwork in their centers. A sigh escapes your lips. All this time, you thought you were encouraging the flowers to grow, when, in fact, they were waiting for you to break through. It's one of the consistent surprises of magic: that which you put into your work comes back to you, challenges you, awakens you.

Perhaps you're drawn to hellebore because it's such a mercurial flower; it can heal or poison, depending on the circumstances. It must be handled with care and firm intention. In Greek mythology, it was used as a cure for the maenads, driven to ecstatic frenzy by Dionysus, and to heal the madness of Heracles. That must be why it casts its gaze toward the ground, away from the moon glow: the moon, of course, works magic and mayhem on the minds of men.

You lean back on your hands, inclining your face to drink in the cleansing moonlight. So bright, so full and heavy that it looks to droop, to sag toward the earth, the moon agitates the tides of the ocean and the inner tides of human bodies. You have half a mind to cast a net around it like a butterfly, bring it inside, and keep it as a nightlight.

But the moon is only a mirror, you remember. It does not have its own light to shine; it reflects the radiance of the sun just as it reflects the stirrings of the mind. Every culture across the wide world and throughout the seas of time has gazed upon its surface and seen a dazzling reflection. A man in the moon, a rabbit with mortar and pestle, a god or a goddess.

In a way, your garden is also a mirror. It transforms as you look upon it, interact with it. But it only gives back what you put forth. It anticipates your hesitations, embraces your intentions, and reminds you of the march of time. The oft-repeating cycles of life, death, and rebirth are present in the phases of the moon and in the abatement and resurgence of the plants. Even as they hide, dormant beneath the soil, they live—awaiting the return of spring. There is value in spending time in shelter, withdrawing, turning inward. But there is equal value in stepping forth again into the light of the sun or the moon and opening once more.

The garden teaches you to grow. It takes courage to grow.

The east wall of the garden is stone, covered now with rich green ivy. An old fountain in the wall is untouched by the vine; in fact, it grows around it so precisely that the ivy must have known to leave the space uncovered. At present, the fountain is quiet, and no water moves through it. But it's marvelous to look upon all the same. The face of the Green Man adorns the fountainhead. Smiling eyes peek from behind acanthus leaves, which frame the face on all sides. When one of the decorative stone leaves begins to flicker, it turns your head.

Soon, you discover that it's not a stone leaf at all, but a pale green moth perched upon the head of the fountain. A luna moth, named so for the Roman goddess of the moon. Her tapered wings, curved and leaflike, don small colorful patterns that resemble eyes. She twitches, flutters lightly, then returns to stillness, apparently content in such camouflage. So, you think, you're not the only one re-adjusting to life beyond the cocoon.

The whistling trill of a nightingale in the trees beyond the garden. The night grows cool and restless, a chill wind shaking through the leaves. The flowers bend and sway. The moon begins to recede.

Before you leave the garden for the night, you take a deep breath, calling in the fragrance and the fellowship of the flowers. How brave they are, you think, to shine their petals in the open air, whatever may come their way. How thankful you are for everything the plants provide: beauty, food, and medicine. They breathe with you, some of them stretching, lengthening toward you, as if they long to go with you beyond the hedges.

Carrying your shoes in the basket of supplies and the diminishing lantern in the other hand, you tiptoe back up the garden path, up the porch steps, and into the little cottage you call home. It's very warm inside, in contrast to the cool air without. At once, a drowsiness falls over you, making your eyelids heavy. You extinguish the lantern and step softly to your bedroom, the floors only lightly creaking beneath your feet.

Before your climb into bed, you open your windows a crack to let in a light breeze. The welcome air immediately brightens the stagnant atmosphere of the room, bringing the sweet smell of night-flowering plants to your senses. You can see the moon through the window, now with a pale golden veil, swollen and shining over the evergreens.

If only you could, like in the fairy tale, grow a flowering plant so tall it becomes a ladder to the stars. Then, you could climb all the way to the sky and dance on the moon. You could search its surface for the rabbit who makes the elixir of immortality. You could meet the goddess who smiles down on the night. You could ride the moon like a chariot across the sky.

With a softened self, an open heart, and a cleansing breath, you crawl into your bed. You get snug under the blankets, warming your feet and feeling the cool breeze on your face. You imagine that the moon, the light of which streams in gently through the open window, is kissing you good night. Bidding you adieu, until tomorrow night when it returns to the sky, a little smaller, but just as present and powerful.

You dream of deep roots coiled in the earth. Of brilliant flowers unfolding. Of butterflies and beanstalks.

EXERCISE: OSTARA SEED RITUAL

At the vernal equinox, the Earth sits in a delicate balance between day and night, winter and summer. Night and day occupy equal hours—a phenomenon that only occurs in the spring and the fall. At the height of this transition, a cosmic alchemy awakens. Practice this simple ritual on or near the vernal equinox (or Ostara, the corresponding Pagan sabbat) to encourage growth and renewal; or at any time of year when you crave connection to the natural world and her creative capacity.

SUGGESTED MATERIALS:

Pack of seeds or seedlings (consider choosing one with cultural significance or symbolism that aligns with your intentions for the season)
Pot and soil if planting inside
Trowel or small shovel
Scrap of paper or parchment
Pen or pencil
Water

✳ Wait until sundown to begin this ritual.

✳ Choose a space in your garden or home to plant a new seed or seedling. Designate this space as sacred in a manner meaningful to you.

✳ Notice whether the moon is visible. What phase is it in? What does that phase—full, dark, waxing, waning—mean to you in this moment?

✳ Set an intention for the season of spring. Consider how the cycle of the moon might inspire this intention. If you need inspiration, consider the following:

  • *I release that which does not serve me, making space in my heart and soul for new growth.*
  • *I strengthen my connection to—and responsibility to—the natural world and my environment.*
  • *I nurture the projects that bring me joy in this season.*
  • *I shed my winter layers and embrace rebirth.*

✳ Write down your intention on a small piece of paper, or speak it aloud while holding your seeds, as if feeding them with your intention.

✳ When you are ready to plant your seeds, plant your intention as well. You might literally plant the written intention in the ground, in a spell jar, or on seed paper, or you might concentrate deeply on your intention as you place your seeds or seedlings in the ground.

✳ Let your hands get a little dirty. Feel the earth, thank it for its blessings, and let this seed, this intention, be an offering to the alchemy of spring.

FAIRIES OF THE FOREST FLOOR

It rained overnight. You can still feel a palpable moisture in the air and a dampness in the earth. You recall waking briefly in the night before being comforted back to sleep by the sound of rain outside your window, even a low rumble of thunder. The storm moved on well before sunrise, leaving hardly any cloud cover behind. And it allowed the early sun to stream effortlessly through your window, waking you gently and peacefully to the new day. Ordinarily, you would have slept in a little later, but today, you want to enjoy the early hours of morning.

The lingering mist from last night's rain acts as a conduit for the fragrance of flowers as they graciously open their petals to the morning. It's an invigorating mixture of scents, both herbaceous and sweet.

It's good to get away from the center of town; you're purposely renting a little cottage on the edge of the wood to avoid the bustling energy of Main Street. It's overrun with academics this week. They've come from all over the world for a long-awaited conference on the life and work of Emily Dickinson. You might take in one of the public lectures during the week if you're feeling up to it, but you haven't decided yet. For now, a walk in the woods is all you really want. A little time in the peace and quiet. A little time for contemplation.

It may be an unanswered question for those scholars and enthusiasts of Dickinson and her peers, the question of why this part of the country seems to be a locus for literary and artistic creativity, but you believe a walk in this wood answers that question better than words can. As many times as you've traced their paths and wandered their meadows, these woods never cease to enchant you. It's as if there's something in the soil or the water that nourishes these trees—something that also sparks the keen imagination and sets the spirit of poetry alight.

Dickinson. Robert Frost—it's on the trail named for him that you now tread. And others, too, were born here, or called here by some whispering muse. The great novelist Chinua Achebe came here to lecture for a time. The playwright Annie Baker was born here. Holly Black, who wrote such engrossing fantasy novels for young readers, lives and writes here still. And so many others have flocked to this little town in Western Massachusetts. Seeking inspiration, perhaps—or answering the muse's call.

When you were young, you called these woods "magic," because that was the best word you had for it. Now that you're older, you're not sure you'd use that word anymore. It makes it all seem too simple. You've seen more of the world, spent years away from home, learned, loved, and lost. Everything is more complex now.

Still, it's comforting to come here, set your feet upon the soil once more, feel the crunch of leaves beneath you and the kiss of sunlight on your face. You can feel those childhood memories flooding back with every step, as though the trail is unfolding before your eyes, almost unchanged. It's as if your memories inform its very existence.

Is this what everyone experiences, returning to a childhood place after a long time away? you wonder. You'd always heard that those hallmarks of youth—old houses, schools, and the like—seem smaller when you go back to visit. Maybe that's the case with manmade places. The woods, a place of wildness and minimal human interference, feels somehow more expansive. Achingly familiar, and yet less known than ever.

There's a rustling overhead and a chorus of buzzing trills. You look up instinctively to see two dozen or more pale-yellow bellies and gold-tipped tails: a bevy of cedar waxwings flushed from their tree, flocking together to find a new place to rest and feast on berries. They cross your eyeline and settle together in a nearby dogwood tree. Here, their colors are on display, from silky soft browns to blazing yellow, black masks across their faces, and bright red waxlike tips on their wings. Someone once told you the collective noun for these birds is a "museum." A museum of waxwings. And they do look like something out of a painting. You allow yourself a long pause to observe and admire the playful birds before you continue on down the trail.

With the rain having passed and leaving behind only lingering traces of its presence, there's an ethereal, glowing quality to the morning light. A pink shimmer cascades over the tall trees and refracts through the tiny droplets of water still suspended in the air. The effect makes the woods seem to glitter. Blush and peach and lemon and sage. You're grateful that today it should be sunny and colorful instead of gray and haunting like it often is after a storm.

The path splits here—one way leading, as you recall, to a winding country road. The other leads deeper into the wood and down a slope to a little basin, where, if memory serves, you should soon encounter a rushing stream. You strain your ears, eager to detect the sound of trickling water, but it must be a little too far down.

For a moment, you smile to yourself, observing the fork in the path and remembering that famous Robert Frost poem...

"Two roads diverged in a yellow wood," it began. [i]

You wonder when, in his storied career, the poet wrote those words. Had he moved here to Amherst yet? Was he looking upon some divergence in this very wood when the spark of creative genius fell upon him? Or was it some other wood—some forest entirely in his mind, even?

As you make your choice—following the path that leads down the slope into the thickening heart of the wood—you recall studying the poem once upon a time. Your teacher insisted then that the poem is frequently misinterpreted. The sentiment of taking "the road less traveled by," they claimed, has been turned into a simple platitude about non-conformity. "Take the road less traveled by," say the motivational posters, "it'll make all the difference." When really, your teacher said, the poet is not celebrating his unconventional choices, but rather expressing a kind of prescient regret.

"I shall be telling this with a sigh," Frost writes. As though he looks wistfully upon that choice, years ago, which set in motion the

rest of his life, and wonders what might have laid at the end of the other road.

You wonder, briefly and absentmindedly, what roads you've snubbed in your life that might have led to great things. You don't let the thought keep hold of you for long, though. As you turn down the trail, the overwhelming, sweet perfume of milkweed floods your senses and clears your mind. It's such a transportive fragrance, redolent of spring and summer evenings in Amherst. Quiet Sundays with a book by the stream. Counting the butterflies in the overgrown garden. And indeed, there are butterflies to be seen today, brilliantly colored monarchs floating lazily and feeding on the milkweed. You're simply bathed in the honey-sweet scent of the delicate pink and white flowers. It sets your heart aflutter, like the butterflies that abound, such a simple and innocent joy filling you up, so you seem to float a few inches off the ground. How long has it been since you felt this kind of unfiltered joy?

And with the fragrance and the feeling, the years seem to fall away. The memories, scented with milkweed, come tumbling down the gentle slope of the trail and nearly knock you off your feet. These woods. These magic woods.

As a child, you used to come here, to this very spot in the woods, and build fairy houses. Using twigs and foliage from the forest floor to construct charming, rustic cottages, patches of moss to thatch the roofs, and smooth pebbles pulled from the stream to line tiny garden paths, you created whole neighborhoods, whole communities for those winged creatures of your imagination. And as you built their fairy homes and fairy gardens, fairy libraries and fairy tea houses, you imagined stories about the little folk who lived there. You gave them names and brought them to life through songs and tales. Sometimes you did so alone, sometimes with friends, who plunged full into the depths of your fairy tale imagination alongside you. You may not be Robert Frost or Emily Dickinson, but this place ignited your creative spark, too.

You haven't thought of those fairy houses in so long, so their return to your memory on the sweet-scented breeze awakens a sharp pang of nostalgia and emotion. A twinge at the bridge of your nose, and the corners of your eyes feel suddenly wet. Oh, how much can come back to us only from the suggestion of our senses. How much can float back on butterfly wings and the scent trail of milkweed.

The gentle sounds of the breeze through the undergrowth, rustling up the leaves from the ground, bring you back to a place of peace and comfort. There's just a little chill in the air, enough to bring the daintiest of goosebumps to your skin.

How long has it been?

What if? you wonder. *What if something is still there of those old fairy houses?* Even a pebble or two still embedded in the soil from the long-set garden walkways you built for the fairies to dance down? Or a twiggy cottage, standing still, overgrown with moss, perhaps now claimed by a deer mouse?

You look to muscle memory—the hints of ages still carried in your body, your bones—to guide you to the place where you might find evidence of your childhood self. Your feet know the way, and your legs. Your arms know which limbs to hold aside. Off the trail, past milkweed bushes, into the copse of trees.

And just now, as you step beyond the river birch, your feet grow nimbler to avoid stepping on a sprinkling of tiny red toadstools in the grass. You almost laugh when you see them, for they look so precisely perfect, as though they were drawn there by the hand of Cicely Mary Barker or Richard Doyle. Just the size you might have delighted at, when you were young, as a perfect place for one of your fairies to perch and read—or a shelter under which to keep dry during a sudden spring rain. Your eye follows the trail of toadstools, dozens of them, straight ahead and scattered like seeds, until your gaze falls upon a wondrous sight.

Where you had hoped to find only the meagerest proof of your having once visited this place, you find much more. Much more, indeed. The crooked toadstool path leads not to stray pebbles and stranded cottages, but—you can hardly believe it, yet there it is—a thriving, buzzing village of tiny, glowing buildings and gardens. A network of little houses, strung with lights like fireflies. It is no higher than your knee but sprawls to take up all the open space between the birch and elm trees. The buildings are roofed with moss and tree bark, and each one glows from within as if, in each, a tiny fire is lit in a tiny fireplace.

You crouch down, bringing your face closer to the wondrous little village so you can observe it in more detail. The largest building—tiny, still, but monumental among its neighbors—has tall, slender windows from which glow different-colored lights. Turrets and archways make it appear almost like a fairy castle; but looking closer, even squinting to peer through the many windows, all you see are shelves of books lining every wall. A fairy library! And behind it, a magnificent, tiny courtyard, in which grow all sorts of minute flowers and ferns. A fairy labyrinth cut from tiny hedges spirals at the center of the courtyard.

It's a glorious vision, and it so captivates you that your mind clears of any concern to make room for unvarnished delight. Who built this marvel? Did someone come along, days or years after you last left these woods, and find the ramshackle cottages you built so long ago? Did they, too, feel the spark of magic in this forest? Were they so enchanted by the fragrance of the milkweed and the soft flutter of monarch butterflies that they were moved to finish your work? And, indeed, build it into nothing short of a fairy metropolis? Who might that person be, who would toil on fairy libraries and labyrinths in the heart of a New England forest? You'd quite like to meet such a soul, at this time when you could really do with a friend.

You're brought out of this line of thought by the sensation of a nearly imperceptible weight falling on your shoulder and the subtle feeling of breeze on your cheek. Thinking a monarch butterfly has landed on your shoulder and flapped its wings to fan your face, you turn your head slowly and slightly, so as not to disturb the creature.

But it's not a butterfly at all, and when you turn your head, you find yourself looking upon a tiny, pointy-featured face! Your eyes widen as you take it in—a little person is standing there upon your shoulder, clad in purple pantaloons and with auburn hair that sweeps upward and outward as though whipped by a wild wind. He has tiny ears that come to a point and smiling green eyes. Green boots, too, and a green belt around his waist. His cheeks are flushed with life, and his face wears a quizzical expression. He's no taller than your forefinger, you reckon. But most unusual of all are the wings—the two shining wings that spring from his shoulders and flutter restlessly as he regards you. Shimmering and delicate as gossamer.

The little creature places his fists on his hips and squints back at you, then bends his knees and kicks off your shoulder into flight, his wings buzzing speedily like a hummingbird's. He floats out a few feet from your face, coming to look upon you at eye level. He's still eying you with the same curious intensity; your face, you're sure, is slack-jawed and shock-stricken. This must be a dream, you think. You can't really be face-to-face with a fairy.

But the little winged one at last opens his mouth to speak, breaking your awestruck silence. His voice is surprisingly mellow and medium-pitched—maybe you expected a high-pitched squeak, but instead, it's warm and gentle. And to your further astonishment, the word that escapes his lips is your name, rising at the last syllable with the hint of a question.

You take in a long breath, almost a slow gasp.

"How do you know my—" you ask, trailing off as you see the fairy's pointed face split into a wide grin.

"We knew you'd come back!" he cries. "Took you longer than we'd hoped, though!"

And before you can respond to this, he's crying out in joy, calling across the fairy village, flying in wide circles and swooping down toward the buildings.

"Snowdrop!" he cries.

"Foxglove!"

"Bluebell!"

"Honeysuckle!"

On and on he calls the names of spring and summer and winter flora. Holly and Blackthorn and Burdock and Sloe. And with every name he calls, out comes a face and pair of wings, flitting fairies all. Each popping up from beds of flowers where they might have been napping, sliding from underneath toadstools, or coming out from their cozy houses with eyes bright and cheeks rosy.

Soon, the glowing metropolis is abuzz with translucent wings, each catching the morning light and sparkling; the effect is like standing inside a snow globe as flecks of white glitter float, suspended all around you.

The fairy with purple threads and wind-whipped hair comes forward again, and with him come two others: a golden-haired fairy, barefoot in a simple white shift with an angelic face, and a childlike sprite in magenta tights—this one wears, for a cap, a tubular bloom of digitalis.

"Snowdrop, at your service," says the golden-haired girl, bowing her head.

"Thistle," says the wind-whipped one, with a gesture of humility.

"And Foxglove!" says the little one, a flash of mischief in his eyes.

"Delighted to be in your presence," says Thistle, who seems to be a leader of sorts. "And we're here for absolutely anything and everything you need."

You blink your eyes, dumbfounded, and survey the extraordinary vision before you. Really, truly, a score of fairies flutter before you, eying you with admiration and interest. Each of them distinct and beautiful in their myriad ways. One with a daffodil bonnet and butterfly's wings, another clad in a poppy-red gown, one here in a skirt fringed with ragwort, one crowned with wild rose. It's no trick of the light, no detour of your imagination. You even pinch your arm to ensure it's no dream. But how is it they know your name?

Finding your voice, you ask them this. How do they know you?

Snowdrop blushes and hovers forward.

"If I may," she says, her voice demure and sweet as nectar, "We understand your surprise. You may never have seen us, but we have seen you."

This does little to clear up your confusion. Thistle jumps in to add context to Snowdrop's remarks. As he tells their story, the pieces begin to fall into place. He explains that they were once a wayward troupe of fairies, left without a home when their first forest was cut down. They wandered for many days and nights, searching for a safe haven in which to settle down. But no place they came upon seemed hospitable for a colony of lost fairies.

Until one day, they came to this wood, and they saw to their surprise a young person gathering flowers and twigs from the forest floor. Pebbles from the stream. They watched this little one tie together blades of grass and thatch roofs with moss, all the while singing songs of the fairies who might one day live in these charming homes. Some days, the child came alone, sometimes with others, building beautiful, if rustic, abodes for imagined pixies.

The fairies lay in wait each day while the child worked on their fairy village, always out of sight. And then, at sundown, they'd storm the meadow, tuck themselves into the tiny homes for safety, and furnish their new living spaces with the gifts of nature. They loved the child who built homes for creatures of myth, never knowing that each night, a fairy could sleep safely for those efforts.

But soon, the child's visits to the wood grew fewer and farther between, and then they ceased altogether—for many years, in fact. In the absence of their benefactor, the fairies set to maintaining and improving their own homes, always hoping that one day, the child would return—and they could, at last, give thanks.

The story winds its way to your ears, fragranced by milkweed and memory, and it warms you from the inside out. You can see that younger version of yourself, kneeling here on the forest floor, building ramshackle structures of woodsy debris. Sometimes alone, but never lonely. Your memory twists and expands to fill in the gaps between the trees with fluttering figures, light glimmering through fine, wispy wings. How can it be that they were always there? And you never noticed?

But you did notice—somewhere, deep within you, even if you never saw them with your two eyes, you always knew the woods were…magic. Now, there's proof of it before you. But that's the thing about magic, you suppose. Proof isn't really the point.

You're speechless, yet again, as Thistle concludes his tale. The fairies seem to sense that you're overwhelmed with surprise and emotion, and their faces mark empathy toward you.

"Can we get you anything," asks Snowdrop. "A cup of tea, to calm your nerves?"

You stifle an involuntary laugh at the notion; you've imagined a fairy-sized teacup balancing on your pinky finger.

"Come," she says, hovering closer to you and holding out a tiny hand. "A touch of my hand and you can walk with us for as long as you like."

You angle your head, curious, but Snowdrop's smile is innocent and kind. Her outstretched hand, inviting. You hold your hand out, and she gently places her palm on your index finger. At her touch, you feel a cool sensation wash over you from head to toe, a bright kind of tingling. As your gaze fixes on Snowdrop's face, your periphery shifts and folds. The trees, the forest, and the sky are all expanding, growing taller and more imposing before your eyes. No, that's not it. Of course not. The forest isn't growing—you are shrinking. Shrinking down to the size of a fairy.

Snowdrop grasps your hand tightly (you don't have wings, after all) and floats gingerly down to the ground at your side. The rest of the fairies drift down to your level at their own pace. Thistle and Foxglove come over to join you. There's laughter in their eyes as they watch you, gleefully taking in the fairy city from ground level. Oh, that magnificent library at the center of town! The sweet little cottages and gardens. Here, a tiny tea shop, set in what looks like an old beehive. A cobbler's workshop and a bakery, from which the scents of rich, buttery cakes emanate.

"Come on, have a cup of tea," says Foxglove, his voice cheery and childish. "I want some biscuits anyhow."

The three lead fairies escort you to the tea shop. Over its door hangs a garland of lavender and chamomile flowers. Such a lovely, relaxing scent washes over you as you pass through. Inside, the walls are waxy honeycomb, each cell fitted with a drawer labeled with the names of herbs and tea plants. You're welcome to anything you like, the fairies insist—they can even blend any number of teas to suit your mood. You peruse the drawers, selecting orange blossom, nettle leaf, rose petals, and ginger for your tea. You take a seat in a soft, cozy armchair that's just the right size, and the fairies fuss over you. They bring you your tea, and sprinkle it, of course, with sparkling fairy dust before you take your first sip. It smells spicy, sweet, and floral all at once, and it tastes of lazy morning strolls in the garden. You share a plate of macarons with Foxglove, each a different pastel color and flavored with sweet flowers and herbs.

As lovely as the tearoom is, you're eager to see more of the fairy city. So, your escorts, the gallant Thistle, gentle Snowdrop, and prankish Foxglove accompany you to the library gardens you saw from overhead. At this level, the flowers and bushes seem remarkably tall and effortlessly abundant. There's an organic romance to the planting—instead of neatly ordered rows, the fairy-sized wildflowers and shrubs overlap and entwine with one another, appearing at once keenly placed and wildly overgrown.

The mouth of the labyrinth gapes and beckons you within, but you leap lightly past it, saving its call for another day. All about the paths and lanes, fairies flit and hover in their business. There are fairy parents in the park helping their little children, with budding wings, to fly for the first time. A whole, lovely fairy community…thriving here because of you.

The hours slip away as you explore the fairy city. You visit the tailor, who fits you with new clothes spun of fine fae silk and flower petals. You taste mead made from forest honey. You stroll through a gallery of shimmering artworks—iridescent paintings of birds and woodland wildlife by a fairy artist. Your escorts press their fingers to their lips as you pass by a charming cottage; best be quiet as you walk by…it's nap time at the fairy nursery.

As the sunlight grows amber gold and the afternoon comes on, Thistle calls for a feast to be prepared in your honor. You protest, but the fairies are already flurrying to work.

And later, under the slouching sunset, a table long enough for a whole village is set within the courtyard of the library. Fairy lights are strung overhead, and flowers adorn the table's surface at intervals. A feast, indeed, is laid there, complete with ripe berries and puddings, buttery cakes, and splendid pies. Carafes of lavender nectar and honey wine for each section of the table. A seat at the head is decked with lily of the valley and cowslips. This is your seat, of course, as the guest of honor.

You feast among the fairies, drinking deep of the nectar and indulging in sweet and savory delicacies. When you've taken in your fill, you relax into your chair, contented and calm, as a fairy band plays music in the garden. A harp, a flute, and a fiddle play rustic songs that remind you of Celtic folk music. It sets the heart and limbs to dancing, you find. Before long, you lose yourself in the dance. You spare a thought for some imaginary wanderer in the woods at night—what music he might hear floating from between the trees. What lights he might see dancing in the breeze.

Fairy lights bobbing and swaying above, music lilting on the evening breeze, wildflower perfume wafting through the air. And best of all—good company.

Your troubles simply cannot find you here, feasting and dancing among the fairies on the forest floor. What sorrow could breach these festivities, rip through the revelry? Joy alone abides here, nothing more or less.

You'll stay the night? The fairies plead. As long as you like. Anywhere you like—in whatever cottage or bungalow you desire. How could you refuse? Never have you known a place of such harmonic peace.

The plates are cleared, and the band winds down, so the dancers disperse and head to their homes for the night. Thistle, Snowdrop, and Foxglove are there to guide you to a place to sleep. Your bones could certainly use the rest after such a day.

But as you climb the stony walkway to a row of fairy abodes, you turn your eyes toward a patch of sky between the leafy branches above. A full moon, silver and bright, shines down on the village through a mask of clouds. Thick, dark clouds, heavy with moisture.

And the first raindrop falls. The fairy city is built to withstand more than a little rain, but the single drop splashes over the library like a deluge, dousing you and your friends entirely. Foxglove is overcome with giggles. Off in the depth of trees, you can hear a few more raindrops. Thistle tries to usher you inside; "don't want to get drenched, do you?"

But you look to Snowdrop, knowing what you must do. Her eyes grow tender and sad, yet understanding.

"Can you reverse it?" you ask, sorrowfully.

"Of course," she says.

Foxglove's eyes fill with tears. He runs to you like an overeager puppy and throws his arms around your legs. Thistle sighs and bows his head.

"Come," Snowdrop says, her voice like sugar, cool and sweet.

She walks with you to the edge of the village—you can hear Thistle comforting a distraught Foxglove behind you. "He'll be all right," Snowdrop insists. "And besides, you'll be back someday. Won't you?"

Hardly knowing whether you're telling the truth, you ensure the fairy that you will.

When you reach the end of the pebble path, Snowdrop says, "Before you go. A gift," and she retrieves a little pouch from the pockets of her shift. You take it and inspect it with curiosity. The pouch is seemingly weightless—as if there were not only nothing inside but as if the pouch itself were made of an impossibly light substance.

"What is it?" you ask.

But Snowdrop only winks and holds out her hand. You store the pouch in your pocket.

"Ready?" she says.

"Ready," you respond.

When your hands touch, the cool, tingling sensation comes over you again. Rapidly, the fairy city begins to shrink before you. The trees contract down to their regular size. Snowdrop slides swiftly out of your reach.

You inspect your hands, and the trees, and the wood. You look back at the fairy village; Snowdrop is gone, it seems, rushed indoors. And the other fairies too, hurrying inside to escape the rain. A few windows still faintly glow.

The raindrops gather speed and density, falling now closer together and with more force. You chide yourself for not bringing an umbrella—but then you remember that you left the house early this morning when the skies were clear and there was no rain in the forecast for hours.

So the only thing for it is to run.

You dash through the river birch, crash through the milkweed, and climb the gentle slope to the fork in the trail. On down the gravel path you hurry, rain falling steadily upon you. In the dim, cloudy moonlight, sprinting through cool rain, you can't help but laugh. It's a deep, irresistible laughter that bubbles up from the belly and into your throat. It's exhilarating and unrefined. Sheer, impulsive joy.

By the time you reach the cottage at the edge of the wood, you're soaked to the bone and exhausted from laughter. You hurry inside and fall into a giggling heap on the couch. Soon, the laughter subsides into a full-bodied sigh, an exhale upon which escapes years of contained emotion. Your pulse slows down to a tranquil, steady rate. Your breathing returns to normal.

You change into flannel pajamas and light a fire, welcoming the dryness and the warmth. It's all you can do to keep from falling asleep there on the couch, cheeks flushed, with the fire blazing. But there's something you want to do before you fall asleep.

You retrieve the pouch from your pocket—the pocket of the clothing made for you by the fairy tailor—loosen the purse string, and peer inside. Something sparkles there, a fine and glimmering powder like colorful snow or pearly glitter. Curious.

Soon after, you climb into bed, weary and wonderstruck from the day's events. You pull the covers tight and snuggle up to your pillow, listening with soft focus to the sound of rain plummeting down outside the window. A purse full of fairy dust, you think, as a sleepy smile creeps across your lips. Will it allow you to fly? Or give you some gift—some spark of the creativity all those famous people found in these woods? Or simply a spark of that raw, uninhibited joy you felt tonight? There's plenty of time to figure that all out, though.

Plenty of time.

Your eyes float closed, and it's not long before the sound of rain lulls you sweetly into a deep sleep. In your dreams: a yellow wood with roads divergent. Hope, a thing with feathers, perching in the soul. A quilt of snowdrops in the wood. Dew collecting on the blossoms. Cherries in the moonlight. Butterfly wings and milkweed sweetness. Memories of distant times—not happier than now, just younger. There is happiness still. Now and in the future. It's all right.

Exercise: Build a Fairy Garden

With this self-guided exercise, you'll create a sacred space in your home or garden to invite the joy and innocence of the fairies. You may enlist the help of a young person in your life—or connect with your inner child as you go.

Suggested Materials:

Flowerpot, tin, or other container (make sure it has holes for drainage)
Soil or compost
Plants or herbs (consider choosing plants that align with your intentions for the season or the ritual)
Twigs, leaves, bark, moss, and other organic plant material (preferably foraged)
Stones and/or gravel
Assorted miniatures (premade fairy houses, furniture, toadstools, and other accessories)
Battery-operated fairy lights

* Choose a home for your fairy garden. You might find a special place in your garden or outdoor space. Otherwise, you can choose a place inside your home—preferably near a window that receives significant sunlight.
* Fill your container with soil.
* Choose one or two plants to grow in your fairy garden; consider the location and size. Succulents, herbs, and small flowers make great additions to a fairy landscape. Plant these in the soil.
* Decorate the top layer of the soil with stones, gravel, bark, moss, or other material. Get creative by forming paths and walkways through the fairy garden.
* Arrange miniatures and accessories within the garden to create a dynamic landscape. If you'd like to make your own miniatures, consider sculpting with polymer clay, building with sticks and wire, or transforming found objects to invigorate the space.
* While you work, think about the fairies you'd like to invite to live here. What would they like? Which direction would they like their home to face? How would they spend their days?
* Add string lights as a finishing touch and place your fairy garden in its new home.
* Visit your fairy garden regularly to tend to the plants and notice how it evolves with the seasons. Add to it whenever you like. Leave offerings for the fairies (food, drink, seeds, or acorns make nice gifts). Make a point to spend some time with your fairies whenever you feel disconnected from yourself, overworked, or are in need of a little whimsy in your life.

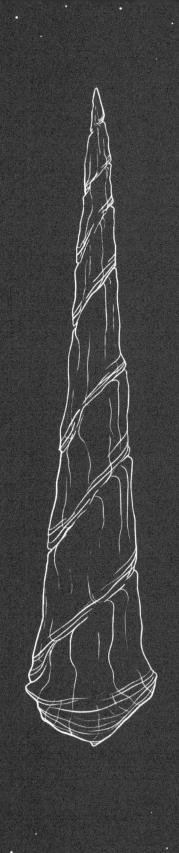

4

THE UNICORN'S BLESSING

The air smells thick, saturated, and earthy. There's a mix of mineral-rich soil and the warm, complex scents of ferns, lichens, and mosses. And here and there, the fresh, herbal fragrance of Scots pine, juniper, rowan. The lingering moisture of recent rain is suspended in the atmosphere. The dampness makes your bones and muscles ache even more. You seem to creak with every step, like an old house or wagon. Your body drags, pulled onward by your commitment; your determination to reach the spring. You've come too far to turn back, but oh…how your weary body would love to lie down and give in.

Still, you push on, unwilling to admit defeat. Miles of taiga already stretch behind you—though, who knows how many miles are still ahead? A map can only take you so far when seeking the landmarks of legend. Since you entered the wood, you've relied not on the map, but on your dowsing twig. You carved it yourself of a forked hazel branch, and you learned the ways of water-witching from a wise woman in your town. Now, you grip it in both hands, holding it steady above the ground, waiting for its end to dip when it discovers a source of groundwater. You must go slowly, and for this, your aching bones both thank you and curse you. You have little strength to move with any swiftness, but the slow, deliberate gait only accentuates the soreness of your muscles. Onward.

The soil is springy beneath your feet. Mossy and soft. Above you, through the trees, you hear the clumsy whistling sound of a capercaillie's feathers in flight. What light penetrates the depth of forest is diffuse and gray. You're not sure if it's early morning or mid-day. You've lost track. Steady, you grip the hazel wood.

But as you concentrate on the tiny, subtle movement (or illusion of movement) in the dowsing rod's end, your eyes are drawn upward by a hint of color ahead, not far off. If the dowsing twig has indeed located groundwater, you can't say—for it could have been nothing more than the twitch of your own hands—but you find you no longer need the water-witching tool. As you move closer to the strange, willowy pops of color in the wood, you realize that they may mark the very spot you seek.

Countless strips of cloth and ribbons—white and blue and bright red, yellow and Lincoln green, tattered and torn, threadbare and knotted—hang from the branches of a hawthorn tree. All tapestried about with rags and ribbons, the tree's own greenery is all but obscured. You remember hearing local folklore about such trees—clootie trees, they're called. Here, someone seeking the healing powers of a nearby well or spring would leave a cloth or ribbon as a means of symbolically shedding an ailment or injury. The goddess or nature spirit who stewards the spring might look upon the ribbon as an offering and, if pleased, grant their healing waters to the supplicant.

For a few moments, you find yourself quietly observing the ribbon-wrapped tree, almost mesmerized by the gentle sway of the cloth rags in a gentle breeze that rustles by. The same breeze shivers through the leaves at the tops of all the nearby trees, producing a brief swell of sound overhead. Each rag or ribbon, you think, represents someone like you. Someone who found their way to the heart of this wood, desperate to taste the waters of healing. A cream-colored rag, seemingly ripped from the hem of a common shift, might have belonged to a young person recovering from injury. A shiny blue ribbon, likely belonging to someone of noble birth, could have been tied there by someone hoping to heal a broken heart. *Every one of them has a story*, you think. You wonder if they all found peace and healing here.

When the rustling of the wind subsides, it's not silence you're left with, or even merely the twittering of birds above. It takes you a moment to realize it, but the sweet sound finally reaches your ears and weary mind. The sound of water, trickling, tripping, lapping. Small and clear. You search the ground nearby, and your heart flutters when your eyes find the source of the sound. A small and steady stream runs through an opening in the trees, just steps from the clootie tree. Hardly a meter wide and shallower still, the stream runs south, its crystal waters tripping over rocks and splashing against tree roots. It's a lovely thing. You feel a crashing of thirst, your lips and tongue parched and longing.

But there's something you must do before you can plunge your hands into the cool water; before you can raise that water to your mouth and drink. You reach to the hem of your tunic and grip the fabric with both hands. The joints in your fingers ache and twinge, but you summon all the strength you can muster to tear a small strip from the end. The threads split and fray at the edges, and the strip of cloth falls limp against your hand.

Approaching the clootie tree, you locate a small branch that is, as yet, free of adornment. You smile to see one of the hawthorn's signature white flowers blooming there. As you tie your cloth to the branch, the frail little flower falls from it, floating to the forest floor, where it joins piles of its decomposing brethren. You hope the cloth from your tunic will be a well-received offering to the spirit of this spring.

Now, body aching but heart light, you kneel beside the laughing waters. If you look closely, you can see the place where the groundwater escapes, bubbling into the stream. You take a deep breath and let out a sigh, on which all your doubts escape. You plunge both hands into the water, which is cold but comfortable. Cupping your hands, you lift them to your lips, drinking deeply.

The water tastes finer than anything you've ever drunk—cool and clear and just a bit sweet, as though it's essenced with the wildflowers of the forest. After you've drunk of it, you splash some of the water on your face. You sigh again, awaiting the sensation of relief. Awaiting the feeling of all pain and discomfort leaving your body. Awaiting the lifting of the fog in your mind, leaving only a pleasing clarity...

But you don't feel any different. You wait by the stream. And wait. And wait. Your heart sinks, nearly breaks when you realize nothing has changed. Perhaps the spirit of this wood, the steward of the spring has rejected your plea. Or perhaps they've abandoned the spring altogether.

You wait, still.

The light changes in the forest. The sheer gray of before gives way to a tender, golden glow, which finds its way through the openings in the trees. The clear water of the stream collects the golden sunlight, then dances on its merry way. You remain. It's hard to think you've come this far for nothing. You're not sure you have the strength to stand, let alone to retrace your tiresome journey. You sit.

Perhaps you will never leave this forest, you think. Perhaps you'll sit here until you grow old in the shade of the hawthorn and the towering Scots pines. Perhaps you'll become a tree yourself, rooted into the ground, and others will tie their ribbons to your limbs when they travel to this place. You'll become the spirit who grants, or withholds, healing.

Your mind wanders. Once or twice, you think you see movement in between the trees. You remember the legends of a great battle somewhere in this very forest, where two great sorcerers bewitched the very trees to dig up their own roots and march into battle. But it's probably just a roebuck you've glimpsed or a mountain hare.

The sunlight falls now on your face and shoulders. The waters catch the golden light and sparkle in response. Maybe you'll get up. And start the journey home.

But something stops you. Something fasts you to the spot. The quality of light is changing again, not in color or warmth, but intensity. And not from above, from the position of the sun, but from within the forest itself, to the north. Perhaps from where the stream originates. You shield your eyes and turn toward the light source; a golden glow pulses through the trees, its rays streaming almost like liquid. You blink and squint against the brilliance of it, and from the shine emerges a silhouette that seems to ring like a bell. Something large and gliding.

As the gleaming light subsides, the silhouette comes into focus with sudden clarity. All at once, you feel your heart fill, your eyes water, and your knees weaken. You're overcome with awe and emotion and an urge to avert your eyes, but you do not turn away. Your senses drink of the spectacle, for it's wondrous to behold but also fragrant and musical and warm. It's an entire sensory profusion.

And there in the wake of it all is the most beautiful thing, truly the most wonderful thing you've ever beheld. A pure white unicorn. More alive and lovelier than in any rendering in books or paintings.

It stands exquisitely still, noble and towering over you in your prostrate form. Yet, the white wisps of its mane and tail flow gently as though disturbed by a constant breeze or as though underwater. Its color, the purest, simplest, cleanest white you've ever seen, is like moonbeams...or fresh winter snow...And its horn, spiraled and impossibly long, endless even, nearly the length of its body, shines like mother-of-pearl. Your breath is caught in your chest.

And then, when you think your heart and senses can hold no more wonder, the unicorn begins to speak. Its voice is neither masculine nor feminine, and somehow both. Booming and incandescent, firm and gentle, reassuring and mysterious. You are almost too overcome with awe to understand the words, but you catch up.

"Tell me," the unicorn says, "in all your life, and in every place upon this earth you've traveled, have you ever seen a creature such as me?"

You want to grovel. To insist and assure the unicorn that they are the noblest and most magnificent beast you've ever encountered. But you cannot muster a sound; all you can do is shake your head. Still, you detect not pride, but a tinge of sorrow in the words that follow.

"I've heard your plea for healing," they say. "I've seen your offering upon the boughs of the tree. I've felt the pain you carry in your hands, head, and heart."

Your pulse quickens. Your hands quiver. The unicorn continues.

"I've waited many long years beside this stream. Waiting for someone with a pure and honest heart. Someone who might give me a gift in return for the magic of the spring."

You feel your face fall into a quizzical glance. What gift could this magical creature need? And yet, somewhere in the depths of your soul, you feel a strong devotion. You feel a wealth of magnanimity you hadn't known you possessed. You have no great wealth or treasure to your name, but if you did, you know you'd lay it all down before the unicorn. What can you offer, though? Besides a strip of cloth from your tunic? And the sincerity of your feelings?

"I have nothing to give," you say, holding your hands out, palms up, in supplication. "I have come many miles to be healed by the spring. All I can offer is devotion and gratitude."

The unicorn's dark eyes seem to sparkle, and you wonder if they feel disappointment. Sadness. Just as you had hoped the spring would heal your ailments, did the unicorn hope you were some keeper of unimaginable riches? Do they feel the same regret as you? But when the unicorn speaks again, it's not with sorrow, but with hope.

"All I ask is companionship," they say. "I have asked it of many a gentle soul who knelt beside the waters. In exchange for the healing magic of the spring. I have a great journey to embark on, and I cannot bear to go alone. I've been alone for so long."

"But why," you ask, "have none granted you this simple gift?"

Now the unicorn bows their head. "Many have made the promise in moments of weakness or pain. But once granted renewed force and energy, they've seized the newfound freedom. I fulfill my troth, but they break theirs." You can hear the heartache in the unicorn's voice, and it sends a pang through you. You can't imagine anyone refusing the unicorn anything they ask for. If you had the strength, you feel you'd go to the ends of the earth for them. But perhaps, you wonder, if you really did have the strength…would you, too, make the choice to part ways? If you felt young and healthy and free, would you still bind yourself to the beast?

Yes.

Yes, you think.

I would.

"I will go with you," you say, confident and bright. Your voice is as strong as you've ever heard it. "I, too, need a friend."

The unicorn lifts their head a fraction. It's such a subtle, almost unconscious motion, as though they refuse to show you any inclination of hope. You can empathize with the feeling. You too have felt lonely. You too have longed for companionship and adventure, despite all that holds you back.

There's a long pause.

The songs of crossbills overhead.

The rustle of squirrels in the branches.

The trickle of springwater.

And then, though it's unspoken, you feel the making of an oath. As though some invisible force binds you to the unicorn. A thousand tiny strings, or strips of cloth, tying together your hearts and fates. The air becomes active, as though all the little particles that make it up are standing on end and spinning through time.

The unicorn, graceful and slow, lowers their head with elegant intention and dips the tip of their spiraled horn in the cool and flowing stream. Where the horn touches, you think you can see a glint of light and liquid gold. The water continues to flow, but its surface quietly changes, a slight disturbance from the horn that ripples outward and resets.

The unicorn lifts their head and looks at you.

"Drink," they say. "Be healed, and let your promise be fulfilled."

Hardly bearing to take your eyes off the creature, you once more dip your hands into the cold running water. You withdraw your hands, cupped, holding a small pool of water within them. You can see your own faint reflection on the surface of the pool. Your eyes are honest. You wonder how this water will change you. Will it change your intentions?

You lift your hands to your lips. And drink.

The water is cool and clear, gently floral and sweet. You feel your throat opening. You take in a deep breath—and at once, you can take in more oxygen than ever before. The breath, whole and capacious, flows into all corners of your body, lighting up muscles and joints.

You feel your scalp and temples soften. All tension, pain, and discomfort leave the space of your head as you unfurrow your brow and awaken your third eye.

On the tip of your tongue, you savor the taste of the healing water, and you become aware of how the mouth feels. The inside of the mouth, the tongue, the root of the tongue, the teeth, and the gums. You release your jaw. Everywhere, tightness is replaced with softness. You feel how releasing the muscles of your jaw and temples releases other parts of the body—how all is connected. One system, all together.

You feel the healing water pass down your throat and into your body. The muscles of the neck and shoulders release and soften, letting go of tension, discomfort, pain—anything that hurts.

You release and soften your shoulders and the muscles connecting your shoulders to your neck, your arms, and your back.

Your awareness comes to your chest—to the space across your heart and ribcage. Breath fills the lungs and belly; you surrender to the natural waves of your breath. Each inhale sends healing energy to all corners of the body, and each exhale carries away stored tension, hurt, and worry.

Your heart feels light. Healing energy radiates from within it. You feel a sense of deep gratitude and trust for how your heart sustains you and carries all your potential. For love and deep, deep feeling.

The muscles of your arms soften, and the joints of your shoulders, elbows, wrists, and fingers become loose, fluid, and smooth. You send the healing breath to the individual joints, carrying pain and stress out on your exhales. It's as though you're clearing away cobwebs and sweeping them outside.

Now, you send the healing breath deep into the belly, releasing discomfort and worry. You allow the breath to gently loosen the knots of unease, unfurling like a lotus to reveal spacious freedom.

The healing breath flows now into your back, untangling the points of tension, relieving the pressure, and exhaling any negative emotions that may cause you to strain.

You send the breath and healing energy into your pelvis and legs. Your lower abdomen softens, and the pelvic floor relaxes. You breathe into the hip points—into any tension, tightness, or strain in the hips. As you send the breath to soften that space, you recognize and release the emotions and vulnerabilities stored in your hips and hip flexors. You carry those emotions out on the wave of your breath.

Now you soften and release your thighs and breathe healing into the joints of your knees. You recognize how much your knees bear, and you thank them, letting them soften and rest.

You breathe into the lower legs and the ankles, sending any strain out and making way for constructive connections and rejuvenation.

You breathe into the soles of your feet, feeling any soreness or exhaustion melt. You send healing breath into the joints of the toes.

The coolness and light of the healing water flush through your body like an exhale—from the top of your head to the tip of your toes, radiating outward from your sweet heart.

You feel mind, body, and spirit moving in concert with the waves of breath, renewing the connections, leaving you rejuvenated.

You find you've risen to your feet, standing taller and prouder than you ever have. You feel many years younger, and a surge of energy and vitality runs through you like a current. The gratitude is enough to bring you to tears. You feel ready to run through the forests, proclaiming your victory. You could lift the trees up from their roots. You could run all the way to your hometown, leagues and leagues from here, in the space of an afternoon. You picture yourself at home, at ease, and the image fills your heart.

But then your eyes meet the unicorn's. Already, the creature looks sad, ready to accept another loss. The image of home dissolves in your mind and is replaced by a hazy, pearlescent glow. You walk toward the unicorn—oh, how swift and smooth is your gait!—and cautiously, you place a hand upon their neck. Their eyes lighten.

"You intend to keep your promise?" they ask. You nod.

"A long journey would do me good," you say. "And I owe you infinite gratitude."

You ask about the nature of the journey, where you'll go, and the object of the quest. To this, the unicorn does not have a clear answer, rather, further questions.

"For all these years, I've been bound to the healing spring of these woods," the unicorn explains. "I cannot say how many years. But I have not strayed beyond the borders of the forest. Once, the wood was abundant with others of my kind. And now, I fear I am the only one."

Your heart aches for the creature. They continue.

"I wonder, in my heart, if others like me still run in other corners of the world. Though, my hope of finding them diminishes with each petitioner's testimony. But, until now, my charge has forbidden me to go looking for them."

"You mean, you've been trapped here?" you ask.

"Waiting for someone to set me free with the gift of honest devotion."

A surge of warmth and compassion fills you up from head to toe. You want to throw your arms around the unicorn's neck. You almost do. Your fates are one now. The love you feel for the unicorn's gift of healing is matched, you imagine, by the unicorn's gratitude for their freedom. You promise, once more, to devote yourself to the unicorn. To search the corners of the earth for others like them.

But as you prepare to depart the wood, a question occurs to you.

"What about the spring?" you ask. "Without you as guardian, what will happen to others who come seeking relief from their ailments?" You cannot bear to imagine others suffering, unable to find succor.

The unicorn explains that now their connection to the spring is broken, and it will flow with healing powers uninterrupted. Now all who seek it shall find their suffering relieved, regardless of their offerings or position.

This pleases you—to know that others in your position might still find relief.

You and your new friend set off under cover of ancient pines, hawthorns, and alder trees. Behind you, the healing spring trickles and bubbles. The rags and ribbons of the clootie trees sway gently in the breeze.

The unicorn lets you ride on their back, and you savor the swiftness of the beast through the winding trails of the forest, over hill and vale. You've never traveled with such speed; your hair whips in the rippling wind. Together, you travel the green glens of the Highlands under skies filled with heavy black clouds. You trudge through grass and mud in a summer rain. You take shelter in the ruins of a forgotten castle, somehow finding the deepest sleep of your life under a broken stone archway.

Across land bridges, you travel to unknown countries. To kingdoms of legend and great citadels. You witness a great many wonderful things: miracles performed by passing magicians, flutterings of fairy lights in distant trees. But you do not see another unicorn.

Your friend's gait slows.

Over hill. Over vale. Over land. Over sea. And again.

You pore over maps of old and new worlds. You consult with traders of rare animals. You parlay with pirates. None have seen the like of your friend.

One winter night, the unicorn says they will return to the wood and become guardian of the spring once more. You've done all you can, and the quest is ended. "I believed," says the unicorn, "foolishly perhaps, that if I could just look...even if I couldn't find them...it would give me peace. But alas."

You try to protest, assuring your friend that their freedom is worth as much as a hundred other unicorns, but their mind is made up. At dawn, they'll return to the spring. You can come along, if you like. The choice is yours.

That night, you dream of the ocean. Of a castle on the cliffside that overlooks the sea. On each crashing wave, in the space between the seafoam and sea sand, you see a herd of running unicorns. Cresting and falling against the shore.

At first light, you prepare to accompany the unicorn back to the wood where you met. You're not sure where you'll go next. Home, perhaps? You know you'll stay by their side as long as they need.

The journey seems longer now. *The way back always feels that way,* you think. *Because the object of the quest is behind.*

Over hill. Over vale. Over snow-covered glens. Over fairy rings.

Under broken archways. Under storm clouds.

And finally, under Scots pines. Familiar and fresh and evergreen. The forest feels like home. This place where you once thought you'd grow roots and become a tree, forsaken by the spirit of the spring. How far you've come. How strong you've been. How much you've loved in the days since you left this place.

The soil springs back with more verve now under thin layers of frost. Your joints bounce with more resilience. You're lighter on your feet. You try to think back to the person you were when you first came seeking the spring. That person seems like a stranger. You make space in your heart for them.

Hazy, golden light falls through the trees. It's the wintry morning light that melts through the chill and warms the heart.

There's a rustle in the trees.

A roe deer, probably. Maybe.

But a whisper of fragrance rides on the cold breeze, and a note of inaudible music.

Something comes alive in the air. It feels charged.

And through the willow and alder trees, the ones that might once have pulled up their roots to fight legendary battles, something is coming toward you and your friend. Something graceful and delicate. On silvery hooves and the fragrance of lilacs and the softness of seafoam and the crackle of taiga frost.

Recipe: Healing Salve

This easy, homemade salve activates the power of plants to moisturize, protect, and heal. I need it most in winter when my hands get extra dry and cracked, but it also contains calendula, which naturally promotes pain relief, reduces inflammation, and cleanses the skin.

Ingredients & Materials:

Dried calendula flowers
Infusing oil (olive, sweet almond, or jojoba oil are great choices!)
Glass mason jar with lid
Cheesecloth
1 oz beeswax pellets (or carnauba wax as a vegan substitute)
Essential oils for fragrance (lavender, lemon, and rose are great, but feel free to get creative! Just be sure your essential oil of choice is safe for topical application in small amounts.)
Double boiler
Small jars or lidded metal tins

* The first step is to create your calendula-infused oil. You can also purchase pre-made calendula oil, but it's easy and satisfying to make your own! Fill a mason jar about three-quarters full of dried calendula flowers. Pour the oil over the flowers, filling the jar (leave just a little space at the top). Tightly seal the jar with the lid.
* Store the jar in a cool, dark place for 4–6 weeks to infuse. Check on the jar every day or so and give it a little shake!
* Strain the infusion through cheesecloth. Reserve the oil and discard the flowers.
* Fill the bottom of the double boiler with water and bring to a boil.
* Add beeswax to the top of your double boiler and heat, stirring, until melted.
* Stir in the calendula-infused oil until melted. Remove from heat.

* Add a few drops of your essential oil(s) for fragrance. A little goes a long way!
* Pour the mixture into tins or jars and allow to cool completely, uncovered. Be sure to label your tins with the date—the shelf life is about one year. You can use the salve topically as soon as it's cool.

THE RUINS OF
ATLANTIS

Vast and unknowable is the kingdom of the ocean. You like it that way. Far beyond the reach of light, deep in the impenetrable darkness—there lies your heart and your quest.

Crystalline structures like sugared castles cling to rock shelves. You slip like a sheet of light through the narrowest of crevasses, expertly navigating the labyrinth of reef. This is who you are. Mover. Diver. Summoner. Whisperer. You know the secrets of hidden places. You swim deeper than most, plumb depths untold, and retrieve treasures unimagined.

Your hair blooms behind you, rippling in the soft sway. You relish the cool calm of the water at this depth. Your eyes feast on the dim blue, edging toward inky darkness, slowly adjusting to the change in visibility. Your mind fills in the absence of light with patterns, inventing images.

How long untouched has this region been by Atlantean hands? you wonder. What wonders might you discover just beyond the borders of the kingdom?

A trade like yours—which is mostly scavenging, no matter how strongly you reinforce the terms "collector," "trader," "merchant," and the like—requires skill, tact, and diplomacy. Since its founding, the Kingdom of Atlantis has held strong, steadfast policies about cooperation and collaboration with the plentiful species and tribes of the sea. More than anything, the kingdom's thriving economy relies on a few strategic relationships and low intervention with the outside ocean. Atlantis endeavors to make no enemies and maintain its friends.

Citizens like you, who operate on the fringes, must work in the gray areas of such philosophies. You must get to know everyone, curry favor with everyone—from mollusk to mammal. You have a widespread network of contacts, allies, and partners in the profession, with whom you barter, trade, and bargain for rare and exquisite wares to sell in your shop. You've traded with oysters for their most precious pearls. You've entreated with an octopus for access to his treasure trove. You've raided shipwrecks—and split the bounty with a school of snapper.

When it comes to searching unexcavated ruins or uninhabited places outside the reach of Atlantean rule, you must be prepared to negotiate. You never know when an uncharted region may have been claimed by some band of dragonfish, a wily Architeuthis, or other dwellers of the deep ocean trench.

But now your eyes have adjusted, and as the darkness subsides, you are amazed by the scene taking shape before you. It's stranger and more immense than you could have imagined. Your lips curl into a smile.

There's a reason you've never come here before—besides the depth, for which you had to train your eyes and body. There are legends about this part of the ocean, beyond the eastern wall of Atlantis. The most commonly told among your circles is of a trench so deep and so wide that its end can never be found. You could swim your whole life long and never find the bottom, but you'd become lost in darkness so black it lets in no whisper of light.

You recall, in your childhood, there was an old woman who lived nearby and liked to scare children with the idea that that trench, so deep it had no bottom, could swallow things up—that it was only lying in wait to swallow up the whole kingdom. But this was just a story. The great scientists of Atlantis debunked the trench tales long ago and put right any mind that feared the swallowing up of the kingdom. Still, rumors and legends persisted—as they are wont to do in the face of such mystery. The legendary area earned the name "the Fissure" for its appearance to those looking down from above.

There is a dropoff in the ocean floor here, even if there is no deep-sea trench, one that looks like a crack down the middle of the ground. As if someone had taken a giant knife and dragged it across the ocean floor, splitting it open here.

The heart of the kingdom lies in a part of the sea penetrated by ample light—ideal for agriculture and a thriving population—so the citizens of Atlantis live their days in warmth. But you've never feared the cold or the dark, so it's almost as if the Fissure is calling to you. Surely, this unexplored cavity, so close to the walls of Atlantis, should hide items of some value.

You haven't chosen just any day to swim deeper than ever before in search of pearls or other valuables. While you slip off to the quiet, untroubled waters of the Fissure, the whole kingdom of Atlantis is aflutter with preparations for today's ceremony. You should be there, too, scrubbing algae from the sides of homes on the parade route or helping your family prepare coral arrangements and food for the feasting. But you have no talent for such things—this, you're convinced, is how you can be most helpful.

An occasion like today's doesn't come along often; in a few hours, the parade will commence, and then a magnificent feast at the Queen's table—set gloriously with enough places for every citizen of Atlantis—and then, by the hand of the Queen herself, a new member will be inducted into the prestigious Order of the Tides. A new Tidemaster hasn't been selected in almost five years, not since before the Queen's coronation. And this time, for the first time, the new selectee is a commoner rather than a member of the Atlantean nobility. Such a thing was unheard of under the old King, who held fast to tradition. But the new Queen has brought significant change in the early years of her rule, and the induction of a common citizen to her highest order of knighthood is a cause for great celebration.

It's personal, too. The new honoree is not just any commoner, but your oldest friend, Alyra, with whom you played as children and listened to the legends of the Fissure before swimming off, shrieking and laughing, into the reef. You can think of no one more deserving of the honor than Alyra. She's brave, noble, and kind—she led a successful diplomatic mission to the Arctic Ocean last year, which strengthened the Atlantean position. She worked her way up to become one of the Queen's most trusted advisors, but she's continued to do charitable work in the neighborhood you grew up in. You've both made names for yourselves since coming of age—in vastly different ways. You became a prominent merchant, and she a highly respected consul on the verge of becoming a Tidemaster. You're proud of her.

And so, it's with Alyra in mind that you take the plunge today. You've wrung your hands for weeks over the thought of not having the perfect gift for her on the day of her knighting. You searched far and wide, called in favors with your most noteworthy connections, but nothing seemed right for the occasion. You rejected a diadem of coral and sea glass, a silver knife with mother-of-pearl inlay, and a harp so sensitive its strings could be played by the gentle sway of the ocean's waters. None suited your friend or the esteem of her position. So, at last, before you give up on the endeavor altogether, you come to the Fissure and dive.

Just as your eyes had taken time to adjust to the onslaught of darkness, your body slowly works to find balance in the shifting temperature—from the sun-soaked warmth of the Atlantean streets to the chill of deep sea. You were ready for it, and with time, your body finds a tender equilibrium, relaxing into the pocket of cold. The wonders and wildness of the ocean never cease to amaze you.

For a civilization so advanced in its technology and philosophy, Atlanteans are still a superstitious lot; beyond the legends surrounding the Fissure, a whole panoply of myth informs the Atlantean mind. It's easy to understand why. The ocean, so vast and seemingly endless in all directions, is home to inconceivable things. The mind grasps for understanding, especially in places of darkness and mystery. There are unknown places, other worlds even, beyond your reach, stories of which spring from curiosity or half-remembered communication with other races.

For instance, though Atlanteans rarely swim so near it, it's known that another realm lies past the barrier of the water above. It's the domain of the sun and moon, those faraway sources of ethereal light. But very little is known about the surface world, and so a wealth of folklore has evolved around it—from its mysterious inhabitants (perhaps very like Atlanteans, except that they walk instead of swim) to a persistent belief that the surface world is reserved for the great warriors, kings, and heroes of Atlantis. A sunlit paradise to which they retire after death. You're not sure what you believe. Some of your merchant partners have been there: whales and dolphins, for example, will breach the surface to satisfy cravings for air. But they bring little insight into the goings-on beyond mere weather reports and sightings of great vessels that glide on the water. Atlanteans, for all their curiosity, have little interest in spying on such a place, if only for fear that the air might be toxic to your kind.

As you descend deeper into the Fissure—for now, it's clear that it is not, indeed, bottomless—you marvel at the eerie quiet of the place. Only a few leagues away, preparations and early celebrations are commencing for a grand triumph. Here, all is peaceful, only a field of ambient sound rumbling low and constant. So constant, in fact, that you only notice it now while searching your senses for sound. The closest thing in the deep ocean to pure silence.

That quiet should descend over such an eerie and serene sight is no surprise. You fall like a pebble toward it, your eyes still drinking in images from darkness. Around you, as though embedded in the deep-sea floor, are strange structures of varied sizes. You must move through the space to make each one out more clearly; you cannot take them in all at once, for as you move only inches, the furthest structures disappear into the black.

From what you can make out, there are pillars, mostly broken, some fallen, but many still standing quite tall. Algae and sea moss cling to the marble, gently fluttering as you disturb the waters. You run a hand across the grooves in the stone; it's weathered and corroded, but you can tell it was once as smooth as the marble pillars of the great palaces and temples of Atlantis. You find, moving carefully through the dark chasm, broken pediment stones so obscured with algae you can't make out the relief. With each piece of the wreckage you find, your mind slides answers into place like a puzzle. The great Atlantean archaeologists will be stunned by your discovery; many ruins have been found on the sea floor, the lost monuments of early Atlantean civilization, but you're sure that never has such an intact and impressive ruin been excavated. You'll make a report soon—after the ceremony. For now, you feel a shiver of thrill; how fortunate it is that for just a few hours, or even a few moments, this impressive and inspiring place should be your secret. Yours alone.

Trembling with the magnitude of your discovery, you feel your shoulder collide with something hard and slippery with moss. The contact and the reaction are instantaneous, as all of a sudden, you must close your eyes against the unexpected onrush of light. Behind your eyelids, blinding gold dots gather in afterimage. You summon the strength to wrench your eyes open once more, and this time, you can take it in much more easily. Oh! All around you are dazzling specks of blue, all blinking and bioluminescent, glowing both tender and bright. They dance, twirl, and spin in all directions. What wonders lie in the heart of the ocean; this twinkling show of light is a school of phosphorescent plankton. You are sorry for sending them into a tizzy of self-defensive dazzlement, but you are grateful for the visibility they bestow now on your exploration. The whole site is lit now, clearly and with a shining blue haze.

You revolve slowly on the spot, taking in the splendor of it all. Beneath the layers of moss and algae, fallen and decaying but still awe-inspiring, are the broken foundations of a palatial structure. Pillars crowned with decorative botanicals, worn stone steps, and crumbled archways. It reminds you of the royal palace at the heart of Atlantis. Older, of course.

Then as you revolve, your eyes fall upon the greatest marvel of all. How such a thing could have been obscured in darkness for so long, you cannot conceive—it shines with tenfold brilliance against the blue haze of the plankton. It is gold and silver and white—and immense.

It's a statue. Tall and towering, unimaginably tall. You crane your neck—then float upward toward its head to look it in the eyes. The face, though worn, is clearly that of a woman, beautiful and terrible, awesome like a goddess. She wears a golden helmet, still shining underneath a thin layer of slippery moss. Her gown is rippled like the sand of the shallow ocean floor, delicately played upon by waves. On her arm, she bears a mighty shield engraved with the scowling face of a monstrous woman whose hair extends from her head in serpentine waves, like eels or anemones. The statue resembles a great Atlantean, and she's adorned quite like the Queen is at triumphs and festivals. But one thing sets her apart from all Atlanteans, whether Queen, commoner, or noble. Where the statue meets its weathered platform, she stands on two legs.

All at once, your mind begins to buzz and rush with revelation. This mighty goddess, or warrior, is a relic of the surface world where they walk instead of swim. Her shining golden helmet must have once caught the direct, unfiltered light of the sun. What a sight that must have been; how it must have glowed, blinding, inspiring her worshippers to kneel before her, averting their eyes from her impossible brilliance. Even now, you feel a slice of that awe, like a holdover from some memory of another life, compelling you almost to genuflect.

Who is this goddess? How did she come to be here, forgotten, languishing in the darkest of caverns in the depths of the ocean? From what ancient civilization does she hail?

Beneath her feet, carved into the platform, is some sort of writing. It's a language you couldn't possibly interpret; the symbols are old, worn, and unintelligible. You don't think you've seen such markings before, but there's something achingly familiar about them. An almost subconscious clarity, despite their indiscernible meaning—it's like the feeling of trying to read text in a dream when you don't realize you're dreaming. The symbols may swim or flicker before you, and though they're impossible to untangle, you know, intrinsically, what they say.

You swim circles round the extraordinary statue, taking in the fine details of her gown, her gesture, and her adornments. Once again, you shiver at the unlikely circumstance of being the only one who knows of its existence. If she really is a goddess, then you are her sole postulant.

You've never been religious, per se; in your profession, you've cultivated a balance of objectivity and awe, finding exaltation in the treasures of all the sea's varied spiritual traditions. You can look at an object with a healthy distance, evaluating its form, technique, and provenance...but in every ware, you seek (and usually find) that seed of the divine. When asked, you claim to believe in everything and worship nothing. But somehow, in the presence of this statue— perhaps it's her sheer size or her imposing expression—you feel as though you've uncovered something lost within yourself. You've come home to something you didn't know you missed.

Now your eye catches a faint glimmer below. Between two broken pillars, almost swallowed by plumes of soft, swaying coral, a metallic gleam. You dive toward it to get a closer look. Long and narrow, tarnished but remarkably well-preserved...your eyes travel to the base of the object, lodged in a heavy stone that appears to be weighing it to the ocean floor. It's a spear. Elegantly fashioned in an unfamiliar style, but recognizable in purpose. This, surely, would be a proper gift for Alyra on the day of her induction into the Order of the Tides. It only needs some restoration and polishing, which you can do quickly in your workshop. This is it.

The glowing blue plankton dance on, whirl, and blink in the dark water. Then, one by one, feeling at last unthreatened by your presence, they blink out. Bit by bit, the Fissure and the ruined temple return to obscurity. Before darkness swallows everything, you grasp the shaft of the spear, hoping it's not lodged too tightly in the stone. But to your surprise, at your touch, the spear slips loose as if it were only waiting for you to retrieve it. You hold it tight in your hand, using the free arm to propel yourself upward and out of the Fissure. You steal a final glance at the face of the statue before the last of the plankton blinks out.

Small celebrations are already beginning in the sunlit streets of the kingdom within the walls. You take the long way to your workshop in the thriving Merchant's Row of Atlantis. You cut through the neighborhood you grew up in, where you and Alyra were children. Your old neighbors are dressed in their best finery, strung with rings of pearls or donning crowns of brightly colored sea flowers. There is music playing round every corner from conch shell horns and tender harps. An exuberant cacophony of song. You can't help but smile as you swim past raucous groups toasting each other's health and crying out Alyra's name. How far you and she have come since you lived among these Atlanteans—but they are still as joyful and proud as they once were. Some of them call your name as you pass through, raising a glass and a cheer to you. You laugh and wave and carry on.

It's wonderful to see the city so alive with your friend's name on everyone's lips. You are so proud of her. You can't wait to see her honored by the Queen. If your gift can commemorate some small fraction of the pride she must feel today, then it will be a success.

Your shop is closed for the occasion, and you breeze past the elegant displays of antique jewelry, ancient weapons, and inscribed tablets. There would be no customers today—the entire kingdom is expected to turn out for the celebration. Your workshop is on the second floor, and it's the exact opposite of what visitors to your shop might see. Instead of pristine platforms, glass cases, and beautifully organized merchandise, it's strewn with objects in need of restoration, left-out tools, bits and bobs you never got around to verifying the authenticity of...This will be an easy job—you'll simply polish off the layer of corrosion.

You assemble the necessary tools and solutions then retrieve the spear, admiring it before it undergoes treatment. As you roll it over in your hands, feeling the satisfying weight of it, your fingers fall into tiny grooves along the shaft. You inspect closer. And there, so small you hadn't noticed it before, is a tiny assemblage of markings. Symbols very similar to those you observed on the statue's platform.

Your shoulders fall, but your heart flutters. In this moment, you know you cannot give the spear to Alyra. It's something more than a rare and exquisite treasure recovered from an ancient ruin. It's a clue to the very foundations of Atlantis—a piece in a puzzle that your kingdom has spent centuries trying to solve. It may be the key to unlocking your past as a civilization. Where you came from. What lies above the surface of the water. This can't be held by one person or hidden away in the collection of even the noblest of royal advisors. It's for everyone. You'll share your discovery and encourage a full excavation of the Fissure. Who knows what else will be recovered? What else you'll learn about yourselves?

It's a bittersweet realization, for now, you must go empty-handed to Alyra's triumph. But no—your hands aren't empty. You'll bring your ever-ardent admiration along with new knowledge. You'll share it first with her, so that it might, for a moment, be a secret between the two of you—sparkling and rare—before you bring it into the light.

Feeling comforted and peaceful, you make your way to the street, where crowds are gathering for the commencement of the parade. You can hear the entire kingdom erupting in cheers, laughter, and excitement. Your eyes flick upward toward the palace, which sits atop a hill at the highest point of the city, visible from all locations in Atlantis. A network of spirals and coral and great marble pillars, shining in the rays of sunlight that reach through the water to kiss its spires. It emits its own inner glow, too, opalescent and soft.

With a marked uproar in applause and cheers, you know the parade has begun—the route commences at the arch of the walled city before winding through the streets of every neighborhood on the way to the palace. It's not long before it reaches your vantage point, to enthusiastic hurrahs. A band plays horns and drums to an old Atlantean tune. Carriages pass by, drawn by hordes of seahorses and bearing important local leaders. There are shoals of blue tang, their brilliant colors catching the light. A smack of jellyfish floats by, their tendrils swaying in the waves like ribbons. A consortium of crabs scuttle past, claws raised to the sky. An audience of squid undulates across your line of sight. As the parade winds down the narrow streets, you can sense its culmination. The young prince and princess, flanked by their escorts, ride by on the backs of green sea turtles with serene expressions, waving to the onlookers. *It must be their first such parade*, you reflect.

Then the final carriage rounds a corner, drawn by silent stingrays, bearing the Queen herself and Alyra by her side. Your chest swells with pride when you see her in the place of honor, smiling from ear to ear and waving out of the carriage. A swell of cheers burst forth from the crowd, who cry her name and utter words of veneration to the Queen. You holler and whoop along with the rest. As the carriage scuds by, Alyra's eyes fall upon you in the crowd, and her smile widens even more, her eyes crinkling around the corners. Then, in the split second that you can hold eye contact, she gives you a kind of expression you expect only you could decipher. It means something like, "How did *I* manage to wind up *here*?"

And then she rounds the next curve, and the parade trails off up toward the palace. There's a palpable buzz of excitement from the crowd, who close in on the narrow street, moving collectively behind the parade's tail. All of the city is swimming behind you and before you as the parade closes. To the palace. To the ceremony. The energy is contagious, but you feel a serene calm wash over you even amid the bustle and noise.

When you reach the palace, it's as though the courtyard and square expand to hold all the citizens within it, like it's drawn in an enormous breath and ballooned outward. You squeeze through to find an optimal sightline. The Queen is at her dais, high above the throngs, resplendent in blue robes. Above her brow is a radiant traditional headdress, reminiscent of the helmet worn by the statue in the Fissure. She wears, you note, a decadent neckpiece, dripping with pink and black pearls...the one you yourself procured at her attendant's request last year. You smirk with some pride at its inclusion in such a day of honor.

The Queen's children flank her on either side, and Alyra attends below the dais, decked in her diplomatic uniform. The Queen's voice carries over the crowds, and a hush falls over all as she speaks. She welcomes the crowds and gives thanks for such a marvelous parade through this beautiful city. Then she angles her head to smile on Alyra. As the Queen begins to praise Alyra's career, her courage and nobility, and describe the deeds that have earned her the place of honor today, you beam with tenderness and pride. What a privilege it's been to see your friend blossom from a timid child into the toast of the kingdom. You feel honored to have known her all your life.

Now the Queen summons Alyra before her, and in a charming move, whispers something to the young princess, who moves forward. The Queen says the words of honor, proclaiming Alyra a Master in the Order of the Tides, but the princess is the one who hangs the medal around Alyra's neck. You know Alyra must love this—and perhaps she even requested it. Then the Queen raises Alyra to the dais for all to see, and the cheering resumes. All exalt this daughter of Atlantis.

What follows is a feast so sumptuous it can hardly be believed. The whole of the citizenry floods in through the palace's open gates toward the great hall, held up on sturdy marble pillars and walls that shine with mother-of-pearl. The chandelier is a bloom of undulating anemones, bright and pink against the white and gold furnishings. The Queen's table is vast and serpentine, winding its way round the hall to make a place setting for everyone. Alyra catches your eye from across the hall—mutters something to the Queen, who smiles—and swims over to you. Alyra takes your arm and brings you back to her seat, gesturing to a place reserved for you, her dearest friend. Together, you sup on delicacies from all across the ocean. You even have the occasion to remark to the Queen that the necklace she wears is from your collection. You whisper to Alyra during a moment of distraction that if she can get away this evening, you have something to show her. Her eyes flash with intrigue, and she nods silently.

The night comes on slowly, the ocean growing dark around the palace and outside the narrow windows. Orbs of phosphorescent light illuminate the table, casting a diaphanous glow about the revelers. The energy wanes as all who dine here become sated and sleepy. The Queen dismisses her guests, and you pour out of the palace gates once more, quieter now, but still mirthful.

As the citizens of Atlantis float drowsily toward their homes, you and Alyra slip away. The city glows at night, a beacon of light in the dark, swaying sea. It's too dark, after all, to take Alyra to the Fissure, but you're happy for her private company after such a day. She's happy too; as gratifying as it is to receive mountains of praise from the royal family and the whole of the city, she prefers the quiet. "You're a tether to reality," she says—you'll keep her from becoming so self-satisfied she floats right up to the surface. Laughing, you both turn your eyes upward. From here, you can see the faint glow of the moon beyond the waves.

You tell her about your visit to the Fissure. The ruins of the temple. The pillars. The strange and yet familiar symbols. The statue of the goddess. The whole story spills forth from your eager lips after holding it to yourself all day. When you finish telling her everything—even about the tarnished spear—you look to her. Her eyes are wide and restless, amazed. She smiles.

"I knew there was something down there. Something marvelous." Then, playfully, "I can't believe you went without me." You give a sheepish smile.

With more seriousness, she asks what you think it all means. Where it came from. You've hardly come to any such conclusions before now, but you feel something crystallizing as she asks the question. Like knowledge that comes to you, intrinsically, in a dream. You're still gazing upward at the glimmer of moonlight.

"I think we used to live up there," you find yourself saying, though you hardly recognize your own voice. "On the surface."

Together, you stare, eyes turned up toward the end of the ocean. Toward that uncharted other realm where mythic figures walk instead of swim. You softly sway with the rhythm of the water, pondering.

Overhead, something is happening. Under the veil of moonlight, trails of colorful light burst and dance across your line of sight, distorted by the waves. It's hard to make out.

You feel Alyra's hand grasp yours firmly, and before you know it, she's pulling you up, up toward the surface. Thoughts flash across your mind—Atlanteans don't go to the surface, the air may be toxic, you don't know what's up there...but these thoughts quickly fade. You feel lucky to swim in the shadow of Alyra's bravery. So up you go. Up, up toward the surface.

When your heads breach the water, an uncanny sensation comes over you. For a moment, you feel intense discomfort as your body yearns for water to breathe. But then something kicks into place, and through your nostrils something just as sweet as water floods in—clean, salty, fresh air fills you up, bringing vitality and peace to you. You can breathe above the water. A miracle.

And above—oh, wondrous thing. Color and light blaze against a black sky riddled with tiny, twinkling sparks. Plumes of light, like weeping anemones burst and spread wide across the night. Again and again, they explode like clouds of ink, violet and red and white gold. You've never seen such things before. You've never dreamt of such things. Eyes up to the heavens, the sky alight. It's darker and deeper and vaster even than the ocean, you think. What wonders lie in that limitless expanse? With your dearest friend beside you, now a Master of the Tides, you feel a new world rush inward on your breath. Your skin prickles. The waves roll on.

EXERCISE: OCEAN BREATH FOR RELAXATION

Practice this simple, ocean-inspired breathing exercise to encourage deep relaxation before sleep, or as a centering practice before ritual or spellwork. Use your imagination to conjure the sounds of ocean waves, play such sounds through a speaker—or, if you're fortunate to live near the ocean, practice this in the presence of ocean waves.

Embrace a slow, easy breath, in and out, like the waves of the ocean.

Feel your belly rise and fall, like the ebb and flow of the tide.

Imagine how the wave swells, unfolds, and breaks against the shore, depositing shells and treasures to sparkle in the sun.

As it pulls back along the undertow, another wave rolls in—an ever-churning motion, perpetual and natural.

Breathe. Feel how your inhales nourish all the corners of the body, bringing sweet oxygen along the bloodstream, lighting you up.

Feel how your exhales remove unwanted or excess tension, signaling to your body that it's time to slow down. Soften. Be still. And rest.

Feel the inhale bring in fresh, clean air and the exhale carry out anything that's not useful.

Feel the softness and the inevitability of the transition between inhale and exhale.

Feel that softness and relaxation travel over your body like a wave, which travels up from the tips of your toes all the way to the crown of your head. Then the wave rolls downward from the crown of your head to the tips of your toes.

As you breathe naturally, keep tuning in to the sensation of the wave, softening and relaxing every part of your body. In and out, like waves.

Find a peaceful, inner sway, as you surrender to the flow.

Know that it's in your nature to look for answers, to seek out the missing pieces of the puzzle—to want more.

Keep searching. Keep stretching yourself. Keep expanding.

You may discover something you didn't know you were missing.

You are a child of the tides, of land, and sky.

You exist in all places, and you walk in multitudes.

Embrace your missing pieces. Relax, and breathe.

6

THE DRAGON RIDER

Ever since you were a child, you dreamt of dragons. Breath of fire that singes cities, leather wings that beat with the sound of thunder, golden eyes, and crimson scales. You've never seen one—they're exceedingly rare, and yet, you are compelled by the idea of dragons. To you, they seem the very quintessence of liberation. With power and might to spare and wings that might bear them to distant lands, far from sorrow and obligation.

Eyes to the evening sky, each night since childhood, you've strained to see those wings in flight or a stream of flame cross the clouds. The village children always say the dragons died out long ago. It's foolish to keep believing in them. But you can't help it; something keeps them on the wind of your dreams, even as you come of age.

Secretly, you've always held the belief—in some unspoken, dimly lit corner of your mind—that dragons are somehow part of you. It's hard to explain. Like a symbolic guide or an emblem of your deepest inner nature. You'd never say so aloud. How silly and presumptuous to liken yourself to a beast of such awesome power.

But a year ago, everything changed. As you were cleaning the stables, like you do each day, your parents brought you into the house to tell you something important. Something they wish they could have told you a long time ago. You can still recall the uneasy expressions on their faces as they struggled to find the words. Even now, you can hardly believe what they told you.

For starters, they were not your birth parents, though they'd raised you from infancy, fed and clothed you, and ensured you received an education. You were, in fact, the child of a prominent family. A very prominent family: you were the sole offspring and heir to the royal line of this kingdom.

A child of the king. The former king, beloved by all the subjects of the kingdom until his death many years ago. It was too outrageous to believe, at first. You've only ever been a farmer's child—tending to stables, milking the cows, feeding the chickens. The thought that you were, in fact, the exiled scion of a line of great kings was preposterous.

Preposterous.

But. Somewhere, in that same secret place where live your dreams of dragons, you've always felt you had some greater destiny. Some fate beyond the farm, the stables, and the chicken coop. You always believed you were meant to do bigger things—to spread your wings, so to speak.

Your parents told you this on your last birthday, precisely one year before you would officially come of age. They told you then to prepare you—because the moment you came of age, you would be eligible to take the throne of the kingdom. But to do so, you would need to summon great strength and courage, for a usurper now rules the kingdom as regent, and he would not easily be deposed. You would need to train your body and mind for such a confrontation if indeed you should choose to undertake it. Your parents—your adoptive parents, who've loved and cared for you all these years—with tears in their eyes, insisted that it was your choice. They were sorry for keeping the truth from you for so long; they only wished to protect you. Whatever you choose to do with this new knowledge, they will support you and love you still as their own.

There is just one problem. On the same day your parents revealed your true identity, they also shared the greatest obstacle to your ascension. You see, when you were born, the king had made for you a ring. It was no mere piece of pretty jewelry, but a symbol of your house, cast in gold and pressed with the royal seal. This was tradition for all those born to inherit the throne of the kingdom; the ring was physical proof of your right to rule.

"So, where is the ring now?" you inquired. With it, you could march into the capitol city, stand before the king regent, and demand he step down.

"But that's just the thing," your parents say. "In the commotion to remove you from the castle on the night of the coup, the ring was lost." The story goes that it was stolen by the fearsome dragon who lives in a cave beneath the western mountains, guarding a horde of treasure.

At this, your heart leapt. Never had you heard your parents, or anyone in the village, speak of dragons with such currency; it was a foregone conclusion to most that the dragons had all disappeared from the known world. But you could hear the ring of truth in this story. You believed it with all your heart, and it incensed your spirit. The injustice of it. From that moment, you vowed to spend the next year training to confront the dragon, so that when you came of age, you could recover the lost signet and claim your birthright.

Now, as the auspicious birthday nears, you feel an entirely different person than you were before you learned the truth. You *are* a different person. You once believed that as you came to adulthood, you'd work toward inheriting your parents' farm—and that thought was satisfying enough. Now, you may stand on the precipice of inheriting the keys to the entire kingdom…and you wonder whether you really have the ambition for it.

You've worked hard to prepare, both physically and mentally, for the challenges ahead, knowing that if the legendary dragons are any guide, they're more than formidable foes for the mind as well as the body. They enjoy riddles, as you know, and are always ready for a battle of wits. You've sharpened yours like an axe upon a whetstone, just as you've trained in agility and swordsmanship.

On the eve of your birthday, you go to your parents and ask their blessing to leave the farm—to pursue the dragon, recover your lost ring, and begin your quest to reclaim the throne. With tears in their eyes, they grant that blessing—though not before cooking you a hearty meal and showering you with love.

As dawn breaks over the village in the valley, you rise with the sun and don your modest, light armor. You carry a sword—of rustic make by the local blacksmith, who agreed to work for a reduced fee—in a scabbard at your hip. Just knowing it's there makes you feel taller, stronger. Still, your belly fills with butterflies at the thought of leaving home and taking on such a massive trial alone.

Just as the sky grows rosy and vermilion in the burgeoning sunrise, and the morning mist kisses your cheeks like dew upon the grass, you take the first solitary steps toward your fate.

The road to the western mountains, where the dragon guards its gold, is long. Three days ride on horseback, but you've never been much of a rider—and the workhorses from the farm are not meant for traveling long distances or over mountains. So, you set off on foot, carrying only the lightest of rations and a pack of simple supplies. The sword is the heaviest thing you bear, and at times, you can feel it weighing you down when you'd otherwise move more swiftly.

But the slow pace, if nothing else, allows you time for contemplation, meditation, and concentration. There's unease, of course—anyone walking away from home with the intent of facing down a dragon would feel uneasy—but there's also something else, harder to explain. A feeling of calm inevitability and a shining confidence that you are being drawn along an invisible string, a quivering cord of destiny. Every step you take brings you closer to your fate.

The road winds through some tiny villages where you're grateful to stop for the night, take in some hot food, and sleep in a warm bed in a tavern. Remembering your parents' advice about keeping your identity close to your chest, you're careful to conceal the sword beneath your cloak whenever you pass through populated areas, and you avoid too many questions about the nature of your travel. But as you draw closer to the mountains, you listen thoughtfully to the tavern gossip, hoping to hear some whisper about the beast's whereabouts or weaknesses. Some morsel of discourse about the king regent. You pick up few conversations of consequence.

Other nights, you camp under the stars, lulled to sleep by the sound of crickets chirping and night owls through the trees. Dragons drift listlessly through your dreams, sometimes made of stars, and sometimes of fire or water. One night, you dream you can see through the eyes of a dragon, and as you soar over lakes and snow-capped mountains, you relish the unbridled freedom before you...your shadow skims the countryside below, so large as to block out the sun and bring night over cities.

It's five days' travel, after all, to the foothills of the western mountains. Mist shrouds the peaks, and an uncanny silence lends a haunting quality to the atmosphere. Your footsteps on the gravel are the only disturbance in the quiet.

The highest summit in the range is that of Mount Arden, which now all but disappears in the descending fog. You're certain that it's there, beneath that skyward mass, that your dragon keeps its quarry. It's there that you must prove your mettle.

To reach the base of Mount Arden, you must weave carefully through narrow crevasses and rocky pathways. Finding your footing on the ever-changing incline is a challenge in itself, but each time your heart begins to doubt whether you've chosen the correct route, your eyes fall upon a cairn—a pile of stones placed precisely and unmistakably by human hands. Whether they're trail markers left behind by other would-be dragon-slayers or tributes to the beast beneath the mountain, you cannot say, but they comfort you, nonetheless. At the very least, they are evidence of another soul who passed this way and chose to memorialize that passage; it makes you feel less alone, as though that unknown wanderer walks beside you.

All the while, your thoughts turn over and over the possibilities that await you. You reflect on the person you were just over a year ago. The modest ambitions you had…the responsibilities that seemed so sacred to you once, and now feel small. Though your dreams have grown dragon's wings, reaching for the grand, sweeping adventure before you, you can't help but ache, just a little, for mornings on the farm. A day of hard work followed by good, home-cooked food and a quiet evening. The company of friends, all in the blush of youth and irreverence. It's such a strange tension, such an unexpected twinge of homesickness, for never before have you held your simple life in any high regard.

Ah, but the promise of palaces. Once again, your heart soars. You'd never dared to dream of such a life. What delights must wait behind closed doors, held only for the elite court? Weren't you born into greatness, only to be spirited away to escape a rebellion? Isn't it the life you deserve? Is it the life you want?

You stumble over the rocks and into the shadow of the afternoon. The day is getting away from you; this final leg of the journey is longer and more meandering than expected. It's as though the lack-adaisical pattern of your musings is reflected in the twists and turns of the path.

But soon, your thoughts are stopped, as before you yawns the mouth of a great and gloomy cave. It's just as you imagined, just as it should look in a storybook. A shiver runs over you, but it's not quite fear you're feeling so much as a frisson of anticipation. Therein lies your fate, should you choose to meet it. You always have a choice.

For a moment, you consider turning back, following the cairns out of the foothills, resting for the night in one of those friendly taverns, and returning to your village to live your life as a farmer. Your parents would be happy to see you safe, and you'd be no worse off. Or perhaps you'll keep walking down the road, find a place to live in the capital, build yourself a whole new life. Perhaps even reveal yourself when the time feels right, ring or no ring. Or—forget everything—you've got enough survival skills to live in the woods. Maybe you'll become a hermit or a mad prophet, doling out advice and fortunes to travelers who stumble through your forests.

But no, you think. If you refuse to answer this call now, then all your life, you'd wonder what would've happened if you earned your crown. Faced your dragon.

There's the shiver again.

At the heart of all this, you realize, is the burning desire, so long kept under wraps, to see a dragon. It's all you've ever wanted. Not thrones or power or wealth. Magic. Proof that there still is some magic in this world, with wings.

And it's with this thought that you step across the threshold of the cave, feeling the instant drop in temperature and the air's moisture rise. It's with this little fire in the pit of your belly that you retrieve a torch and tinderbox from your pack, lighting your way down the dark passage of the cave.

You move carefully through the darkness, your torch rising and falling with your step, throwing its amber light across the walls and floors of the cave. It's as though, you reflect, the dexterity-challenging path through the foothills to the base of the mountains was trying to prepare you for the tests you'd face here, absent the sun's light. You keep your breathing steady, your feet agile, ready for sudden uneven-ness in the ground or unseen obstacles. The torchlight flickers within an intimate radius; beyond it, the unknown. Your mind searches for patterns. Resets when the unseen becomes visible. The slow, deliberate nature of the journey lulls your mind into a calm contentment. There's a subtle decline in the floor; you descend, step by step. Lower and lower, little by little. Your footsteps on the damp stones echo across the cavernous walls. Deeper, you go. Deeper and deeper down.

You might have walked for a mile or more or perhaps descended only a few fathoms. As the resonant silence envelopes you, it's hard to tell time or distance. But at last, there's another change in the atmosphere. The moisture in the air thins, stretches out; there's an earthy scent listing on the air that wasn't there before. Even without seeing it yet, you can sense that the close walls of the cave are becoming more spacious, opening into a vast cavern.

Now, the reservoir of your torchlight falls on something other than slate gray stone; limestone stalagmites materialize before you like great accumulations of melted wax. Stalactites cling to the ceilings; water drips in hollow, musical tones, like tiny mallets striking tiny bells.

And there's another texture, too, in the cavern. The torch casts its amber light on crimson scales, blackened and armorial. Slow, unconscious breath and heaving motion. Your eyes begin to adjust to the darkness in the immense cavern, revealing more and more of the beast as though your light grows in size and throw.

Oh, and a magnificent beast it is! All covered with those black and scarlet scales, leathery wings folded by its side. Its eyes are closed, and its nostrils flare as it breathes heavily, sound asleep. Twisted ivory horns extend from its head. Your heart swells, and your breath catches. The sheer size of the thing is enough to make you lightheaded, but you can't help but find it beautiful. Rapturously so. Curled and coiled… vast as the chamber is, the creature hardly fits within such confines. Why, oh why, would this majestic animal choose such tight quarters for a lair when it could have the world—the skies, the sea, all of it? This place is fit for hoarding treasure but not for living.

But it's funny…scanning the floor beneath the dragon's mammoth figure, searching with your light for the faintest glimmer of gold, you fail to find any trace of treasure. Curious.

And now, tracing your way along its length with a thousand questions rising to your mind, you notice something you hadn't seen before. There around the beast's neck—and yes, on its forelegs and hindlegs too, you see—are thick iron rings connected to thick, rusting chains. A feeling like pity rushes over you, sorrow like water, to see such power and freedom chained up, stifled. Who would, or even could, subdue a dragon so?

The weight of the sword at your hip brings you back to yourself. Perhaps now is the best chance you've got to defeat the dragon. Strike while it sleeps, then find your signet, which must be here somewhere among the dragon's things. Perhaps within its very grasp. Then, signet or no, you could march into the capitol with proof of a slain dragon— and be lauded as a hero by all the subjects of the kingdom.

Summoning all the courage you can, you unsheathe the sword and step into an advantageous position. You take a deep breath and prepare to strike.

But your mind cannot let go of the question: *Who would chain up a dragon within a mountain? And why?* Despite your body's readiness to go ahead with the task, your thoughts will not allow you to bring down the sword. After a few moments—and a battle between head and heart—you relax your shoulders and allow the sword to fall at your side.

At this very moment—perhaps caused by the slashing of the sword through empty air, a ripple of wind, or the subtlest of sounds—an eyelid lifts. The breathing quickens, and soon, the chamber is all alive with coiling and uncoiling movement. Your torch seems to brighten to behold it all as the dragon, awake and inquisitive, unfurls to its full height, gaze intent and fixed on you, small and trembling in its wake. You've gone and woken the dragon, and now your fate must be faced.

Your first instinct, though it might seem foolish, is to kneel. You drop to a knee and avert your gaze from the creature. Then you speak, as you imagine princes or princesses from your storybooks might: infusing your voice with a noble purpose, you state your name, your house, and your intention. For you are heir to the throne of the kingdom, here to recover your birthright and that which was stolen from you.

When there is no response—neither growl nor fire—you dare to lift your head. The dragon, gathered up still like a great mountain itself, is looking down at you with an expression of unmistakable...

curiosity. You hadn't known dragons were capable of such expressiveness, but there it is. There's something so human about it.

You hold your ground and try not to flinch as the beast retracts its great neck, lowering back down onto its forelegs and bringing its face as close to your level as possible. Its head might be the size of the stable house on the farm back home. You feel so minute, so unthreatening—your sword a mere strand of straw against the dragon's full might.

But nothing can prepare you for what comes next—the dragon opens its mouth to speak. And the voice, though it sounds as if it hasn't been used in a century, is clear and distinctly feminine.

"What is it you believe I've stolen?" she asks.

At first, you're too stunned to respond. You can feel her breath, warm on your face and limbs. Observing your shock, she withdraws, curling herself up again, though still watching you expectantly. The chains click and clatter in her wake.

"I can't very well hand it over if you don't tell me what it is you're looking for."

You find your voice again, though now it sounds weak, distant.

"A ring," you say, clearing your throat. "A signet. The symbol of my house and my rightful claim to the throne."

"Can't say I've seen it," she responds with an air of nonchalance. "So, I suppose you'll be on your way."

"But…" you stammer, "it must be here. It was stolen when the old king was put down. You must have it."

"I haven't much," she retorts, angling her head in a gesture toward the emptiness of the cavern. The chains drag along the floor as she shifts. There's so little slack—she can't move very far at all, you realize. You should press her about the ring…but you can't get your mind off it.

"Who did this to you?" you ask, pointing to the chains.

She releases something like a sigh and slouches. "I don't know," she says. "All I know is that someone sends a goat or a sheep in here every so often, so I don't starve. I never see anyone. For all I know, it might be you who did to this me."

"Have you never…have you never left this cave?" you ask. The sadness in her eyes tells you everything you need to know. You feel immense tenderness and pity toward the creature.

Thoughtfully, deliberately, you lay your sword down upon the floor of the cavern. You ask the dragon if she has a name. She does… but it's one she's chosen for herself, so she's not even sure if it is a name or only a sound she remembered from long ago before she was imprisoned here. "Night" is her name. You like it. She begins to warm to you, and you to her.

You learn of Night's long imprisonment and the few happy memories she has of freedom. When she hatched, she was kept by kindly humans, and from them, she learned the art of speech. Though she's had no occasion to practice it with anyone listening, she's spent all this time telling herself stories. They're her only escape from the darkness.

"I was supposed to have a different life," she says. You feel a pang of sympathy. You, too, were robbed of the life you were meant to have. Though there's love and fondness in the one you ended up with. That you can't forget.

You tell Night your story. Your humble upbringing, and the shocking revelation of your true parentage. She listens patiently, seeming to hang on your every word, delighted for any company outside the stalactites. How you ever could have feared her, you don't know. Why anyone would want to imprison her is an even bigger mystery.

If you could see yourself now… you think. The child who dreamt of dragons, now conversing with one like an old friend. There's a warmth and a kinship kindled between you and Night already, a bond that feels, to you, stronger than any you formed with your peers in the village. It's as if the two of you were bound on this path toward each other, as if it were she, and not some figment of a fairytale imagination, who visited you in all those dreams. As if you saw through her eyes when your slumbering spirit took wing.

"This ring," she asks, "what did it look like?"

"I guess I'll know it when I see it. All I know is it bore the seal of my family," you say. "But I never even knew them."

"I'm sure they were good people," says Night. Her voice is disarmingly gentle. *How could anyone see dragons as monstrous?* you wonder. In your eyes, they're miraculous.

The conversation turns to the future. The possibility of your reign. Night jokes that she could simply give you one of her teeth and let you carry it into court—a stunt like that would make all the barons swear fealty to you in an instant. You'd be known as the Dragonslayer in all the history books. You confess it's not a title you've ever craved.

"Do you really wish to rule?" she asks, cutting to the core of your ever-questioning heart. You've struggled, so far, to come up with an answer to this.

"I don't know," you respond. "I've only ever been responsible for myself. A few farm animals. I think I know right from wrong, but I've never had to decide it for an entire kingdom."

Night receives this and looks pensive. Really, so wonderfully expressive, dragons are.

"Can't you break out of those?" you ask, gesturing to her chains, which still preoccupy your mind. "Burn them to ash, or simply break them with brute strength?"

"Alas," Night responds. "No breath of fire have I, after all this time in the cold and damp. Only thick skin, though it grows brittle. Sharp claws, though they are overgrown. And wings, though they've been folded and weakened for many a year."

"I wish I could break your chains with my sword," you say. "I'd set you free in an instant, only so you could see the world. It's a pity to chain up someone with wings. It's a pity to chain up anyone."

In Night's eyes, you see something almost inscrutable—a kind of disbelief mixed with warmhearted gratitude. You doubt she's ever heard a word of sympathy for her plight.

"I think you'd make a good ruler," she says. You feel yourself blush.

Then Night, the mighty, if weakened, dragon unfurls herself, chains scraping against the floor of the cave.

"I kept something from you," she said. "But only because I've kept it secret for so long, and I didn't know if I could trust you."

In unfurling, she brings round her strong, spiked tail to the front of the cavern, where it falls right into the spill of your torchlight. There, sparkling at the end of it, hanging loosely on one of the ivory spikes, is a speck of gold.

"Go on," she says. "Take it."

You reach out, hardly believing it, and carefully remove the gold ring from the spike. It's heavier than it looks—solid gold and finely cast. It glimmers in the firelight. Set on its bezel is a raised image, delicately engraved. You have to squint to make out the minuscule details. A coat of arms. A shield, in which stands a dragon, wings spread, a crown upon its head.

"Is it really?" you ask.

Night explains that she hatched on the same day the old king's heir was born. She's younger than she looks. The ruling family, whose symbol was the regal dragon, intended to raise her as a companion to the heir. Their fates were intertwined, and their lives should grow side-by-side.

But it wasn't meant to be, it seems, for the old king was displaced by a rebellion. Night was captured by the rebels and chained up within a mountain—and the heir was lost. Until now, she'd thought forever. But it turns out the king's child was only spirited away until the day they might return and claim the throne. Luckily, Night held onto the signet, wishing that one day her valiant friend would come looking for it.

All those years you spent believing dragons were only fairy tales, here a dragon believed the same thing about you. Your heart aches for the lost time, but it soars with gratitude at having reunited with a friend you didn't know you were missing. Your eyes sparkle with tears.

You thank the dragon for telling you the truth and for keeping the signet all this time. You ask her what she remembers of your real parents. All she recalls is that they were kind. She was young, then, too. She never knew much of court or kingcraft.

But why, then, you wonder, *did the rebellious forces imprison her so? Why do they still send food into the cave? Why not raise her up to serve the king regent?*

Night knows the answer to the last question. By the time of the coup, she was already fiercely bonded to you. "Nothing can break the bonds of fate," she insists. "Not between hatchlings." You smile, thinking of Night, now, as your sister. Scales and wings and all.

But, she supposes, the king regent must believe that if you were still alive somewhere, someday you'd come looking for your lost ring.

"And if he kept me alive," she muses aloud, "he must have hoped we'd finish each other off in some final confrontation. He always underestimated us both. He didn't know you'd show kindness to a lonely dragon."

You try the ring on, finger by finger. It doesn't fit quite perfectly anywhere. But that doesn't matter.

"What now?" you wonder. Amusingly, you imagine moving into the cave with Night, hunting food for her, sharing your lives as the companions you were supposed to be.

"You'll go to court," she says. "And you'll be great." Her eyes are smiling. "I've done my part."

"We've been separated before," you say. "But I don't think I can do it without you."

Then, a thought occurs to you—an outlandish, far-fetched thought which blooms madly and swiftly into a fantasy.

"Night," you say. "You say you haven't got any strength or fire left. But have you actually tried?"

She cocks her head at an angle, and for a moment, you're reminded of one of the dogs on the farm. It's rather endearing.

But she understands. You're here now. Together, your resolve is so much stronger. There is so much more to fight for. Night gestures with her head for you to climb aboard her back. At first, you step back in surprise. But she insists. Carefully, using her tough scales to maintain your footing, you climb the magnificent dragon and rest at the nape of her neck. You leave your torch behind on the floor of the cave, where it flickers and crackles still.

"I believe in you," you whisper, so quietly you're not sure Night can hear you. You're not sure if you even want her to hear you. But it must be said. You feel her muscles tense as she strains to break the shackles about her legs and neck. You hear the iron groan against her power, resisting but yielding ever so slightly. Night catches her breath and tries again, straining harder.

"It's no use," she says. "They're too tough. I can't break them."

Just breathe, you want to say. But you find you don't need to say it—for at the moment you think it, you feel a soft harmonic pull. Like the tensing of the atmosphere into a taut string—a cord—connecting your mind and the dragon's. You feel her breath synchronize with yours, and it's as though you can see through her eyes, feel the strength and fatigue in her muscles. You're one.

Deep in your belly—her belly—you can feel a kindling heat. It tumbles and roars like a rush of water through the mouth of a cave, building and intensifying until it can no longer be caged. You feel an eruption, a release, an exhale of fire, billowing and beautiful. You feel cleansed from the inside out, and you feel powerful.

The stream of flame melts the links in the chains to molten iron. Night tugs once more at her shackles, and they disappear into liquid and ash. Then she's off and running, lumbering unevenly on feet that haven't traveled in a lifetime. You cling to her scales and hold on for dear life as she moves, thirsty for sunlight and fresh air to breathe. You find yourself laughing, even as you clutch at the dragon's hide.

When you break out of the cave, the clean air floods your lungs with such a sweetness. For you, only hours underground has you gasping for the freshness of it—for Night, decades underground. You squint against the sun's brightness. She must be nearly blinded by it. But she's laughing too—it's all too wonderful.

She topples the cairns in her giddy clumsiness, scraping her claws against rock and cliff. She climbs swiftly, you aboard her back, to the peak of Mount Arden, where the mist has lifted and the skies are effortlessly clear. You can see for miles around. Far off on the horizon, the stone walls surrounding the capital city and the palace.

"Shall we go home, my friend?" Night inquires.

But you're not ready for that just yet. There's a whole world your dragon has never seen. There's a whole sky she has yet to explore.

Taking flight for the first time since her imprisonment, Night cries out with delight to feel the full expanse of her wings. It's such sweet release. You can feel it too, as if she's an extension of you. As if her wings are your wings, her muscles your muscles, and as they unfurl, you grow more spacious. More free.

There's a kingdom beyond the western mountains, waiting for you. But it can wait a little while longer. There are oceans to skim. New foods to taste. Lives to be lived.

You have a choice. You always have a choice. To rule a kingdom? To learn the ways of justice and strive to make the world a better place? Or to live untethered, unfettered, unkempt, and wild? To taste the sweet freedoms of the world, unbothered by the machinations of court?

There's time to decide.

Night soars with sunset on her heels. The wind dances through your hair. You catch a wave. If they do write history books about you, they won't call you the Dragonslayer. They'll call you the Dragon Rider.

Onward. Into the endless sky.

Exercise: Fire Magic for Cleansing the Spirit

Fire is a powerful element—an agent of transformation. Often, we think of its capacity for damage and destruction, but fire can also clear away that which we no longer need. It can be a cleansing and clarifying tool, making room for new growth. With its steady, natural heat, fire is also an engine of creativity, motion, change, and magic. Practice this simple fire ritual when you need to clear your mind, awaken creativity, and find your foundations. Consider performing this ritual seated at your dream altar and/or making it a part of your nightly ritual.

Suggested materials:

Candle (preferably a new candle, never-before-lit)
Matches or lighter

* Begin by delineating your space as sacred in a manner meaningful to you. Darken the space as much as possible.
* Set an intention for your practice. If you need inspiration, consider the following:
  * *I create meaningful change in my community.*
  * *I am free to write my own destiny.*
* Light your candle. Look into the flame and soften your gaze as you observe the flicker and the brilliance of the fire.
* Deepen your breath, allowing it to gather up from deep within.
  Concentrate on the base of your spine—your foundation, your root—as the origin of your breath.
  Feel warmth kindling from your foundation.
* Imagine a ball of energy or a small, constant flame that powers the breath.
  Think of that inner heat, like the flame of the candle before you, as an engine that animates, cleanses, and heals.
* Continue to observe the flicker of the candle flame. Does the color change? What patterns emerge? How does your breath, or any draft or disturbance in the air, change the course of the flame? In the deepest, brightest core of the

flame, what can you see? How quickly does the wax melt? What patterns can you see in the melting wax?

* Breathe deeply and imagine how you might nourish your inner flame—in the way the air feeds the candle's flame.
* Stay here as long as you like, with your focus soft and your mind open to receive whatever messages the fire has for you. If you're working with a small enough candle, let it burn almost all the way down.
* When you're ready, extinguish the flame (feeling the power of your breath again as you blow out the candle).
* Record your experience in a journal, as a stream of consciousness, poetry, or simple notes.
* Close your sacred space.

THE HOLLY KING
& THE OAK KING

The fluting call of a nightingale dances on the warm summer wind. A chorus of crickets joins in, creating a low landscape of symphonic underscore for your evening ride. The sun droops, full and fat and low in the sky, but seems in no hurry to set beyond the distant mountains. A night like this—with excess light and warmth—begs for a long, leisurely ride. Let the home sit vacant and the tea grow cold. Much like the sun, you are in no rush to return.

The evening breeze runs its fingers through your hair and provides only a slight resistance to your horse's canter. The gentle bay mare, Winifred, snorts and saunters through a speckling of poppies, tossing her head with pleasure.

Much of the land that surrounds your home is still a mystery to you—as yet unexplored by you and your Winifred. To the west lie emerald green mountains, which stage glorious pink and orange sunsets most evenings. Just north of your home, according to locals, is an Iron Age hillfort. You've seen it from afar, with thick grooves carved in concentric circles round the hilltop. Locals debate its history—whether it housed the defensive armies of King Arthur in a bygone era or was a seat of resistance to Viking invasions. A local man once told you that the hillfort's defenders buried objects imbued with charms and spells in the earth to ensure it would never be overtaken, even long after they were gone.

Just past the hillfort is a vast, dense woodland, which you've not yet explored. To be honest, you've always sensed that the forest holds something powerful and unknown; it's at once deeply alluring and impenetrably wild. Someday, you're certain, its charm will draw you in.

And to the south, the ruins of a great stone abbey decorate the rolling landscape. Years of abandonment and disrepair leave only desolate archways, broken pilasters, and crumbling foundations; robust grasses, moss, and ivy threaten to reclaim the stone for nature. You visited the abbey once at sunrise, and you marveled at the golden hue held by the green moss in the early morning light, the dew that hung suspended in the air all around, the picturesqueness of the dereliction.

This land hums with history—and you can hear it, feel it, most potently at first light and twilight, when the sweet sun bathes the green mountains, hills, and mosses with a gilded glimmer. At times like these, when the wind sweeps through the grasses, whistling a low song, the whole world feels connected, alive, and attuned to one single spirit. One essence.

Tonight, though the sun persists into the late hour, the scent of wild campion and lavender from beyond the hills wash over you, summery and sweet. The air is warm but mild, succumbing slowly to a cool shade as night creeps across the land, lingering behind you lazily. Indeed, there is no haste about you tonight—the sun, the moon, the wind, the stars, the land, you, your horse…all surrender to the golden impermanence, sliding along each moment like a leaf, dancing upon the wind as it tumbles to the ground.

As Winifred sidles along the grooves in the grassy hillside, your body sways with the rhythm of her gate. Your muscles feel loose, relaxed, and languid. It's as though you move through crystal-clear water. Your eyes slip out of focus for a moment as you let go, but you blink a few times to return to yourself, wondering if you should call it an early night. But as you regain focus, a flash of red and white catches at the corner of your vision.

Yes, there is something, moving across the grass. It's too distant to make out clearly, but there are white forms—animal—ahead. They move without clear direction, and at first, this leaves you confused until you realize…they're playing. One of the forms stops suddenly, standing at attention, and you imagine it must have seen you and Winifred. You slow your pace so as not to intimidate the thing. But after a few moments, it bounds toward you. Then it's followed by two others. You pull back on Winifred's reins and pat her neck gingerly, calming her. She seems undisturbed, which is a good sign. She's always been a strong judge of character and danger.

The first of the white forms bounds into view, and with a smile, you recognize it as a mid-size hound. He bears a wide, infectious smile, his tongue hanging out of one side of his mouth. The dogs are sleek and muscular with short white fur. Their pointed ears, however, are the bright red of the holly berry. The three hounds play and vocalize joyfully; Winifred snorts and shakes her head, showing kinship with the creatures. You've never seen anything like these hounds, but you feel instantly as though they've always been with you. They project astounding warmth and familiarity. You find yourself laughing.

Then the first hound, recognizable by his eyes—one brown, one blue—stops his playful cavorting and utters a cheerful bark. His fellows stand at attention and follow him as he trots off in the direction of the hillfort. Curious, you watch the trio of hounds leave as quickly as they came. You're about to continue your ride, dismissing this as a brief, charming interlude, when you notice the leader stop and turn to you, still smiling. His fellows do the same before all three turn again and scamper north. It's as though they want you to follow them.

You stroke Winifred's mane as if to say, "What do you think, old girl?"

Winifred utters a snort and, before you can even give your signal, begins to walk in the footsteps of the dogs. *Very well, then*, you think. Tonight, under the waning warmth of the setting sun, you'll let the animals be your guide.

By the time the hillfort comes into view, large and looming over the grassy scene, the sun is surrendering to night's advances. It's still light enough to see clearly, but a translucent plum pall has fallen over the land. The air is cooler than before and rich with the campion musk. The sound of swift wingbeats overhead signals the night flight of a corncrake or nightjar. Somewhere, insects are humming beneath blades of grass.

The hounds move apace, checking every so often to ensure you still follow. Deep shadows accentuate the grooves in the hill's earth that endure from the Iron Age. Strange to think how long ago they were dug; you wonder if the diggers, defenders of the hill, considered how long the fort would stand after their absence. The world is very, very old, you think—and yet, it bursts forth with things anew each day. All is alive and in constant motion under the endless waltz of planets, moons, and stars.

For a while, you think the dogs must be leading you to the hillfort; perhaps they've dug up some forgotten treasures of a lost civilization. And it wouldn't be a bad place to watch the final wisps of sunset on this long-lasting day. But to your surprise, they lead you past and around its girth toward the wood.

At last, you think. You'll stumble at last into the unknown forest at the behest of these strange guides. Seems fitting. You approach the treeline, and sensing Winifred's weariness, tug gently on her reins to signal that she can take her time. You are, after all, a bit wary of stepping into the wood just as night falls.

But the hounds sally forth, unafraid. The lead dog stops to look at you and barks jovially. If you're not mistaken, he even jerks his head as if to beckon you onward. These are more than average beasts, you wager.

You spare a moment to look back toward home. You've ridden a considerable distance, but you can see puffs of smoke from various chimneys beyond the slope of the earth. Your neighbors are surely enjoying their tea or reading, soaking up the last rays of the sun's lingering presence. To the southeast, a pale pink moon already floats in the darkening sky. A sigh issues, almost involuntarily, from your lips. You feel a sense of deep surrender, as though you might, like a fallen leaf, let the wind sweep you onward toward whatever your destiny holds.

So on you ride. Into the wood.

Your concerns about the lack of light beyond the treeline are immediately allayed when, to your astonishment, you notice that the white fur of the hounds carries a sheer luminescence. They glow like moonlight, just enough to light the path a few feet ahead. Winifred keeps pace with them; her hooves land in the gentle spill of light which dances through the emerald darkness like a fluttering moth.

In local legends, woods and natural spaces like this are often inhabited by fairies and elves. You wonder now how much those stories of enchantment originated with travelers who spotted these glowing canines from a distance on a dim night. But then again, you reflect...there's nothing so natural about these hounds, is there? They might be spirits or harbingers, escorting you to the land of faery.

The hounds lead you deeper into the heart of the forest. From somewhere in the trees, a night thrush twitters. Pale light splashes against a bevy of arbors. Mighty oak trees ribbed with ivy. Alder trees with ghost-white bark. The path, if you can call it such, twists and turns, but your guides seem to know the way. Something calls you onward in their footsteps.

Soon, the darkness dissipates, and the dogs lose their luster as you perceive a light source ahead. You, the hounds, and Winifred step forward into a vast clearing. The sight is dizzyingly picturesque. Golden fireflies sparkle across your line of vision, dancing amid what must be a stone circle. The stones, of various heights, are overgrown with moss and vines, protruding like natural growths from the grass. Primroses and toadstools speckle the ground as though they were painted there by an unseen artist. A full Strawberry Moon bathes the glade in its rosy glow. It all seems at once carelessly wild and impeccably placed. You watch the hounds prance into and among the stones, resuming their play. It would seem you've reached the place they intended to bring you—and indeed it seems like a gateway to another world.

You dismount Winifred and stroke her neck; she gives you a friendly nuzzle. You're comforted by her apparent lack of apprehension. Giving her an assuring pat on the nose, you move toward the stone circle to investigate further.

The largest stone, which stands directly across from where you entered the clearing, is wildly overgrown. It's of an unusual shape, as well. Where many of the others stand straight, narrow, and monolithic, this one has a high point and a lower level with greater width. The lead hound follows you over to it and noses some of the ivy that lies across its width. Something about it compels you to stare fixedly, unblinking, as though you might miss a clue if you look away.

And also...

Somewhere, under the vegetation and vines, in the gaps that allow you to see the stone material, there's a pattern. Something hand-hewn or carved into the head of the bluestone, right at your eye level. Hesitating for just a moment, you reach a hand out to tug at the ivy. With a few minutes' work, you pull away enough vines and scrape away enough moss to reveal something marvelous. Carved into the stone is a human face. Smiling and joyful, its features resemble those of Father Christmas or Yuletide spirits. He's old and wrinkled, but his eyes are smiling too. You pull away more greenery to reveal more around the face. Adorning his brow are carvings of a crown made of holly leaves and berries. Carved pinecones and spruce needles are strewn through his long hair.

More and more vines and moss come away under your hands, down to the shoulders, about which you reveal a robe carved to look like rich fabrics and furs. Now it occurs to you that the odd shape of the stone resembles a chair. A throne, more likely. You tug away at the vines to uncover the figure's right hand, in which he bears a goblet carved to look like it's encrusted with rich jewels. You scrape at the moss to expose the length of the figure's fine stone robes. Then you uncover his left hand, empty, but clasped in a gesture that makes your heart leap. With one rigid stone finger, the figure points straight ahead.

It's now that you notice the lead hound has vanished. You rotate slowly to face the direction of the figure's gesture—the opposite side of the stone circle. The hound is there, sitting dutifully beside another large, oddly shaped stone directly across from your carved, holly-crowned man. Your heart flutters. Something very strange, surely magical, is afoot. You glance at Winifred, who grazes peacefully.

It seems you already know what to do as you make your way across the circle, feet falling between primroses on the soft, moon-washed grass. You make short work of uncovering the counter stone. Just as expected, another carved figure lies beneath the greenery, seated on his bluestone dais. But unlike the holly man, this figure's face, though human-esque, looks more like that of a tree with human features. His eyebrows, whiskers, hair, and beard are a tangle of carved oak leaves and twisted branches, which sweep upward and outward from the center of his face. A few acorns stick out from the twists of his beard. He too smiles with a frozen twinkle, but you think you detect an expression of sadness or longing behind his stone eyes. His robes seem hewn from rough tree bark.

You take a moment to marvel at the sheer craft of the carver—for the style between the two is so similar they must have been made by the same hand. The realistic, intricate detail is ages beyond that of the rudimentary stoneworkers who might have inhabited the hillfort. But the circle feels immeasurably ancient. By whose ingenious hand did these exquisite artworks take shape? And why were they placed here in such a remote, untraveled place, left to be overgrown and obscured, with no passersby to behold their beauty?

You begin to feel a prickle at the back of your neck and a strange tension in the air with both figures now uncovered, as though the atmosphere is made up of vibrating threads, each with little hooks upon their ends, stretching the night taut across the summer moon. The lead hound pads to your side and rubs his head against the inside of your palm. You respond by patting him gently, your hand moving against the tension in the air.

Looking from one stone figure to another, you have the distinct impression that their gazes are locked. Another magnificent feat by the artist: these monumental men hold eye contact across the ages.

With a low utterance and a nudge, the hound seems to be ushering you toward the outside of the circle where his fellows stand together. You've placed your trust in them so far, you think, and you follow the hound back toward where Winifred rests.

You notice all three of the hounds' red ears perk up suddenly. A moment later, you hear something, too. The sound of cracking, breaking, shifting rock. What happens next leaves you nothing short of awestruck. The pale pink moonlight seems to effuse more brilliantly as the two figures—one decked in holly, the other in oak—begin to move. Bluestone splits, pried apart by shining light as the two towering men emerge from stone like a fragile shell, each in full, resplendent color and texture.

The holly man, whose face you were first moved to uncover, is bright and saturated, face pink and plump with ruddy cheeks and sparkling golden eyes. His long hair and beard are white as the sparkling snow, making the brilliant green and vibrant red of the holly at his brow even more dazzling to look upon. His robes are lush fabric, trimmed with furs, and threaded with spirals of gold. The cup in his right hand gleams a burnished copper, and wine splashes from its rim. At the crown of his head, you marvel to see a halo of white candles topped with living flame.

Simultaneously, the oak man bursts from his stone seal, green and brown, and all the colors of the earth. He is all twisting, coiling ringlets of tree and vine, leaf and fruit. About his face, the oak leaves blend seamlessly with butterflies and Luna moths. His legs are trunks twisted about with ivy and datura, mossy at the ends and gloriously alive. From his head grow the antlers of a great and mighty stag, and wisteria falls lazy from the antlers. His ribs are not so knit, and where his heart might be, in that open, rooted cavern, you can see a small, suspended crystal—glowing, gleaming.

They are wondrous; strange and beautiful. The night is scented with unidentifiable flowers and spices, mingling in such incongruous but appetizing mélange. Perhaps cinnamon and marigold. Juniper and violet. Sparkling berry and apple blossom.

The two kings rise, together, from their thrones; their movement is slow and deliberate. So slow, in fact, that they seem to move against the arrow of time. The fireflies, winds, and birds of the glade move faster the further away they are from these two magnetic centers. You can perceive halos, rings of moving light encircling the full monument. Nights and days and nights pass perhaps, before your eyes. Or is it an illusion?

The kings—one of holly, one of oak—travel clockwise round the inner edge of the stone circle, keeping equidistant from each other in their careful movements. The earth groans under the weight of their footsteps. They seem to have grown to the size of giants—or gods.

Now they stand facing one another again, having shifted a quarter way across the inside of the circle, moving along its edges like a wheel of time. On the night wind, you can hear the tiny palpitations of the moths and butterflies, the crackle of the flame atop the candled crown.

The Oak King raises his right arm, and in from his open palm grows the oaken handle of a great axe, its blade formed from the ether of shining green-hued steel.

The Holly King holds his cup aloft, and where there was wine, now blue and white flames erupt and crackle.

The tension burns behind the eyes of the rivals. They awaken, you realize, to do battle. You sense—and perhaps the back of your wonderstruck mind kindles a legend you once heard—that this has happened before. That this happens over and over. Or that it is always happening. As the earth turns along the Wheel of the Year, its spirits wrestle for dominion, fertilizing and decaying.

The Oak King raises his axe, but he does not try to land a blow against his opponent. Instead, he drives the blade into the earth. From the wound erupts a thousand birds and butterflies, a rush of wings catching the glitter of moonlight. The winged army rises against the

Holly King, but as they cross an invisible equator at the center of the circle, they instantly turn to flurries of snow that catch upon the breeze and dance through the night air.

The Holly King returns the advance, drawing a deep inhale and blowing from his lips a blast of blue and white frost, sparkling in spirals toward the Oak King. The frost lands upon the Oak King's shoulders, face, and branches, resting there like a coating of sugar for just a moment before melting into him. The two kings smile; *this is an old ritual*, you think. It's more game than battle. Perhaps they sit in stasis for the better part of the year, clad in bluestone, imagining what tricks they'll play on their nemesis at the next meeting. The next rematch.

The battle carries on, each king making more and more marvelous advances, calling the elements against each other. From your vantage point, protected by the trio of hounds, you feel only the slightest chill when the Holly King strikes. Only the lightest breeze when the Oak King parries. The night is alight with awesome sights and sounds and smells.

Winifred blows air against your shoulder. You cradle her head in the crook of your elbow, grateful for the presence of your dear friend as you witness such mysteries.

As the moon climbs to its peak and midnight falls on the glade, something shifts in the battle. A new slowness sinks in. The candle flames adorning the Holly King burn brighter than ever. But the glowing crystal at the heart of the Oak King seems poised to dim or even burn out completely. Now you understand.

The Oak King rules the earth for a time each year. He cultivates the land, deposits minerals in the soil, brings riches and fruits to the limbs of trees. He is the warmth on your cheek on a summer evening. He is the reluctance of the sun to set on a night like tonight. He sows, and his brother, his rival, the Holly King, reaps.

Bearing the sad, mournful smile you saw in the stone, the Oak King slowly kneels with the sound of yawning branches. He lowers his head. He holds out the axe. The Holly King takes the weapon in his free hand; he does not strike but rather affixes the axe to a belt around his middle. He cups the Oak King's face in his hand. At the touch, the Oak King's branches seem to shrivel. His leaves turn red and yellow and orange and brown and drop suddenly. He grows old before your eyes. Then, with patience and pity, the Holly King watches his rival stand and cross the circle to take his seat—the Oak King sits in the throne where you first uncovered the Holly King. The light of the crystal at his core goes out…but the same sad smile rests upon his lips as he returns to stone.

The Holly King, triumphant, surveys his kingdom. He will let his brother's labors unfold for a few months more. Trees and grasses will green, for now; and some will stay green through the winter, too. Creatures will have time to gather their stores before they must find warmth and shelter. The water will flow freely for a bit longer, before the first frost. There's tenderness in the Holly King's role, you think. He guides the earth toward the inevitable winter. He softens and prepares it for the chill, the freeze, the decay, which must occur, each and every year, for the earth to be reborn.

The Oak King sows and the Holly King reaps, preparing the earth for a time of cold and darkness.

Seemingly satisfied, the Holly King, too, moves toward a throne— the one originally occupied by his rival. A mighty axe at his hip, a crown of holly at his brow, and a cup of flames in his hand, he looks powerful, grand, and benevolent. He takes his seat, and like his brother, returns to stone.

It's a long time before you can move; you hold the two kings in a dazzling afterimage before your eyes for many moments. Your limbs feel almost like crackling stone as you finally shift in place.

Something has shifted in the night. The tension in the atmosphere is gone, no more little hooks in the blank spaces of the evening. Looking upward, you notice that the moon has shed its strawberry veil for a corn-hued glow. Then, glancing around for your guides, you realize that the three white hounds have gone. You and Winifred are alone in the forest clearing. Where the lead hound last stood, there's now a brightly lit lantern on the grass. Stranger still, when you look back to the opposing thrones in the circle, both are once again overgrown with thick moss and vines.

Dazed, you gather up the lantern and mount Winifred once more. She remembers the way through the forest. The lantern casts more than enough light to illuminate your path. You retrace your winding steps through the wilds and finally emerge from the wood. The yellow moon is immense atop the hillfort.

Winifred bears you home. She's earned a reward, surely, and you feed her plump, ripe apples from the tree outside your door before leading her to the stable.

Later, as you lie in bed under a light blanket, enjoying the fragrant breeze from your open window, you can almost feel the earth turning beneath you. You close your eyes and allow your muscles to relax, to surrender to the earth and the arrow of time.

Somewhere in the distance, the moon casts its amber glow on the ruins of a great abbey. Moonbeams fall through a preserved rose window of delicate stained glass, throwing splashes of pale color onto grass and stone.

Deep under the earth of an Iron Age settlement, stone tablets and earthenware, carved with arcane symbols, pulse with ancient protective magic.

And in the heart of an emerald forest, a circle of standing stones languishes under ages of growth and greenery, guarded by crimson-eared heralds. The earth turns and the old gods battle for their thrones. Trees flower. Leaves quake and consider surrendering to the seductive pull of gravity.

Exercise: Ritual Walk for Summer Solstice

Growing up, my dad would often take my sister and me on what we called "nature walks." Considering we grew up in the downtown neighborhood of Austin, Texas, "nature" was sometimes a minor player in these adventures. But, even in a major city, there were always parks, preserves, and hidden trails to discover. Our nature walks kindled my connection to the natural world and deepened my intuition. It's a practice I've maintained all my life: seeking wild spaces, moving through space without urgency or predetermined destination, and observing nature (even in urban settings) with openness and curiosity.

I especially love to take long, contemplative walks near the summer and winter solstices. There's such a special feeling in the air on those days when the light and energy are poised at the edge of a powerful shift. The portals to new seasons.

Practice this mindful walk on or near the summer solstice (or Litha) in any place that sparks curiosity within you—and where you can feel the immediacy of the natural world. During your walk, intentionally observe your surroundings, looking for ways in which the earth signals the changing of the seasons and the turn toward the darker half of the year. Try to keep your phone on silent, avoiding the distractions of our busy modern world. Allow this walk, though active, to be a practice of rest.

Consider performing any or all of the following actions during your adventure:

* Notice how the ground feels under your feet. How does this change when you walk on different surfaces (grass, gravel, soil, cement)? What thresholds, natural or humanmade, are present?
* Notice plant life—especially that which is in transition. New growth, dying flowers, or changing trees.
* Spend some time sitting beneath a tree. Touch or talk to the tree, if you like.
* If you arrive at a forking path, allow your intuition to guide the choice you make.
* Observe local wildlife—birds, squirrels, rabbits, insects…What behaviors do you notice? What sounds? Do they notice you?
* Retrace your steps. Notice how different a space may look or feel from another perspective.
* Imagine who else may have walked this path today, this week, this year…or many, many years ago. Imagine their story.
* Consider the history of your land. What do the place names, street signs, or other indicators tell you of this history? Who are the Indigenous inhabitants of this place? Does this land have a history of war or violence? How can you honor this history today, even in a small way?
* Narrate your walk in your mind. Imagine how you might tell the story of this walk to a listener. Think of this simple walk—and every interaction you have with nature—as important.

When you return home, reflect on your experience, and if moved, record your reflections in a journal.

You can adapt this meditative walk to suit any point in the Wheel of the Year. Walk with intention, intuition, and inquisition. Notice the time of year, connect to the spirits of the land, and offer gratitude to the spaces and thresholds through which you move.

8

DREAMS OF THE BLUE LOTUS

Hints of sweet jasmine and citrus whisper on the warm breeze. Through the trees and low-lying vegetation wakes a symphony of sound: the rustle of ferns and leaves, the chirrup of a quetzal, and the hum of dragonflies. All woven through like a tapestry by the gentle wind and the murmur of the river.

The wooden raft floats gently down the narrow river; you gingerly navigate with a smooth pole to avoid running aground of the bank, so thick with mud and vegetation. *Every inch of this forest is alive*, you think. From the rich soil to the leaves of the canopy. Beneath the raft, in the lazily running water, swim blue and yellow fish. They draw your eye each time they flash near the surface, dazzling and colorful.

You've come from far away, and you have farther still to go before you reach your destination—if indeed the place exists. For generations, it's lived only as an ideal—a figment in the minds of storytellers and audiences gathered round the fire in the cold, dark night. A promise of hope and restoration.

Your home, the legends say, was once a flourishing oasis. Verdant and abundant with food and water enough for everyone. Wherever you stood, you could close your eyes, reach up, and pluck a ripe fruit from a tree. The people lived in harmony with the land and all its diverse flora and fauna. The birds in the trees, the fish in the stream, even the tigers that roamed the land. It was a paradise. Until the last blue lotus died.

It was the blue lotus that sustained this haven, made its waters safe to drink, and its trees plentiful with fruit. It once grew wild in your homeland—the river at night would shine like a blanket of stars with its blue luminescence. The lotus had the power to heal, rejuvenate, and strengthen not only the land itself but the people and animals living there. An herbal tea made from its leaves could lengthen life and youth. A salve made from the oils of its petals could quicken the healing of wounds. Its root could purify toxins.

But such magic never lasts, the storytellers say, because of the greed of mankind. Over time, your people harvested the blue lotus more quickly than it could regenerate. People simply longed to look young or hoard the healing benefits for themselves. Long before you were ever born, the last blue lotus withered on the surface of the dwindling river, and the plentiful trees withered with it. The birds migrated, and the tigers moved on. The soil, once rich enough to bear many crops, became dusty and infertile. Soon, the river was only a trickle.

Now the land, once a paradise, is mostly dry and barren. Your people remained only because of a prophecy: that one day, someone would restore the blue lotus and make your home prosperous again.

Each year, however, the river floods. It brings fish and mineral deposits to the banks, and for a short season, the soil is rich enough to till. There's enough—just enough—for your people to survive, though they wait patiently for the permanent return of the vibrant oasis, telling tales of the prophesied hero. You always tried to picture them—the savior who would bring back the magic flower. Their face never quite materialized in your mind, but it was like you could see them in silhouette or through rippled glass, their specific features moldable, changeable, rearranging like a reflection in the river when the tide is high.

Each year, just before the river is expected to flow fast and deep once more, the whole village gathers to make offerings to the land. At this festival, they choose a hero: someone to try their hand at fulfilling the prophecy and restoring the land. Dressed in the finest garments, fed with the best of the year's salvaged food, and readied with traveler's tools, this hero prepares to ride down the flowing river in search of a land where the blue lotus still grows. In all the years of your life, despite the hopes and prayers of your people, no hero has ever returned with the blue lotus in hand. Nevertheless, every year, the tradition continues.

This year, you are the hero chosen to undertake the quest. You were robed in fine linen and presented with a meager yet heartfelt feast of preserved foods from the fertile season. You were anointed with oils to bless your journey. A raft was made for you by a gifted craftsman. The local wise woman, in a cloud of incense smoke, whispered prayers for your success. The whole village danced round a fire in the cold desert night to honor you and send you off splendidly.

You've never thought of yourself as a hero. Only as part of a whole—part of your community. To be singled out thus and given special attention was so far from your usual experience that you now truly cherish the solitude of your raft on the river. It's given you time to think, time to recharge after the overwhelming celebration.

There's no map for an adventure such as this. Though you know, to an extent, what kind of terrain you'll face, for those who've undertaken the journey before have told you a little about their experiences. They've remained tight-lipped, however, about their reasons for returning home empty-handed. *Is it guilt?* you wonder. How will your journey be different?

The river flows north and downhill from home—you were told of this forest, which sings day and night in manifold voices. "Keep your wits sharp," the others said, "for you'll see things you never dreamt of between those trees. The forest itself plays tricks."

Aside from your minimal efforts to steer away from the risen banks, you are little more than a piece of driftwood, surrendering to the directional flow of the river. The raft, steady enough and finely built, bobs evenly on the moving water. From time to time, you catch yourself nodding into an almost trancelike state, eyes slipping out of focus with the hypnotic sway of the vessel.

You come back to yourself each time, like a ball tossed into the air, returning to the hand that tossed it. For a moment, you float into a sensation of weightlessness, selflessness, dissolution from the body... then you float back down, reclaiming the stability and security of your physical self. Up you rise. Out you flow. Down you sink. Up. And out. And down. The weightless sensation is pleasant, liberating. It's tempting to let yourself glide on the breeze, up through the canopy, and into the night sky beyond your body. But each time you slip into that reverie, you feel the familiar, safe tug of your body beneath you, pulling you back, keeping you close.

The river widens, and your raft catches a regular current. The vegetation is so thick in this part of the forest as to nearly obscure the light of day, though threads of it still squeeze through tiny partings in the leafy overgrowth. What light makes it to you is enough to reveal the striking colors of the flowering plants: the vibrant flush of the heliconia and buttery yellow blooms of plumeria, all against the thousand shades of green—oh, such green as you've never seen in your homeland. Green and wet, pooling with water that seems to trickle from all directions, up and down and sideways, pooling on the caved surfaces of fronds and sinking into the soil.

Why can't we just live here? you find yourself wondering. *Perhaps the oasis didn't dry up so much as drift down the river...*Like you're doing now. Your thoughts meander and coalesce into an image of a floating island, green and alive with flowers and birds...simply gliding across a desert like a mirage. Or floating atop a cloud like a dream or a melody.

But a place like this isn't meant for human interference. It is unutterably wild, its vines and leaves growing without interruption, its trees inhabited by innumerable species. Even now, tossed along the river on your raft, only exerting the faintest touch against the water and the riverbank, you feel yourself an intruder in the exquisitely untamed jungle.

Night follows swiftly behind you. You departed in the early hours of morning when it was still mostly dark and only the faintest glimmer of pink dawn disturbed a peaceful azure sky. You wonder how many leagues you've traveled—how much further till you reach the land where the blue lotus still blooms.

Those who came before you, seeking the mythical flower, told you to be on your guard when night falls, for the forest comes alive at night. As you float downstream, you find it hard to believe that this place could come more alive than it is at present. The undercurrent of sound and song, the constant movement of water and wind, the ever-present sense that everything around you is actively growing, reaching. But as darkness comes on—and thankfully, the vegetation thins overhead to allow in shafts of moon and starlight—you begin to understand what they meant.

The sounds of insects and owls are no more a distant fugue but a concert close at hand. The noises melt into a kind of unified hum, which washes pleasantly over you, rising and falling in irregular patterns. All around you, night-blooming flowers unfurl their petals before your eyes, yellow and pink and blue, seeming to generate their own hazy light—or perhaps absorbing and reflecting the opal moonlight. And from those supple-leafed flowers come a network of fragrances: earthy musk, exotic spice, and narcotic amber. Intoxicating, all. Your head swims, your muscles relax, and your eyelids droop. You once again drift toward a trancelike state, but this time, you feel yourself collapsing inward as though sinking deep into the center of the earth rather than buoyantly floating upward. Lulled by the gently bobbing raft on the river and softened by the union of sound and aroma, you feel yourself completely relax. Settling deep within yourself.

Still, you endeavor to keep your senses awake should you meet a bend or a fork in the river. You expect a divergence soon, for those previous adventurers warned you that you would reach it in the early hours of night.

On you drift, mind and body soft, reclined on the surface of the raft. Somewhere, a night heron buzzes and calls through the trees. Aided by moonlight where the canopy briefly opens, you think you can see the fork in the river ahead. You stiffen and clutch the pole you've been using to steer. Sitting forward now, you squint to better make out the path ahead.

There in the middle of the river's widening berth, something—a tree, certainly—is protruding straight out of the water. It's tall, certainly, but the most extraordinary thing about it is its color. Its color and…something else, hard to put your finger on from a distance. As far as you can see, the tree is a glowing, phosphorescent blue. A pulsing, gleaming cerulean. It's as though the very trunk of the strikingly blue tree has a heartbeat. As you draw nearer, angling your steering pole to slow the raft and give you time to avoid colliding with it, the tree seems to shift and rise and fall gently like waves. Like breath. That's what has you so mesmerized. The tree—just like everything in this forest, everything that's so miraculously alive—seems to breathe. In and out.

Without effort, without any thought of it, you feel your breath naturally synchronizing itself to the slow, deliberate undulation of the tree. Slowly in. And slowly out. Your breath slows and deepens to meet the pattern. With each deep inhale, you take in more of that hypnotic fragrance. With each deep exhale, you feel your muscles relax. Indeed, the breathing, luminescent tree must mark the fork in the river; this may be the very choice that determines whether you find the land of the blue lotus. Have so many before you come home empty-handed simply because they chose the wrong path at this juncture?

No, says a lazy, yet clear voice, echoing from somewhere inside your dizzy, tranquil mind. *It wasn't because they chose wrong. It was because they* chose.

You loosen your grip on the pole and rest it beside you on the raft. Your breath and heartbeat are steady, still slow and deep and harmonizing with the oscillation of the glowing tree. You drift toward it, straight on—but there, now, the raft is listing left. Ever so slightly and then definitively. The river, constant and confident, is choosing for you. All you need to do is surrender to it. Trust it. A feeling of lightness and liberation; sweet relief, too, as the raft corrects against the current and narrowly slides to the left fork.

The rush of water brings you within arm's reach of the breathing tree, and at last, you can see the source of its fluid flutter, its supernal hue. From root to branch, the tree is covered round with blue morpho butterflies, twitching and shifting in a smooth, rising-and-falling motion. It's not one organism but many, moving as one.

And as you float by, the butterflies notice and take wing. A thousand of them or more, at once launching from the trunk of their home tree and swirling, fluttering through the open forest. They carry their blue incandescence over the surface of the river, lighting it up. They circle around you and your raft, their gentle wingbeats kicking up a wind on your face. One alone wouldn't so much as disturb the air, but together they simulate a fierce gale. And then, leaving only traces of their light and flutter behind, they disappear into the dark between the trees. For a few moments, you hold the sight of them in your mind, but soon, you're left to question whether they were ever there at all.

The forest thickens, sealing out the moonlight. Fireflies blink here and there, providing brief glimpses of patches of shrubbery. But your eyes savor the darkness, and your other senses awaken.

As the night ages and curlews whistle their tremulous calls, your tributary narrows. You become alert once more and agile with the staff. The river is just wide enough for your raft to move through without scraping the banks—but only with nimble steering and care. Reeds tickle your shoulders and the sides of your face. There's more visibility now; moonlight streams downward in a milky cascade, splashing against the water.

You lean over the front of the raft, thinking to take a drink of the cool water. In the wash of moonglow, you can see your reflection, dimpled by the river's rippling. You look changed somehow. You can't quite describe it. But there, in the lines of your face, the curve of your mouth—it's you, no doubt. But this face has echoes of the legendary hero you see in your mind whenever you hear tales round the fireside. This face is closer to that face.

You cup your hands and take a drink. The water is cold and soothes your dry throat. When you look once more on the surface of the river, your reflection is once again the face you've always known, rippled and moonlit. The river bends sharply now; you lean strongly to one side to stay afloat but the raft hardly wavers.

Somewhere above the woven threads of night birdsong and insects floats another sound, perhaps created of the intricate harmonics of all the other sounds of night, or perhaps its own individual sound. A high tone, like music or…no, not like music at all. As your ears search for it, attempt to isolate it, it slips away, only to return atop the breeze when you let it go. Finally, you stop trying to hear it, and simply let it wash over you, harmonize with your tranquil state of mind and the languid, lolling raft.

And as you turn the twisting bend, the forest of reeds abates, revealing soft grasses and moss-covered stones. The river narrows suddenly, so the sides of your raft scrape the banks. Soon, the channel tapers all the way to a tiny stream, and the raft, at last, runs aground. Your body, accustomed to the hours of constant, flowing motion, takes some time to adjust. It's as if you can still feel yourself swept along an invisible current. Beneath the raft, a trickle runs into the tall grasses ahead.

You sit for a few moments, somewhat stunned. None of the ones who came before you ever described something like this—the river coming abruptly to an end. Should you stay in the raft? Wait for a sign? Or should you leave the raft and the river behind, take to the jungle on foot?

There's something through the trees ahead. Something that gleams. Your mind flicks back to the tree covered in iridescent blue butterflies. And indeed, whatever light emanating from between the branches is of a similar quality to the light of those winged creatures. A similar blue, too, pulsing with soft luminosity. This is your sign to get up from the raft.

You move slowly, allowing your legs to acclimate to solid ground again. The grasses collapse beneath your feet; the soil is spongy and pillowy. You follow the trickle of stream toward the radiant blue light. The closer you get, the more it seems to shrink—from a nebulous cloud of blue incandescence to a concentrated sphere.

You climb cautiously over the exposed roots of a walking tree, clinging to its trunk for stability. Then you step through a tangle of limbs, and you find yourself in a moonlit glade. It's surprising, at first, to see so much sky—your eyes are drawn naturally upward to drink in its light. Oh, how many stars there are! How bright the moon is, waning just short of full tonight. But there are two skies here in this clearing, for a great and glassy pool below reflects the moon and stars, adding its own glittering essence to their beauty.

You're so captivated by the dual skies—their infinite dazzling allure—that you forget, for a moment, why you came this way at all. Until, that is, at the corner of your eye, a blue-white orb shimmers. You turn your head to see it, but then—it's gone. No, not gone. It's only moved—hopped or flown—out of your line of sight. You scan for it once more, and this time, you see it leap—from the branch of a distant tree to a closer one. Fixing your gaze upon it, you realize the little glowing orb is moving closer to you with every jump. Until it lands, at last for good, on a twisted vine that encircles a rubber tree just before you.

You blink against its brilliant blue glow, shielding your eyes to try to take in more detail. You're unsure whether your eyes adjust or the glow actually dims, but whatever the case, you can now see the organism to which you were drawn. You'd thought it might be another blue morpho, but it's not so.

No, clinging to the twisted vine is no butterfly but a little frog. Its shiny skin is a rich, iridescent blue dappled with amorphous black spots. It's so small, so dazzlingly blue that it looks like a tiny gemstone fixed to the tree. Its moist black eyes seem focused on you. You return the concentrated, curious gaze.

Then, though you don't know what compels you to do it, you utter a simple, "Hello?"

The frog's throat pulses, and it angles its head.

"You again?" the frog says.

You're taken aback. Certainly, when you embarked on your journey down the river, you hadn't expected to meet a talking frog at the end of it. You merely blink, mouth agape. Then you process what it was the frog said.

"Me again?" you reply. "But I haven't…"

"Oh, you have," the frog says. Its voice is calm and confident; the mysterious, not-quite-masculine-nor-feminine tone makes you think of the wise woman back home. "Every year, at this same moon, you come this way."

"Oh, but that wasn't me, you see." You're beginning to understand. "Others like me, yes, have come down the river before. For generations."

Maybe, you suppose, the frog can't distinguish between you and the others, dressed in similar linens, driving similar rafts. But why did none of them tell you of the strange creature at river's end?

"You seek the blue lotus?" the frog says, expectantly.

"I seek the lotus. Yes," you respond, mustering a tone of assurance. "Can you take me to it? Or tell me—is there a land where the blue lotus still grows?"

The frog is silent for a moment. You watch intently as it leaps from the rubber vine to the mossy surface of a boulder. Here it can look more directly upon you, into your eyes.

"Why do you seek the lotus?" the frog asks. The question hangs in the warm night air, seeming to twist on the breeze.

"To restore my land to its former vitality," you say. "To enrich the soils, bring back the birds, and let the river flow freely all the year round. To heal the sick and protect the aging."

"That's what you always say," the frog says. It still believes you and all your predecessors are one persistent pilgrim. This time, you decline to correct the frog; what difference would it make?

"I've come a long way," you say. "Please, do you know where I can find the blue lotus?"

The frog does not reply—at least not in words. In a blaze of blue, it leaps across your eye line. A magnificent leap that defies belief, out across the still and silent pool of water. You watch the arc of its jump as if in slow motion, how it bolts across the sky and delicately falls toward the water. But when it breaks the surface of the pool, you hear no splashing or crashing. No, only a kind of humming, high tone—that sound you could never quite isolate. It now subsumes all the other sounds of the jungle, falling on your ears like the sweetest song.

And there on the surface of the pool where the frog landed, a flare of blue light. Like fire, almost, the way it leaps upward and unfolds. No, not like fire at all. It's as if the very surface of the pool has been made solid and peeled back in layers. In petals. There, unfurling slowly in the center of the water is a gleaming blue lily flower. A lotus. You feel a tremendous exhale escape your lips—a sigh of wonder and awe. That streaming note—that hum—is issuing, you realize, from the center of the lotus.

And before you have time to think, to consider—you've leapt into the water yourself. It's not so deep; you feel your feet graze the silty bottom before you start to swim toward the center. And it's not quite cold either, not like the river through the forest. Your heart beats an elated rhythm. To think that you, after generations of others who've taken on this quest, generations of rituals and prayers, you will be the one to achieve the lotus and bring it home to your people. The tears of joy they'll cry! The admiration with which they'll shower you. Already you can see, smell, and hear the land coming back to life. The birds singing once more in the flowering trees. The tigers prowling, purring. The river, running wild. All of it alive and vibrant with blue lotuses!

Now you're nearing the breathtaking blue flower at the center of the pool. Your eyes drink of its dazzling hue. You feel warmth radiating from it like a low flame. It's so beautiful, so luminous, you almost can't bear to look upon it. But then, neither can you bear to look away. And the closer you come to it, the more the light from the lotus and the frequency of sound seem to expand, intensify, until the sound and the light envelope you.

You can see that, like before, when you floated past the tree enfolded by blue butterflies, the lotus dilates and contracts, making it appear to breathe. In and out. Unfolding. Folding. Swelling. Collapsing. Inhaling. Exhaling.

You stop swimming and let your toes touch the bottom of the pool. Will you reach out and take the blue lotus? Swim back to shore? Hike back to your raft and find a way to row upstream? Or make the journey home on foot through the forest?

You find that your arms will not reach; they are content to float by your sides, swaying gently amid the reflected stars. It is enough, for now, to bathe in the soft light and the song of the lotus. To watch it breathe, and to let your breath align with its soporific rhythm.

The lotus uncurls its elegant, curved petals.

Inside, at the center of the lotus, you see a burst of pale yellow you hadn't seen before. The heart of the lotus shines like the sun, hidden within the brilliant blue enclosure.

The petals close, obscuring for a moment that golden center.

Open.

Close.

Breathing in.

And out.

You stay this way for a long time, breathing with and through the lotus. Swaying softly in the water. Your mind clears, empties, of all concerns. Whenever a thought comes to disturb the peace in your mind—a question of the time of night or of what you should do next, for instance—you simply breathe it out as the lotus petals curl inward. Letting it ride on down the river.

In the exquisite emptiness, the clarity of your mind, one thought surfaces—like a lily sprung from the mud to float atop the water. The thought blooms, too, and breathes in time.

Ah, you think. *Now I understand.*

You remain, a little longer.

Breathing.

Swaying.

Softening.

Relaxing.

And then, when the time feels right and the waning moon is lost over the trees, you turn. And you swim back to shore. From the banks, you look back. The whole pool from here seems to be awash in lotus blue. With a glow-like bioluminescence, you can see the stem and root beneath the fluttering flower. How it reaches down like an umbilical cord to the center of the world. *To think that you might once have wanted to sever that connection.*

The path home through the forest is not a straight line but a long and winding one. Your linen clothing dries under the morning sun, which you follow in its arc across the sky through partings in the trees. Southward.

The walk gives you time to think.

All the while, your breath remains steady, your heart soft. For you carry with you now something of greater value than a single sacred flower. You hold within you the seed of secret knowledge, a boon to bring home to your people.

It was never about the blue lotus, you know now.

You were never meant to seize it, possess it, give it to your people. It was never yours to give.

The frog asked you why you sought the lotus. Your answer, you understand now, was simple and insufficient. The blue lotus is not a magical cure for illness. Nor is it the key to revitalizing the land. The land already does this once a year when the river floods, depositing enough rich minerals in the soil to sustain your people until the cycle begins anew.

The lotus is life. And breath. And ritual. It opens, shining like the sun. It closes, beaming like the moon. It rises and falls like the water and generates itself anew. Just like the earth. Just like the year.

It was never about the lotus. It was always about the ritual. The flood. The journey. Each year, when your people feast and bless a hero, they exalt the life-giving, life-affirming cycles of the natural world. What true hero would pluck the lotus from the mud and break that ritual? That respect?

How many of your forebears came to this same realization by way of the raft on the river? Did they, too, converse with a jungle frog? Or did it appear to them with another face? A blue morpho butterfly? A tiger with sapphire eyes?

By day, the jungle sings with the rattle of kingfishers and the buzz of insects. The river is always at your right hand, even if the path may stray now and then.

And soon, the forest is behind you, a wild and beautiful thing. Hidden therein, a sacred pool mirrors the sky and nurtures the great secrets of the universe. A place of private revelation. A place of self-investigation. The heart of the jungle, and indeed, the very navel of the world—pulsing and dazzling and bathed in lotus blue.

RECIPE: LAVENDER & MUGWORT DREAM TINCTURE

Lavender is widely recognized for its calming effects and can be used as an herbal remedy to improve sleep. Mugwort (*Artemisia vulgaris*) is another herb prized for its sleep benefits and as a powerful herb for dreaming. Mugwort may improve dream recall and support lucid dreaming.

This simple, homemade tincture recipe, using the folk herbalist method, combines these two medicinal herbs to support relaxation, better sleep, and create a portal to your dreams. It can be ingested sublingually or diffused in hot or cold drinks. Be thoughtful about where you find your herbs, and ensure they are safe to ingest before making this tincture.

INGREDIENTS & MATERIALS

Dried lavender buds
Dried mugwort leaves
Vodka or 80–100 proof grain alcohol (use high-quality, neutral-flavored spirits)
Mason jar with lid
Cheesecloth
Dropper bottles (preferably amber or dark-colored)

* Rinse lavender buds and mugwort leaves. Allow to dry completely.
* Fill the jar about halfway with dried herbs.
* Cover the herbs with alcohol, leaving a little space at the top for the soaked herbs to expand. Seal the jar tightly with the lid.
* Store in a cool, dark place for up to 6 weeks. Check on your tincture every day or two and give it a little shake!
* After 4–6 weeks, strain the tincture through cheesecloth and collect in dropper bottles, preferably dark glass. Label

your bottles with the date (though alcohol-based tinctures can have a very long shelf life!). Store in cool, dark cabinets, especially if the bottles are clear.

How to Use:

The recommended dosage is 2–4mL, taken up to three times per day. Place a few drops under your tongue before bed or when you need to relax. Alternatively, add to your evening cup of tea, your water bottle, or soda water (a squeeze of lemon is a beautiful addition, too!).

Mix it Up:

Consider combining other herbs to create tincture blends, or using this recipe as a base to create future herbal remedies. A few suggested herbs to try are below:

* Chamomile, lemon balm, or valerian root for relaxation and sleep
* Ginger or licorice root for digestive support
* Dandelion for energy
* Motherwort for menstrual pain, menopause, and post-partum recovery

Note: Always consult your physician before taking an herbal tincture and be sure to research the plants you use in your home-brewing. Some plants may be toxic if ingested. Mugwort may gently induce the onset of menstruation and should not be consumed by pregnant or nursing people.

9

Tales by the Tavern Fire

What a comfort and a wonder it is to enter warm quarters out of pouring rain, to find pleasant and welcoming company on the unknown road. Indeed, it is one of the chief miracles of this life, were it put to you—finding anchorage at the very moment it's most needed. Shuffling off your rain-soaked boots and shaking free of your damp cloak, you care nothing for the stale, musty air of the rooms. They're dry enough, and warm plenty, and a safe retreat from the storm. In truth, you'd hoped to travel well into the night and make it at least a few leagues further down the road, but the storm moved in quite suddenly and without warning. As if by providence, just as the rain began to fall, you perceived a light, fuzzy and orange, in the dale.

The innkeeper is kind—the sort of friendly fellow who works in the trade for the love of people and deep curiosity about differences. You were met, on entry, with a thousand questions; from whence you came, to whither you travel, and what news you have from lands to the south. Hot supper, the innkeeper said, would be ready soon, and you'd be most welcome to a mug of ale or cider by the fire. All of that sounds infinitely tempting to you now. Swapping out your wet socks and muddy boots for another pair from your traveling bag (oh, it's such a comfort to put on dry socks!)—and hanging your cloak on a hook to dry—you turn back for the door and make your way to the tavern on the ground floor.

Where before there were only a few patrons huddled over pints at solitary tables, now several more have taken up residence on benches and around the blazing hearth. The innkeeper, a rag slung over his shoulder, brings frosty steins to a table of weary-looking folks in gray-green cloaks. You overhear his jovial greetings to the three of them.

"Not too often we see half-elves this way," he says, beaming. "All are welcome here, o'course. And my Mary's lamb and leek pies are just out of the oven, how many for you?"

Most of the patrons are human, like you, though there's a somewhat surly-looking dwarf at a table in the corner. The whole place is lowly lit, with candles dripping wax that pools in brass and copper holders on every table. Wooden crossbeams on the low ceiling and slab stone archways reflect the candlelight and that from the fireplace, which offers a pleasing crackle. You find yourself an open table, close to the half-elf party, and a perfect distance from the fire—where its warmth is enough to comfort you but not so intense as to flush your cheeks. The innkeeper is glad to see you freshened up and ready for company; his rosy face, plump and pleasant, splits into a welcoming smile. He'll have one of those pies sent to you straightway—unless you'd prefer stew and fresh-baked bread, of course. He can rustle up anything you like. You hadn't realized how hungry you were until you sat down; now you're even more grateful for this port in the storm.

Though the inn and tavern are relatively small, the rain seems miles away within this cocoon of warmth and welcome. Just as the innkeeper plants a mug before you, the door to the inn swings wide, and a flash of lightning illuminates a figure in the doorway. Happy words of welcome greet her—a dark-haired lady who looks to be of high birth by her dress and manner. She sits down straight away at a table very near the fire, which illuminates her features plainly: about her neck is a deep green amulet, wrought with a silver chain. As the room fills, guests entering from the rain or coming down from their rooms, there's a fair bit of shifting glances as you take each other in. Not surprisingly, the innkeeper remarks that it's the fullest his place has been on a given night in many years, and with all sorts of people, and what a delight. Just last evening, he was here alone in the barroom while Mary made pies in the kitchen for no one to eat.

"Just me, my Mary, and the cat, it was," he says to no one in particular. The food he brings you is hearty and delicious, seeming to feed your very soul. You feel stronger, more resilient, and energized as opposed to the road-worn self you first dragged through the door. And those around you clearly perk up after a few bites, too. As if there's some magic seasoning sprinkled in the pie crust and stew that wakens the heart and stirs courage in you.

Soon, the quiet conversations, isolated between tables and traveling companions, begin to overlap. Heads turn, bodies lean back in chairs as guests begin to compare weather conditions, the obstacles they've met on the road, and the destinations in store for each party. Coincidentally—though perhaps this should not surprise you at all—you are in the company of a dozen or more others on their way to the same place as you: a festival honoring the crown prince's coming of age. The whispers throughout the kingdom—though they may be greatly distorted and exaggerated—suggest that the king regent will install this nephew of his upon the throne during the festivities. There are rumors that a lost heir to the old king's line has surfaced, and the king regent must act swiftly to secure his family's place, crowning the prince before all the public so there's no question to the validity of his rule.

By your measure, it's never much mattered who sat at the high throne of the kingdom. You answer mostly to the local lords, who provide protection and benefits in exchange for taxes and work. What draws you to the festival is a chance to sell your wares to a wealthier clientele and those who might find your crafts novel and exotic. You hail from the southernmost tip of the kingdom, where the air is crisp and salty, and a mulberry tree grows that produces the richest and most elegant dyes. You're well-respected in your region as a dyer of textiles and producer of fine pigments; with luck, you'll be able to sell bolts of fabric and wool to noble lords and ladies at court who've never worn such a lush palate of golds and greens.

It seems every guest at the inn has a different reason for traveling to the king's festival. You learn that the trio of half-elves intend to seek an audience with the regent; they've long paid tribute to one of his dukes and wish to entreat him for sole sovereignty. The dwarf, whose surly expression melts to a serene one after a few mugs of ale, brings gifts for the crown prince, mined from the old mountains.

Only the lady by the fire, about whose neck hangs the strange amulet, remains reticent with her motives.

Though the hour grows late and bellies are full, the atmosphere in the tavern is so warm and companionable that no one seems eager to retire to bed. A twosome sitting in the corner near the kitchen reveal themselves to be traveling minstrels, and the rest of the guests persuade them to play a merry song for the gathering. It doesn't take much convincing for them to produce a harp and a flute and to begin playing a charming melody that floats in the background of continued conversation. The innkeeper is mightily pleased; how nice it would be, he remarks, to have such passing sweet music here all the year-round. You learn that his name is Hal, and he and his wife, Mary, have owned and operated the inn for nearly twenty years now.

"Built it with me own hands," he insists, displaying his rough, calloused hands as proof, "at the crossing of the three great roads. Knew we'd always have guests from one way or another. Though a night like this we don't see often. Get all types, mind you. Just not always all at once."

Hal's laughter is booming and infectious, and he has a way of coaxing stories out of even the shyest of the guests. He longs to hear stories of the further duchies and petty kingdoms or stories of the road. Hasn't anyone a tale of adventure or excitement to share?

"We have a tale to tell," ventures one of the three half-elves, the one named Erin Brightbuckle. Her fellows give uneasy glances, but with a tilt of her head, she seems to reassure them that the company is trustworthy. "A tale of a strange occurrence on the road from the north."

The fire's blaze and the pummeling rain form a curtain of fuzzy, crackling sound as the music ceases and Brightbuckle begins her tale...

"It was three days ago we set off from our village, deep in the green forest. Our guide was the river Durendal, which flows southward to the edge of the wood, then breaks easterly. From time immemorial, a bridge has stood over the river just before its bend, leading to the king's road. But when we came to the forest's edge, we found the bridge had fallen into the river. Only a few stones remained, with crumbling mortar. We know not how long it was in such disrepair, for our kind rarely leave the forest.

"And so," the story continues, this time the half-elf called Whistle picking up the thread and weaving the narrative, "We followed the river east, hoping to come to another crossing. But by nightfall, still, we had found nothing. Not a village, or a footbridge, or anything. We were ready to settle and make camp, to continue searching in the morning, when we saw a fire a little ways off. We drew our bows and approached the fire—a little thing, only—and found, sitting beside it, a hermit in humble robes, with long silver hair and a beard that nearly reached the earth."

Now the third half-elf, the one called Thorn, picks up the tale. "When he saw us, he begged that we put away our weapons and join him at his fire. Stay a while, he beseeched us, and share a crust of bread, for the night was cold. We asked him if he knew of a crossing nearby or of a harbor where we might find a boat. But he would not answer, only insisting that we sit with him a while and bring our warmth to the fire. At last, we put away our bows and acquiesced, for the old man seemed weary and hungry for company. But the moment we sat round the small, feeble fire, the flames leapt high into the air and turned every color of the rainbow in succession. The old man, seeming to swell from within, cast off his shabby cloak and rose to his feet, shining bright as the fire itself. He was grand now, robed in fine emerald threads, his tattered beard now smooth and shiny. In one hand, he clutched a magnificent staff, and from the other came sparks and mist."

"We had to shield our eyes against his light," says Brightbuckle, reclaiming the tale. "He was one of the old sorcerers of legend, I say. The ones they say left this realm for distant shores in the last age. He looked like a star fallen to the earth, grown wise and aged. In his eyes burned a blue intensity, and yet—through everything awesome and terrible about him—he smiled with a kindness that made us weep. For our act of compassion, the simple act of stopping to sit with a weary old man, he raised his staff to the sky and uttered an incantation I cannot repeat, for the words were in no tongue I've heard before. And from the staff and the gesture of his hand, a twining of stone and mortar unfurled. Stone by stone, at his command, a bridge lay itself across the rushing river. It shone there in the moonlight, gleaming like gold.

"When we'd caught our breath and the gleam had faded, we found the old man gone, only embers left of the dying fire. Shaken as we were, we crossed the sorcerer's bridge. But on the other side, we found three newly fashioned bows of shining birch wood and quivers full of glittering arrows. One for each of us."

There is silence for a little while, save only for the outward sheets of rain and crackle of fire in the hearth. It's as if the story has cast a spell upon the unlikely gathering; as if the tale has struck each heart, whispered a secret in each ear. There are wide eyes all around, an audience held within the story's enchantment. You, one of the spellbound, feel a dreamy sense of déjà vu, as if the half-elves had repeated an old folktale, one you hearkened to in your youth, forgetting as you came of age. But then, you also had a mysterious encounter on the road hither, did you not?

It's Hal who breaks the silence at last.

"Strange wonders lie on the road these days, I reckon," he says. "Come to think of it, not a fortnight hence, we had a visitor in these parts. A farmer, young one, only just come of age. Had a rather unique sword, as I recall. Asking questions about dragons in the western mountains, of all things. And wouldn't you know? Not a few days later, there's talk of a dragon sighted again, first time in living memory."

This sends a bout of whispers across the tavern, blending into a natural susurration. Dragon sightings? Hermit sorcerers? These are marvelous times, indeed...

"I, too, witnessed wondrous marvels on the road," comes a low, husky voice. It's the woman beside the fire, speaking at last.

"I was older then when I left my village," she says, her tongue tracing the first of many riddles. "Wiser, too. My neighbors came to me for charms and remedies, potions and tinctures. I worked with the water and the moon and the plants and was called wise woman. But before the harvest, a blight came. All the crops of all the villagers and all the healing herbs in my garden withered—and my magic with it. I left to seek an answer to the sudden dying of the land; they say the king regent receives counsel from a wise magician. Nothing like the sorcerers of the past, but a learned sage with wisdom of the cycles of the world. So it was of him I sought guidance."

As the lady speaks, her raven-dark curls in silhouette against the fire, you sense a presence at your feet. Peering discreetly under the table, you meet two bright green eyes. A cat, black with white paws and chest, winds its way around your leg, gently butting its head against your shin. Then, swiftly deciding it's finished with you, the cat leaps away and into the lap of Mary, the innkeeper's wife, who now sits and hearkens to the tale.

The lady continues: "It was a perilous journey for a woman of my age. My bones were not what they once were, and they sorely ached as I traversed the land. Yet my quest spurred me on. Only I could save my land and the magic it held."

You glance about the room and the puzzled expressions of other guests mirror your confusion. The storyteller appears to you in the prime of youth, and yet she speaks of old age and frailty. You listen on.

"On the second night of my travels, as I searched in vain for shelter—for the night and the moon rose full overhead—a sudden chill took me, and I could go no further. I sat beneath a hazel tree as the cold closed in. But as I sat and shivered, I felt, at once, a shower of warmth and light upon my face, then upon my shoulders, and my whole body. By the light of the moon, a young man approached me, and from him seemed to come a glowing warmth that then enveloped me. He took me by the hand, and I rose to my feet as though I were weightless. I moved with a swiftness and an ease I had not known in years. I followed him through the wood, and it was as if we passed through a kind of veil to another world where the sun shines as though through a dense fog. In this strange country, the food tasted sweeter, and the earth yielded herbs I did not recognize.

"With each day I spent in his ethereal kingdom, I felt the months and years fall away. I grew younger each night and rose freshly each morning to a new flush of youth. A year and a day I spent there in the other world, living among its people and learning to cultivate these strange herbs. At times, I forgot the plight of my village and indeed forgot that there was any world outside of this one. I knew love and friendship there, and I was cherished. But soon, the cries of my people I heard upon the wind, and I knew I must depart and continue my journey.

"The people of that other world dressed me in fine clothing and wished me well. The beautiful man who brought me thither—a fairy man, I'm sure of it now—blessed me before I embarked. He gave me the gem you see here," and she gestures to the amulet around her neck, which glows with a virescent depth in the flickering fire. "This gem, imbued with a charm of protection, would also safeguard the youth his land had restored to me. Should I ever remove it, he said, the years would swiftly return to me. When I left the fairy realm, I found that, indeed, no time had passed in this world, but I was young again and eager to bring my findings to the king's mage."

The lady's story hangs upon the warm tavern air like ice crystals melting upon the skin. You feel a mixture of emotions toward her: a slow, kindled tenderness and compassion. A feeling of protectiveness and concern for a woman traveling alone and carrying such a valuable item in plain sight. Also, a sense of pity; for you never saw age as a weakness, but something to be admired. There's a wisdom in the lady's eyes that's unmatched by her countenance.

Behind the stirring feelings, a curiosity awakens within you. The lady spoke of strange herbs in the world beyond this one, plants that do not grow on the green earth. You must speak with her further, for perhaps there are plants in the fairy realm that produce even rarer and more exotic dyes than the ones you peddle. Colors only dreamt of and never seen under the sun.

"A fairy man, you say?" comes the voice of one of the minstrels. "And was it the fair country in which you passed the year, lady?"

"I cannot offer proof, save for the certainty in my heart," the lady replies. "In that country, food was plentiful, all were eternally young, and illness and disease were unheard of. I might have stayed all my life were I not called to a purpose in this world."

There is great interest among the guests as to the location of the doorway to the other world; even you harbor a longing to find the fairy country. But the lady insists she could not recall the way—a year in the company of the fay has blurred her memories of the path she walked. And even if she could find that hazel grove once more, the doors to other worlds rarely appear in the same place twice. At least, and the minstrels here agree, that's what the old songs say.

In the wake of dragons, fairies, and sorcerers, at last, you feel moved to tell your story of the road. You feel struck by the same poetic spirit, just as you were clearly visited upon by some similar strangeness.

"I have a tale to offer," you say, your voice clear and confident. "I, too, encountered a marvel on my journey."

Hal pours another round for those guests who wish it. Your eyes focus on the fire in the hearth as you weave the tapestry of your tale.

"It was mid-day when the road from the south brought me to the edge of a dark wood," you begin. "I was prepared for this, as those who have traveled to the castle before have brought back warnings of this place. It is a vast forest of confused and entwined paths, earning it the name of Tanglewood…"

At the utterance of its name, many of the guests around you nod or mutter sounds of familiarity with the wood.

"Many a traveler has become lost in Tanglewood, and dangers lurk in the shadows there. But I was unafraid when I entered. I made, of the stories and songs of the wood, a kind of protective shield. I wrapped myself in the rumors—for that was all they were—and turned the dangers back upon themselves with every step.

"But the wood was dark. The afternoon sun strained to reach between the brambles, and the path was winding and difficult to follow in the dim light. My resolve began to fade, and my invisible shield of songs and stories with it. With every snap of a twig or sound of a scurrying creature through the trees, I became afraid. I worried I would lose my way and be lost in Tanglewood forever.

"But as I reached the densest part of the forest and the canopy closed in, sealing out the last of the sunlight, I perceived a silver glow straight ahead through the trees. It was bright as the harvest moon and almost seemed to sing, to hum toward me. Indeed, it seemed to me that I could hear, in that quivering song of the silver light, my name upon the lips of a gifted bard. It called to me.

"And so, I followed it, this gasp of light in a forest of darkness. My eyes and feet found clarity in the path, and the light guided me onward through the thicket. The faster I moved toward it, the more it pulled away, as though I were chasing a playful child.

"Finally, the traveling light slowed, allowing me to reach it. And when I was close enough for my eyes to grasp the detail, I discovered that at the center of the glow was an animal. It was a white hart generating this abundant light. The creature was so beautiful, an expression of such profound innocence that I nearly wept at the sight of it. I was so spellbound by its loveliness that I did not, at first, notice its injury. But there, in its hind leg, was an arrow. The poor creature was wounded, and yet it still led me safely through the wood with its light.

"I endeavored to help the creature. I carefully removed the arrow and dressed its wound with a scrap of fabric from my pack. I hoped that this small gesture would convey my gratitude to the hart. Then, to my surprise, the wounded hart began to transform before my eyes. Its shining coat became skin, its forelegs stretched outward into arms, and its body stood upright. Before me, there was no more a hart, but a child, with moon-white hair and a clean white shift. She looked no older than seven or eight, but as I beheld her, it seemed she flickered between multiple states, as though superimposed here with the pale image of a grown woman, there with the specter of an elder. Briefly, she was all three at once, but as my eyes grasped for the full picture of her, she returned solidly to the little child, barefoot in the dark forest.

"She stayed by my side and walked with me till we reached the far edge of Tanglewood. And there, before we parted, she insisted I accept her gift. Then she plucked three platinum hairs from her head and sealed them in a small glass jar, which I now carry close to my heart. It is like bottled starlight, she said, and I only need open the jar when I find myself lost in the dark. Her gift will always light my way."

Even now, as you conclude your tale, you can feel the presence of the tiny jar in your breast pocket. Your bottle of starlight. With your words on the air and your story in the minds of others, you feel a rush of amity—of fellowship. It's as though by offering your tale, like a kind of communion, you've formed a sacred bond of kinship with the people in this room. You have exchanged memories and marvels, creating an intimate community of travelers and storytellers.

Many an hour passes before anyone is ready to retire to their rooms. Guests change their seats, and tables are pushed together, moving close to new friends who were perfect strangers not moments ago. Hal and Mary beam at the new connections made under their roof. Before the night is over, you have shared a toast with Brightbuckle and the wise woman, and you've resolved to go forth together, as a company, to the king's festival.

The storm is quieting outside the inn, the rain only a gentle pitter-patter against the windows. At last, the ache and weariness of long travel overpower the exhilaration of new friendships and discovery. The harper in the corner is lazily picking at the strings, composing out loud a song of powerful hermits, fairy kings, and magical harts. Dragons in the night sky. Arranging to meet your party at first light to set off toward the capitol, you bid Hal and Mary a grateful good night and make your way up to your chamber.

One by one, you extinguish the lamps. You shuffle carefully to the bed, feeling for obstacles in the darkness. There's a small window by the bed, against which beats the last gasp of the evening's rain. Gray clouds obscure the stars and the moon tonight. *But it's all right*, you think, settling into the soft embrace of the mattress and letting the night's darkness close around you like a blanket. You've got bottled starlight at your fingertips.

Exercise: Journal Practice for Lucid Dreaming

Tales by the Tavern Fire, like many of the stories herein, draws heavily from universal mythemes and archetypes. In this sustained practice to encourage lucid dreaming, you'll work with various archetypes to create portals to the dream world. Lucid dreaming occurs when we, as dreamers, become aware that we are dreaming. In some cases, a lucid dreamer may be able to control the circumstances, master supernatural powers, or access hidden wisdom within the dream.

For some, lucid dreaming happens spontaneously or naturally, but it's also a skill that can be developed and advanced through a consistent practice.

Keep a Dream Journal

Begin by keeping a regular record of your dreams. Stash a journal and pen by your bedside. Every morning, before you start your day, make a point of writing down everything you can recall from your dreams the night before. Don't analyze or edit yourself as you write;

just let all the details, images, or scenarios you remember fall onto the page. You may be tempted to rationalize the output by inventing or guessing certain details. Try to avoid that. If you don't remember how you moved from one dream space to another, make a note of that discrepancy. Don't force meaning onto a dream. Practice objectivity as you write down your recollections—you can look for the meaning later.

Be consistent. Record your dreams every morning.

EXPLORE ARCHETYPES

Once a week (or once per moon cycle), at a time of day when you have some distance from your dreams, revisit the most recent journal entries. What potent symbols stand out? You can consult a dream dictionary if you like, but first, try to look inward at the personal meaning these symbols might convey to you.

Do you notice any patterns in the content or emotional impact of your dreams? Do you recognize any narrative archetypes in your journal entries? When you dream, who are you—yourself? Or someone else? What archetypes do you recognize in your dream self or other figures in your dreams, and how does this change from night to night, or season to season? Write down your reflections.

Consider the following archetypes; do you recognize them in any of your dream journal entries?:

* The Hero
* The Child / The Innocent
* The Father / Mother / Caregiver
* The Maiden
* The Crone / The Sage
* The Magician
* The King / Queen / Ruler
* The Outlaw

What are the qualities of the archetypes you recognize? What is aspirational about them? What can you learn from them? Record your reflections.

INCORPORATE YOUR LEARNING

Revisit the nightly sleep ritual you developed at the start of this book. Consider adding a meaningful interaction with one or more of these archetypes to your bedtime activities. This might look like:

* Rereading the previous night's journal entry or the periodic reflections and meditating on the archetypes you recognize.
* Writing a short story or poem, or creating a piece of artwork inspired by the archetypes and symbols that spring up in your dreams.
* Adding an item to your dream altar that evokes positive symbols, archetypes, or patterns you'd like to reinforce.

In time, as you continue to journal and untangle the mythic archetypes in your dreams, your dream recall will improve. By noticing patterns in your dreams, you will become more adept at spotting dream signals when they occur. Continue this practice as you deepen your connection to the dream world, and soon, you may be able to recognize when you're dreaming.

Combine this exercise with other rituals and recipes in this book (particularly the Lavender & Mugwort Tincture on page 117 or Sleep Spell Sachet on page 159) if you'd like to use ritual herbs to augment your interactions with dreams.

10

Cauldron of Cerridwen

Wind shakes the leaves and catkins of the alder woods, a rustle faint and flowering. You feel the breeze disturb the grasses and send a tingling down the back of your neck and shoulders. It seems to you that the breeze almost sings, soft and sweet with the touch of evening, with a voice at once familiar and foreign. You catch yourself humming, trying in vain to harmonize with the near-inaudible notes of the wind. Would that you were a harp, and the breeze might play your strings with its tender hands. Would that you could make such beautiful, otherworldly music. A word forms soundlessly on your tongue but lingers there and dissolves; you can hear it almost echo in your head, but you cannot bring it forth. Not yet.

A sigh escapes your parted lips, and you return your eyes—which have drifted toward the tops of the alder trees—to your task. Your hands never stop their toil, of course; the goddess forbade you to let your arms fall or to slow your speed or forget your task. Now your gaze falls again upon the simmering surface of the liquid. Funny how it changes color and consistency as you stir...how you do not seem to recognize the change as it happens, but if you turn away for even a moment and return to the sight, it seems to you a wholly new thing. Moments ago, you could swear its color was a deep and opaque purple, its consistency thick and resistant. Now it bubbles crimson with an edge of shining gold, and it moves like weightless water against your paddle.

You've found a constant rhythm of stirring, your paddle hardly touching the rim of the cauldron, moving smoothly sunwise through the bubbling potion. How many nights have you toiled? How many more lie before you in your task? The ache in your shoulders from the first few hours of labor has dulled to quiet relief; your body surrenders to the repetition of the task. Round and round you stir.

The goddess—the Lady—honored you with the assignment. She foraged the herbs and berries from the hazel grove. You were not by her side for the harvesting; she went alone, as she often does to yonder woods. She passed, you think, beyond the veil of the world even. Into that unknown country, where there are herbs and simples and flowers unfamiliar to those who walk upon the green earth.

When she returned, you watched her from the window of your quarters as she prepared the ingredients and set the mixture to boiling over a blazing fire on the shore of the lake. You are only a low attendant to the Lady of the castle, but she dotes on you, giving you a chamber of your own with a view to the lake.

There are some in the village who whisper about her ways—her affinity for magic and the healing arts. They call her sorceress, enchantress, witch. But to you, she will always be the goddess. In the spring, she blesses the groves and fields of grain. At the harvest, bearing her willow staff, she oversees the cutting of the corn and barley. She sings and plays the harp as beautifully as any bard, rules the land fairly and justly alongside her husband, and does kindness to the unfortunate. She took you into her service and treated you with compassion and curiosity; to you, she is like a mother, a teacher, and a friend.

The Lady Cerridwen has her own children: a daughter, bright-eyed and well-loved, and a son, lacking in beauty, charm, or wit. It's out of tenderness for him that she set about making the potion you now stir. If brewed carefully and administered properly, the potion holds the power of poetic inspiration—and the potential to make the drinker wise beyond measure and possessed of divine poetry. A coveted gift indeed, and one that would bless Cerridwen's son to a charmed life and immortality through song and poetry. With such gifts, he might be happier, more loved, more accepted by his peers. Cerridwen loves her children and laments to see them suffer; thus, she undertakes this most difficult and precise of potions with your valued assistance.

The heat from the fire tickles your toes. The potion, somehow right before your eyes, has gone all gold and sparkling. Spirals of steam curl upward from the surface, carrying whiffs of herbal scent to your senses. There's a fragrance you recognize—the mysterious perfume of wild poppy, you suppose—but all else is unfamiliar, either blended into the unknown or produced by plants salvaged from that Otherworld. The one your queen tiptoes into from time to time.

And now, you realize, for the first time, that you can see your own reflection on the surface of the liquid. You wonder how long you've stared down at yourself, unaware, not seeing or recognizing your own face. For a brief moment, the reflection shines—gleams, radiant as the sun. No, like the moon when it's full and golden at the harvest. Your brow shines bright as though a coronal were placed there. This task has a way of playing tricks on you, and surely the hypnotic perfumes of the potion do you no favors. But you keep your pace, slow and deliberate, eyes fixed on their pale mirror below. Funny how the ripples and bubbles in the liquid distort your visage slightly, stretching and resetting, and yet it remains your face. Unmistakable and true. You think of how your face has changed as you've grown, so different from the face of your childhood and yet recognizably yours. How your body has stretched and settled, yet carries the same soul.

An assemblage of words floats distantly in your subconscious, rippling like water or wind.

I have been in a multitude of shapes,
Before I assumed a consistent form.

You hear the words, dull and echoing from somewhere else, and you feel them aching to be said aloud. They do not come to your lips, but you can almost taste them.

You feel the dimming of night creep across the land, curling around your shoulders. The next time you steal a glance at the sky, away from your toiling, the moon is bright and waxing nearly full. You mark the phase in your mind and search your memories for how many moons like this have hung in the sky. How many months have you stirred the cauldron now? How many until your task is complete? You imagine that by its end, you will know the movement of the earth and stars, the phases of the moon and sun, as well as your own countenance. You'll feel the sun and moon tides within your veins.

A year and a day—that's what the Lady commanded.

How long has it been? You stretch your mind to count the moons and months. By your estimation, only a fortnight remains. Your shoulders loosen at the very thought, but the task seems all the more challenging for the promise of looming release. The potion appears dark and shimmering green in the night, and its surface catches the pure white reflection of the moon, rippling and flickering so.

At midnight—moon big and bright and straight overhead—the goddess comes, as she does every midnight. She brings you fresh-baked bread, ripe fruit, and clear water to break your fast. She drapes a warm cloak over your shoulders against the night's chill. She looks upon the cauldron with quiet composure, casts another armful of foraged herbs into its belly, and sets you back to your work.

It seems the moon shines brighter when she's at hand. As if, just as the tides are drawn to the movements of the moon, so is the moon tied to her. It sinks close to be nearer her presence. And, as she departs, it slowly shrinks back to its corner of the sky, having drunk its fill of her beauty.

You like the night. The hum of crickets, the call of owls, and the rustle of night breezes. The crisp evening air is a balm to your sore muscles and perspiring brow. Before you undertook your labor, the Lady Cerridwen worked her enchantments so that you would need little nourishment and not a wink of sleep to disturb your yearlong effort. Still sleepless, each night, you dream. Shapes and images take form out of formlessness on the surface of the potion. From whence they come, you cannot say. Whether from your own mind, searching for patterns in the darkness, or from that Otherworld where dreams are made. They are strange, sometimes, and often delightful.

You recall one dream—or vision—that came to you in the cauldron many months ago. It was, you think, at the Flower Moon, not long after Beltane. It seemed that petals of broom, meadowsweet, and oak flowers fell delicately into the cauldron, though none of those plants grew nearby. And as you watched, they fell into the pattern of a woman's form—a flower maiden, who then sprang to life as flesh and blood.

Another night, it seemed to you that night that a fleet of boats sailed across the surface of the potion, miniature but so real to the eye you could have reached out to touch them. In the bow of the boat at the head of the fleet was a king, crowned and robed in finery. You stirred the cauldron still, and your movements created the gentle waves upon which they rode. Then, before your eyes, the tiny ships passed through a shimmering veil and vanished. And then, upon the water, a mist seemed to hang, shining and golden under your moon. Three boatfuls of men stood in the mists, and another world took shape in the shifting winds. The men were fierce of face—warrior stock—and you watched them lay siege to an unknown kingdom. The people of that country in the mist went not quietly, but fought bravely and without restraint until the invading forces claimed a hard-won victory.

And then you watched as the surviving force—the king and a mere seven men—returned on their boats, now laden with the spoils of war. Pearls that shone with inner light. A brindled ox, richly adorned. And most prized of all, riding in the boat with the King—the cauldron of the chief of the Otherworld. A cauldron that brought forth wine and food aplenty, never running out.

When you recall the dream now, once again some distant verse is there on the wind or in the recesses of your mind. Words that find no voice.

I have been a sword, narrow, variegated,
I have been a tear in the air,
I have been in the dullest of stars.

You stir on, round the rim of the cauldron. The potion, though low-lit, is a pale silver-green now. Your paddle sends gentle ripples through the liquid. For a moment, your eyes slide out of focus, your vision blurring. When you blink them back to concentration, you find your head is drooping toward the liquid—your nose mere inches from the surface. You pull back, careful to maintain your effort.

But there are, again, shapes and movement in the cauldron. It's time to dream again. You wonder what visions the cauldron will conjure for you tonight, so close to the Hunter's Moon.

There are shapes indeed on the surface of the cauldron, but they are only the dim reflection of the alder and willow woods cast in moonlight. Perhaps no dream awaits tonight. You stir.

And then you see the trees, reflected as shades on the liquid, sprout and grow upward from within the cauldron. The alder. The willow. The rowan. Cherry trees and birch. Pine trees, elm, and hazel too. Holly and hawthorn. Chestnut. Oak. Before you, a full forest grows in minuscule form but exquisite detail. The round and round movement of your paddle astir sends waves of wind through the tiny leaves. An undulating dance of breeze and bend and sway. Leaves whisper. Trunks groan. Roots sigh.

But it is more than the small disturbance of your labor, your endless stirring. The whisper, the groan, and the sigh all build to a chorus; you can almost hear the voices of the trees, each varied and distinct. The alder's voice you recognize, for the woods near the lake sing with that timbre. You feel it resonate in your body, as though you were a harp string.

Now the trees, all swept into song and speech, are pulling up their roots from the depths of the cauldron. With slow movement, like the gait of herons on the marsh, their branches twist and bodies sway. They move with deliberation into formal rows and groupings, readying, you realize, for battle.

Transfixed on the slow and steady spectacle, you watch the very trees assemble armies. The wood—so like the alder forest and hazel grove in your own country—is at war. Perhaps enchanted to enact some ancient conflict between gods and sorcerers. Or—and this thought gives you some amusement—what you see is a reflection of reality. As if the trees and woods of your world are always moving toward war, but they move so slowly that their efforts are imperceptible to the mortal eye, their conflict playing out over the ages, unseen by man.

As slowly and deliberately as their warring began, the trees plant their roots again and ease into stasis. Soon, the only movement left in the forest of the cauldron is the windswept shaking of leaves. The alder, sacred king of the forest, is the last tree to resume stillness.

And, sometime later, the liquid is clear and rippling again, the forest gone and dissolved into mist. Again, you question the source of the dreams on the water. Are they gifts of the goddess to pass your time without tedium? Shadows of history or prophecy—things that have been or things that have not yet come to pass? Or visions born of the cauldron itself—born of the potion of poetic inspiration? Are they poetry made solid? Somewhere in the chamber of mind and memory, you hear in your own faraway voice…

I have been a word among letters,
I have been a book in the origin.

You turn the paddle round the cauldron's edge. Soon it's dawn again, the sun breaking with golden crest over the forest, which sparkles with dew. In the chill of early morning, you're warm beside the cauldron and the low flame. The dawn chorus, led by the blackbirds and thrushes, swells amid the trees.

And so the cycle begins again—as you stir, it seems you keep the wheel of time turning. The arc of the sun powered by your mechanical movements and the travel of the wind spun in your hands. You turn the earth and wake the moon. You set the moon and call forth the sun. Should you stop your labor, let the potion simmer unstirred, you'd be surprised if the world didn't halt in its tracks, frozen in stillness and unmoved by time.

I have been the light of lanterns,
A year and a day.

The moon changes to full then wanes, night by night, to the faintest of glimmers. If your attention to the moon phase is right—though after all this time at work, you do not know if you can rely on your memory—at the dawn after the new moon, you will have completed your task. One year and one day. The potion and its power will be activated. You expect the goddess will fly to your side at its moment of readiness. You look forward to putting down the paddle at last, and you wonder if you will be handsomely rewarded for your effort. A castle, perhaps. Or a great feast in your honor. Gold and titles.

Though as tempting as the thought of riches and recognition may be...a part of you, buried somewhere under devotion and loyalty, would be most satisfied by no more than a drop of the potion itself. You long to enjoy the fruit of your labor and to feel in your own body and mind the effects of Cerridwen's magic. To taste the spark of divine poetry.

But you must shrug off this dreaming—of all the rewards that might await you, this is the only one the goddess cannot, and will not, grant. The art of her magic is precise, with no room for error. Only the first three drops of the potion will grant its gifts to the drinker. The potion is intended, as you know, for the Lady's son. No drop will go to waste on you.

Still, you think, what a bard you'd be, were you given the skill and savvy. If you could find the words and string together the songs, you'd bring to life the visions that float upon the surface of the cauldron. You'd call up the very roots of the trees and wake the rocks of the mountains to sway to your songs, like that ancient bard, Orpheus.

And indeed, a gifted bard is always met with praise and honor at Cerridwen's court. Would that she'd honor you so and listen to your voice and harp at the great feasting days. What a poet you would be.

I have been a continuing bridge
Over three score rivers

On the eve of the new moon, as the sun sinks out of sight over the lake, clouds gather to shower the country with gentle rain. While the water coats the grasses and the treetops, Cerridwen's magic protects you, forming a kind of canopy over your head, shielding you from the rain. With no moon to light the night and black clouds blurring the sky, there are no stars, even. The rain passes quickly, but the darkness remains, falling over the lake and forest like a light blanket. The only light is the fire beneath the cauldron. Your eyes, accustomed to night, search for the movement of wind on the water of the lake or the rustle of the trees. The darkness is comforting, somehow, as though in its near-total blackness, it opens you to new sight—just as when you close your eyes, you still find light and image in the void. You drink in the darkness like a healing elixir. It smells sweet and smooth, fresh with the specter of rain.

At midnight—you feel the moon swaying the tides of your body, though it cannot be seen overhead—Cerridwen comes one last time to check your progress and bring you nourishment. Her features are lit only from beneath by the dim flames, but you can tell she's pleased. Only hours remain till the potion is ready. She'll be back in the morning to relieve you from your duty, at which time you'll be escorted to your chambers for rest and recovery. You've done good work, for which the Lady is eternally grateful, and your efforts will be generously repaid.

After she goes, you wait for the dreaming to start—for the mists to rise on the potion or the figures to skate across its surface. But no vision comes. The potion grows thick and resistant to the paddle, but you keep up your pace and strengthen your resolve. You're nearly there.

The clouds clear soon after, and a dazzling array of stars smear the sky. By their light, you suspect the potion has taken on a hue of deep copper. It bubbles, seeming to sing or vibrate on a familiar frequency.

I have been a drop in a shower;
I have been a sword in the grasp of the hand
I have been a shield in battle.

Among the stars is the form of the hunter, with bright belt and bow strung. By his progress across the sky, you track the hours of night in the absence of the moon. Soon, he too sinks out of sight, and dawn's blush blooms over the alder trees with the choir of birdsong. You expect the goddess will return at any moment. The potion is thin again, a rosy gold color, and it bubbles vigorously within the cauldron. At last, you allow yourself to feel the ache in your arms and shoulders, for you are very nearly at your long effort's end.

But in letting the soreness break through your steely composure like the re-heating of a blade once tempered, you feel your whole self loosen and relax. Your hand slips against the shaft of the paddle and your stirring slows. At once, just as the sun breaks full over the forest, a great bubble on the surface of the potion bursts and lets fly a small splatter of liquid. You release the paddle against the brim of the cauldron and pull your arms away from the sputtering potion; and just then, three drops of rosy liquid, hot as bright coals, land delicately upon your hand.

Feeling the sharp heat of the potion on your skin, you instinctively raise your hand to your mouth to soothe the tiny burns. And, in an instant, you know what you've done—the three blessed drops of potion land effortlessly on your tongue. The potion tastes of sweet orange and honey-scented elderflower. Light and elegant as moonbeams. Some part of you nearly succumbs to laughter, for the irony is as delicious as the solution; that you should have toiled here for so long, limbs stiff at the cauldron, for the promise of the goddess's reward, and now you are the recipient of the unintended gifts of her magic.

Only the first three drops grant the power of poetic inspiration.

The taste lingers on your tongue as your lips curl into the start of a syllable. A great *ahhhhh* that starts a word you do not know—did not know—until now. A word that hums like a string in a harp as great as the wide world, strung from the stones of Salisbury Plain to the sunken city of Atlantis into the stars and beyond the known world. The word, "Awen." It's like a shiver on the water or a groan of ancient trees. It's hot like fire and bright as the sun on your brow.

And it seems your limbs are lengthening, stretching into the branches of a great alder tree, then weeping like the tendrils of the willow. As you take in a sweet breath, your body yawns into expansive greatness. And as your breath flows outward, you contract to the size of a tiny seed or grain of wheat. You feel your boundaries—the edges of your physical presence—soften and become indistinct as you reach outward to incorporate the swaying forest and the glittering lake.

You thrum like a harpstring—you *are* a harpstring—plucked and played by the morning breeze. And now you are the whole harp, the slope of the willow wood carved by loving hands. You feel the music and poetry deep in your belly, vibrating on a clear and ringing note. Now it seems you are the willow itself, your feet dug as roots into rich soil and your trunk solid as stone. You are the seed of the willow. And the fallen leaves. And the willow harp. You are past, present, and future.

You move with graceful languidness, unbothered by the spinning of time's wheel. You move faster than the lightning in a spring storm. You run with the deer of the forest, and you roll as a boulder over the sides of mountains. You are the drop of water in a shower of rain, and you are the shield and the sword of the king. You are the boats over the waves, and you are the mists of the unknown country.

Before you, the cauldron overflows with the finest foods you've ever seen. It cracks and spills forth into the lake. And it sparkles as a basin of clear water, in which your reflection—familiar and unrecognizable—shines back at you. Your brow, crowned with light and radiant like the sun. Or the moon.

The new word comes to you again, "Awen," powerful and musical in a voice that's your own and is also the voice of the singing winds and trees and water. You understand now that this word, and the sensation of expansiveness, is the spark. Is the flow. The inspiration. The breath. The poetry. It is the river through which you, a mere fish, swim—have always swum. Only now, thus awakened, do you feel the water on your scales.

Now comes another word. A name. Your new name: *Taliesin*. A name that means, you understand, "radiant brow." You are a poet now. A bard, inspired. You are *awenydd*. And it's through this Awen—inspiration, breath, poetry, spirit—that your eyes see now beyond the veil to what has been, what shall be, and what might be. Your mind, unfolding and opening to new feeling and understanding, burns bright with shining inspiration.

All at once, the visions of the cauldron move with elegant clarity through you, and they climb your harpstrings to become words and songs. You can reach through the visions to pull forth the epic songs of great kings and warriors of a distant past. And you can reach forward to pull into song the shadows of things to come. Past, present, and future dissolve into a constant march of poetry, folded into your mind.

> *I have been an eagle.*
> *I have been a coracle in the seas*
> *I played in the twilight,*
> *I slept in purple;*
> *I slept in a hundred islands*
> *I dwelt in a hundred castles*
> *A golden gem in a golden jewel.*
> *I am splendid as the stars.* [ii]

You spare a moment's apprehension for the fury of Cerridwen, in whose name you've toiled these many moons. You've tasted the spoils she had long promised to another. But you do not fear her wrath, for as you call up her image in your mind, you see her face radiant with love in the presence of your gifts, shining with tears and devotion as if you were the child of her own womb. It was your fate to stir the cauldron, to receive the visions, to drink the potion. Cerridwen is the mother of your poetry—the mother of Awen—and she remains the goddess, the muse in whose name you will sing, always.

Carrying forth your new gift and your new name, you rise from beside the cauldron. You'll leave this place to seek the promised willow tree, wherein your harp lies raw and uncarved. It already exists; you've seen it, just as you've seen the seed from which the willow grew. But someone will have to give it form, string it with horsehair and silk, and tune it to the music of Awen.

EXERCISE: AUTOMATIC WRITING FOR INSPIRATION

Where does inspiration come from? Does it lie behind a locked door, to be retrieved by the worthy? Is it woven through encounters with the Muse? Or do we swim through it like a flowing river, each and every moment, invisible unless we awaken to it?

This divinatory scrying-writing ritual can be performed at any time and in any space you're comfortable, but consider performing it in open air under a full moon. Just as the tides of the ocean are governed by the moon, so may your unconscious be.

SUGGESTED MATERIALS:

Cauldron or dark-bottomed vessel, filled with clear water
Journal and writing utensil

* Arrange your vessel before you, find a comfortable seated position, and designate your space as sacred in a manner meaningful to you. Have your journal at hand.
* Take notice of your surroundings. If you are outside, acknowledge the climate. How cloudy the sky is. The quality of the light. The flora and fauna surrounding you. Can you see the moon or any stars? Wherever you are, listen attentively to the sounds of your environment. Notice individual sounds, close up and far away, then reflect on how they blend together into a backdrop of noise. Feel the sensation of your body at rest. Notice how you are supported by the earth beneath you. Take as much time as you need to feel aware, grounded, and comfortable in the space. Use this awareness to quiet the mind and enter a receptive state.
* When you're ready, begin gazing into the vessel. First, focus on the qualities of the water's surface. Is it absolutely still, or does it ripple slightly, disturbed by your breath or the deep rumbling of the earth? Can you clearly see the bottom of the vessel, or does it merely fade into darkness?
* Now, move beyond perceiving just the physical nature of the liquid and notice with more clarity the environment and objects it reflects. Your own face, for example. The sky

or ceiling above. Soften your awareness so that you do not fixate on any one detail, but instead, remain open to receive any message or vision that rises to the surface. Let all your senses be open. Notice thoughts, patterns, reflections, memories, or flashes of inspiration that arise from the act of gazing.

* Take your time. Aim to spend at least fifteen minutes here, gazing into the water (especially if you are a beginner to scrying and/or meditation).

* When you feel ready, gently move your gaze away from the water. Let your eyes refocus briefly by gazing at an object far off.

* Immediately retrieve your journal and begin recording everything you felt or experienced during the scrying session. Take all your senses into account. What images did you see in the water or in your mind? What did you hear, either in the environment or in your mind while you gazed? Did you experience any notable physical sensations? What could you smell and taste? What thoughts or intuitive flashes crossed your mind during the session? What emotions woke within you?

* Write down everything—*everything*—in a stream of consciousness. Don't worry about completing your sentences or proper punctuation. Just write. If it's more helpful to doodle or sketch a particular experience, do that! Write until you have nothing left to share; wring out your memories of the experience like a rag until every last drop is on the page before you.

Repeat this ritual whenever you need to awaken yourself to inspiration. Try practicing at different moon phases to discover which part of the cycle is most potent for you.

phrases in any order. oughts? Use this framework to begin a new writing project, song, illustration, or any other creative endeavor.

THE MIDNIGHT CARNIVAL

A sharply defined oval of light pools over the pages of your book. As the bus rattles over a patch of uneven road, you struggle to focus your eyes, which, in your drowsiness, have read the same sentence over and over a few dozen times. *Perhaps now is the time to give up on reading,* you think. You'd hoped to bite off a sizable chunk of this substantial novel on the trip, but it seems sleep has come for you early.

The sparkling city lights of Albany are well behind you on the interstate, and the bus barrels now over the Mohawk River into the mountainous hinterlands of Upstate New York. You haven't spent much time in this part of the United States, but as you move further north, away from New York City and toward dense forests and sprawling lakes, something in the energy of your surroundings shifts. Perhaps the darkness of night lends a little mystery to the atmosphere too. But there's something about this part of the country that feels wild and ancient—like the vibrations of the land are on a different wavelength.

You close your book and reach up to click the light above your seat off. Only a few lights—three or four—are still on at seats around you. But there aren't many passengers anyway. A dozen, maybe. The rest of the bus, and now your seat, is dark and quiet. You recline your seat somewhat. There's no one in front of or behind you. You stretch your legs forward, leaning your head against your plush neck pillow, but you're not quite ready to close your eyes. From the window—you always like to sit on the right side of buses or trains so you can see the open country instead of the other side of the highway—you can just make out the silhouettes of tall conifers. What might be Douglas firs or white pines...you might be able to tell in the light of day.

There's something mesmerizing about watching the tops of the trees, the shining black bodies of water, and occasional small town centers whizz by outside the window. You've always found this kind of sight comforting. It reminds you of childhood—cross-country road trips with family. Counting windmills, cows in pastures, or red cars on the road.

The travel bug bit you late last week. You were at odds with the mundane routines of your life, craving a change of scenery, even for a little while. You've always liked the idea of visiting Quebec, and with heat wave after heat wave arriving this summer, you're anxious to escape somewhere milder. So you packed a few belongings, found a cozy-looking rental in Montreal, and booked the overnight bus. You're not sure what you'll do once you get there besides enjoy the greenspaces and historic neighborhoods. But you've decided that it's just what you need: a last-minute adventure.

The bus's movement is smooth and swift. Outside the window, you can make out fewer and fewer features of the landscape as the area grows dimmer and sparser. You allow your eyelids to sag, then fall closed.

What feels like only a few moments later, you're awoken by a sensation of movement, a lurching motion as the bus slowly grinds to a stop. You flutter open your eyes to see not inky darkness, but artificial, yellowish light through the window. It takes a few moments to remember where you are, where you're headed. You inhale deeply and roll the kinks out of your neck, then look around at the other bleary-eyed passengers.

The bus driver stands and announces that you'll be parked at this rest stop for twenty minutes. "You can leave the bus, stretch your legs, get something to eat...but be back at precisely..." he checks the clock on the dashboard and gives an exact to-the-minute return time.

You contemplate simply closing your eyes once more and waiting out the break in your seat. But you feel a rumble of hunger and the beginnings of a charley horse in your calf, so you opt to leave the bus for a few minutes. It's nearly midnight, and you've been asleep on the bus for a few hours rather than a few moments.

You try to get your bearings in space, but the name of the rest stop tells you little about your location. According to the GPS on your phone, you're somewhere outside of Saratoga Springs. The pin on the map sits in the middle of a largely vacant swathe of Upstate New York. This rest stop and a squiggle of highway are the only landmarks in the empty green of the image. The nearest town looks to be Fort Edward, a good ways away.

The vacuity in the map is reflected in your surroundings. Beyond the pale wash of fluorescent light, the landscape is shrouded in murky darkness. Every few seconds, the swell of headlights on the highway floods the scene with momentary illumination, then passes.

You are just about to head into the all-night convenience store to purchase a snack and something to drink when a faint glimmer off in the darkness catches your attention. At first, you think it's only a mirage, a reflection perhaps, of car lights on a distant reservoir or pond. But that's not right. There's something out there generating its own light. Something very irregular—not a blinking signal tower or power generator.

It's nothing, you think, even as your mind invents strange and fantastical explanations for the light. You've always had an active, wild imagination.

Oh, but it's not nothing.

Before your eyes, which are fixed on whatever it is, the light is shifting and growing. Expanding or extruding until it's not just one single light source but a network of them, shimmering like gold glitter in the dark of the night. *Can anyone else see this?* you wonder.

The lights—some of them static, and some moving in curious patterns—have grown to a large constellation out there. And you think you hear—is it your imagination again, or do you really hear it?—a faint spiral of calliope music issuing forth on the night breeze.

Before you even realize what you're doing, you're walking away from the rest stop, away from the bus, toward the spinning network of lights like a moth to flame. It's as though an invisible string draws you inexorably forward—one that's wrapped around your heart.

The closer you draw to the lights, the more the spectacle ahead comes into focus. Indeed, that was calliope music—jaunty and expressive—on the night air. It grows more present in your ears, along with the sound of laughter and shrieks of delight.

A bevy of scents fill your nostrils—something rich and animal, but also the fragrance of a thousand delicacies. Sweets and salty popcorn and fried foods and funnel cakes. Under string lights and floating lanterns is, to your awe and wonder, a red and white big top circus tent, its curtains drawn and inviting. And beyond it—impossible that you couldn't see it before, but there it is—a brilliantly illuminated Ferris wheel. Rows and rows of stalls for games and food vendors, all appearing as though they've stepped out of the early twentieth century.

It occurs to you that you might be dreaming. You might have, in fact, chosen to close your eyes back there in your bus seat. You might already be en route once more to Canada. For surely, only steps away from the rest stop, you would have seen the attractions of a carnival more sharply; they couldn't have burst into being before your eyes. And what would such a thing be doing out here, in the middle of nowhere, in the middle of the night? But the sounds and smells and sights are so infinitely clear now, so textured, bright, and alive with authenticity that it can't be a dream. It must be real.

There's a bunting-covered archway that marks the threshold of the strange carnival, and you hesitate to step through it, drawn as you are toward the mystery of it all. First, you look at your phone—it's just now midnight. Then, you turn to look back at the bus and the rest stop. Rather than a few dozen steps away, it seems miles and miles off, as though the distance has stretched through time. It feels a world and a half away. Only sixteen minutes until the bus departs to tackle the stretch of highway still ahead. Perhaps you should go back.

But something swells deep within you, growing with a breath that carries the scent of carnival fare. Something wild and adventurous. Whatever lies beyond the archway—this curious mirage in the sticks of New York—might be just the thrill, the escape you've been so desperately craving.

Feeling light as a balloon and letting all thoughts of the road fall away as you turn your head from the rest stop, you step beneath the bunting and into the carnival grounds.

At once, the sensory experience heightens. The smells are more enticing, the lights are more colorful, and the sounds are more musical. A rush of childlike giddiness comes over you. You feel small and silly, frivolous, like a child with a pocket full of quarters and an insatiable sweet tooth. Everything around you is sugary sweet and overwhelming. You hardly know where or how to begin.

Eyes wide, reflecting the floating paper lanterns—wonderful how they seem to hang and bounce on the air as if held there by magic, you wonder what the trick to it is—you stroll through a line of wooden stalls at which people of all ages stand, cheer, and play games. All these people, you think, in the middle of nowhere, in the middle of the night. All these children, out of bed. What a strange phenomenon.

One of the games catches your eye for its bright, vibrant colors. The backdrop of the stall is painted with a thick, bold rainbow across its corners. Your eyes follow the rainbow to its end, in an illustrative pot of gold. There's also a cartoonish image of a leprechaun, smiling and rubbing his hands together as he eyes the pot of gold.

The game being played, you recognize, is a sort of ring toss. A coin toss, rather. The participants, three children of varying ages, are attempting to throw comically large gold coins into their designated pots, each pinned to the back of the stall and painted with a dollar sign. You remember a parent once telling you that all carnival games are rigged, and you suspect that may be true with this one. The children are laughing and shouting, and each misses every toss they make.

You glance at the game operator. Like the cartoon leprechaun in the backdrop, he's dressed up in green and gold, with a funny top hat and a shamrock at his lapel. He looks over at you, and you hastily avert your gaze. When you look back, he's still smirking in your direction. Beneath his hat, you think you see—how curious—that his ears are subtly pointed. He winks at you and, to your surprise, tosses you a coin. *A souvenir,* he calls out. It's about the size of a quarter and looks to be of real gold. On one face is an engraving of the rainbow and a pot of gold; on the other is an image of something like a winged pixie.

You continue to walk through the stalls and observe the goings-on. Your focus is continuously drawn upward with the revolution of the brightly lit Ferris wheel. Incandescent and pluming from the center of the wheel, its lights blaze in rippling patterns. Once you stand directly beneath it, you're amazed at how monumentally tall it is. The highest point seems to disappear into clouds and stars. You're certain now that you should have seen such a thing from the highway. This carnival is much more than meets the eye.

The rumbling of hunger is still present, so you approach a food stand. There's a short line, only a couple of people ahead of you, and they come away carrying armfuls of popcorn and corndogs in moments. A freckled young woman with a bright purple pixie haircut asks for your order, and—feeling a craving for sweets—you cautiously point to a few menu items with enticing names. "Fairy floss," you assume, is cotton candy, so you order some. And, to quench your thirst, you ask for a "sprite lemonade," which must be extra citrusy and carbonated. The young woman tells you, to your surprise, that it's on the house, and goes to retrieve your items.

The fairy floss is indeed cotton candy—puffy wisps of spun pink sugar whipped onto a paper cone, that is. But it shimmers and glints in the carnival lights as though it's run all the way through with sparkling rainbow glitter. It has an otherworldly quality, seeming to disappear and reappear in strands before your eyes. And the lemonade, though pleasantly bubbly, is flavored not with citrus soda but with something like tart hibiscus or elderflower nectar. You enjoy both, feeling pleasingly light-headed as you tear off pieces of the fairy floss and let them melt on your tongue.

You check the time on your phone, and you're surprised to see that it still reads twelve-midnight. But you think little of it, sipping happily on your lemonade. You don't even notice that with each bite of fairy floss you eat, your feet hover another centimeter off the ground—until you step not across grass but buoyant thin air.

Now you arrive before a most marvelous sight—a carousel, fashioned like one of the antique steam-powered ones with an ornate canopy and warm, bright bulbs. Finishing your refreshments, you marvel at the smooth movement of the jumping mounts, which glide up and down with amazing, near-lifelike grace.

The carousel slows to a stop, its calliope tune winding down, and you see that the mounts are not only horses but the most marvelous creatures. Winged horses. Unicorns. Horses with fins, and long, fishlike tails. Dragons. Gryphons. Winged lions and tigers. Animals and hybrids that seem to have stepped from the pages of myth. You step eagerly into the line to ride the carousel as the previous riders stumble out—if only to admire the mounts up close.

Once you step aboard the platform, you're even more impressed with the craftsmanship. The level of detail, texture, and realism in the creatures is astounding. Each is more creative than the last. You hurry to select a mount as children scurry toward the unicorns and tigers. You find a beautiful, unrecognizable animal that seems to call to you. It's not unlike a horse at first glance, though elegant horns grow from its head, and it's covered from head to toe with silver and blue scales. Its hind parts are more reptilian, with a serpentine tail curled behind. It has wings, too, which are folded by its side. It resembles the union of a horse and a dragon—something powerful, loyal, and, you sense, lucky. The operator calls for all riders to board their mounts, so you climb onto its back and grip the metal pole. A sense of electric anticipation builds as the gears and cranks begin to turn, and the music begins to crescendo.

And you're off. The merry-go-round turns, slowly at first, then gathering speed. Your surroundings become a blur, and the breeze feels cool and invigorating. You feel lighthearted, carefree, and boundless.

Sometime after the ride begins, the stiff fiberglass and shiny varnish of your mount—the dragon horse creature—softens beneath you. You're not sure when it happens. It's as though a hard outer shell has melted away to reveal the truth underneath. You look down to see that the dragon horse, scaled and silver-green, is gracefully galloping and whipping its head in the wind. It snorts, and little spirals of smoke escape its nostrils. It is alive and soft and real. You hold tight around its neck and look around to the other carousel mounts. All are alive—the unicorns, the winged bears, the other chimeric wonders—and all are running, galloping, flying in place. Your dragon horse unfurls its silver wings and soars, treading the air in line with its fellows on the carousel platform.

Laughter, music, whinnies, and roars spin round the axis of the carousel. It's exhilarating—unlike anything you've ever experienced—and yet, you feel no fear, only an innate sense of trust in your steed. You want the ride to last forever or to break off from the platform and fly off into the dark sky. You and the dragon horse feel connected, moving as one through the night. It's blissful.

But after some time, you feel the gears and the cranks and the motors slowing down. The world outside the carousel becomes less blurry, more static. The sounds of the carnival become louder than the diminishing music of the ride. And beneath you, the soft scales of your steed begin to harden once more into lacquer and fiberglass. Before it's too late, though, the creature turns its head to look back at you, and you think you can see a smile—or a twinkle in its eye.

You dismount, pat the dragon horse on the muzzle, thinking how silly you must look, and depart the carousel. Your legs quiver a bit as you readjust to solid ground.

The fairgrounds seem to stretch impossibly onward in all directions. Endless games, rides, and stalls. You stop to play a game that looks like a balloon pop. You have a handful of darts, for example, but it's not stationary balloons at which you aim. Instead, there are floating orbs of soft, colorful light that move languidly about the stall. Will-o'-the-wisps, you might have called them, had you come upon them in a moonlit wood. Try as you might, and your aim is good, you can't seem to hit one. Though they move slowly, they always jump an inch to the left or right when your dart comes flying.

The operator takes pity on you, however, and offers you a consolation prize: a simple but lovely tin ring. A strange prize, you think—and curious that the workers of this carnival seem so eager to give you things for free. He urges you to try the ring on, but some hushed instinct tells you not to. Instead, you pocket it, assuring him you'll find a chain to tie it round your neck.

As you continue to explore the grounds—checking the clock on your phone once more and noting that it's still just twelve-midnight— you catch the fragrance of sandalwood incense on the air. Your head swims as you look around for the source and see a small dark purple tent nestled between larger food and activity stalls. Over the beaded entrance to the tent is a humble sign, with handwritten curlicue letters reading "Fortune Teller."

Usually not one to seek out such things, you find your curiosity impossible to ignore. You part the black and purple beaded curtain and enter the tent. It's tiny—only large enough for two people to fit comfortably inside—and there's one person already seated at the small round table in the center. An embroidered black drape hangs over the edges of the table, and on the drape sits a crystal ball, a deck of oracle cards, and a burning candle.

The seated person—presumably the fortune teller—wears a sheer, dark veil over their head. You can see the shine of a pair of dark eyes, but not much more. With a gentle voice and a gesture of delicate hands, they beckon you to sit down.

It's funny—once you sit at the little table, a hazy silver mist seems to settle about you. The outside noises and music of the carnival grow quiet, muffled, distant. It's you and the fortune teller.

They wonder if you have a question. Something you're seeking answers or guidance about. You open your mouth to speak, but they assure you, you don't have to say it out loud.

You try to think of a question. In truth, you have many. About the direction of your life. About your choices. About your relationships. About risks you want to take. About things you want to change. It's hard to find just one simple question.

You take your time. Until the right question emerges. Not the ultimate question—but the right question for right now on this leg of your journey.

When you're ready, you look into the fortune teller's veiled eyes and nod.

They reach for the oracle deck, shuffle it fluidly, and reveal the top card. It's a vague and abstract, but appealing image. On a deep blue backdrop, you see what look like dandelion seeds, white and wispy. From the seeds grow long wisps of gauzy light, which stream toward the bottom of the card, almost in the shape of a flowing gown.

"The threshold guardian," says the fortune teller.

"This card represents your current state. The card indicates that you recognize the immeasurable hugeness and wildness of the world. That you see life as an adventure—or the potential of one. But you may feel lost or torn in a world of infinite possibilities. You may feel overwhelmed by choice or afraid to take a first step toward something real and life changing."

They turn the next card over. The image on the card is of a bluish fairy, hunched over and covering their face. From between its slender fingers, one green eye peers out at the looker. The fairy's hair is dark and wild, frazzled. Pointed ears and what might be horns or tree branches stick out from the tufts of it.

"This is the obstacle," the fortune teller explains. "This card can represent sudden, unexpected change. The breakdown of routines and structure. The loss of one's footing. It may mean you've settled into something comfortable in life, only to suddenly lose that sense of equilibrium. Or, it can be read in a more global...or even cosmic sense. That the world you know has broken down around you, and you are one of many attempting to adapt to a new order. It can signal the need to reevaluate your life, shuffle off any baggage you may be carrying, and start on a new path."

The fortune teller turns over one more card. Behind the veil, you can see their eyes glittering with what might be interest or excitement. You too feel your breath catch when you see the illustration. It's of a fairy woman, with wings spread and luminescent in a bath of moon and starlight. She's crowned with tiny, glowing flowers and surrounded by little sparkles of light. Above her open right hand floats a gleaming orb. On her face is a serene, peaceful expression. Her gown is luminous and delicate as gossamer. You look between this card and the first one—the threshold guardian—and recognize that the sweeping gown shapes reflect one another almost perfectly.

"The weaver of dreams..." the fortune teller says, their voice tinged with awe and mystery. "A very special card indeed.

"This is the lesson," they continue. "With the knowledge of the situation and the obstacle"—here they gesture to the first two cards— "the Dream Weaver is trying to tell you something. She is a kind of guide—but more like a flash of intuition, creative inspiration, or otherworldly revelation. She might be reaching out to encourage you to trust the flashes of instinct or inspiration you receive, even if they feel like they're coming from out of nowhere. For just as she is self-illuminating—generating her own light—the energy is coming from within you."

You sit with the cards for a little while, exploring the intricacies of the illustrations. The fortune teller seems in no rush to dismiss you. *The threshold guardian. The change in routine. The weaver of dreams.* The situation. The obstacle. The lesson. All the cards seem to call out to you, but you're not quite sure the message they're trying to convey.

You thank the fortune teller and begin to ask how much you owe, but they—like the food vendor and the game operator—insist that your first reading is on the house. You give them a puzzled look, but they sweep the three cards into a neat pile and hand them to you. To keep. You're bemused, but you accept the gift, knowing you can contemplate the message further. How generous the workers at this carnival have been.

Before you leave the tent, the fortune teller asks your name. You turn, and you're about to respond when you see that she's lifted her veil. There are the dark eyes, along with delicate, childlike features and a sly grin that gives you pause. Something deep within whispers to you—an instinct or a flash of intuition—that you should not give the fortune teller your name. You don't feel any sense of danger or trepidation, but you listen to the voice. All you say to the fortune teller is… "I'm a traveler."

When you leave the tent, the sounds return—of laughter, song, and popcorn popping. You pass beneath the towering Ferris wheel again, craning your neck in the attempt to see its zenith, which disappears into a passing cloud far above you. Your pocket is heavy with your gifts: the coin, the ring, the cards.

Though there's still much to see, experience, and explore on the fairgrounds, you begin to feel like it's time to go. You can't explain it. But somehow, you understand that you should leave soon…before you become lost in this place. You check the time again—still, it's only just turned midnight, but that doesn't seem strange to you at all.

You breeze past the food stalls, games, and rides. You pass through a row you think you've been through already, but there are attractions now that you don't recognize. Perhaps they set up, or changed over, while you were having your fortune told. Never mind. A laughing, blindfolded child attempts to pin the tail on a cartoon dragon.

A sparkling haze gathers at the corners of your eyes as you move toward the exit. You can see the archway and its bunting from here, but as you walk, it doesn't seem to get any closer.

You overhear a man calling for folks to gather round. The crier stands before the open flaps of the circus tent. He stands on a decorative platform and ushers attendees into the tent for a marvelous presentation. He's small in stature but bears a mustache so thick and black and heavy you're surprised he doesn't topple forward from the weight of it. Upon his head sits a towering black top hat, and he wears a red coat with elegant tails that fall well past his feet.

As you pass, he looks directly at you, pleading for audiences to go and see the fantastical attraction before it's too late. You consider heeding his call to go inside and witness whatever wonders lie within. But no, you've already decided to make your way out. You continue toward the exit, ignoring the calls of ride operators, food vendors, and game attendants hocking their wares and attractions in your direction.

Finally, after what seems like hours and miles of walking, the exit is within reach. You almost turn around for one last look at the magnificent carnival, but you resist. Something tells you to resist. You pass under the bunting once more. A strange sensation passes over you, a sort of rush like wind or water, and your feet thud against the dark grass as though you've fallen from a not-so-significant height. You catch your breath, and only now, you turn back.

The bunting, the archway, the red and white tent, the stalls, the carousel, and the Ferris wheel have vanished. With them, the scents of popcorn and sweets and the sound of the calliope. You stand alone in a dark field. There's no moon, but there are many, many stars overhead.

You can see from here the uncanny yellow of the rest stop's light. The bus hasn't left yet, you realize, with a sigh of relief. You check the time. It's 12:01. Curious.

You walk back to the rest stop, feeling less nimble, less light on your feet than a moment before. *A dream brought on by delirious exhaustion and inky darkness and gnawing hunger,* you think. You purchase some sustenance from the convenience store and reboard the bus with a few minutes to spare.

The bus pulls away from the stop and gains momentum on the dark stretch of highway through lake country, the Adirondacks, and coniferous forest. Before long, swayed by the gentle rocking of the vehicle and the pale white shine of headlights on black pavement, you close your eyes.

In your pocket, there is a coin engraved with the symbols of flight, lightness, and air.

There is a ring forged from the metals of the earth.

There are three cards reaching out to deliver you a message: a guardian, a seismic shift, and a dream weaver.

You won't realize they're there until morning breaks over Montreal.

Exercise: Sleep Spell Sachet

Assemble this small sachet of herbs and crystals to support better sleep, meaningful dreams, and relaxation. You can use the suggested materials or adjust to suit your preferences and intentions.

Suggested Materials:

Small sachet or cloth bag (preferably with a drawstring or other closure)
A few sprigs of dried lavender, or a pinch of dried lavender buds
Dried valerian root
Moonstone

Other Suggested Ingredients:

Dried rosemary (for dream recall)
Dried mugwort (for lucid dreams, vivid dreams, dream recall)
Dried mint (for relaxation, clarity)
Lemon balm (for relaxation)
Amethyst (for deep sleep, calm dreams)

Optional:

Small piece of paper or parchment
Writing utensil

✳ Mix dried herbs in a small bowl, adjusting measurements to your preference. Add crystal(s) to the sachet, then fill the rest with dried herb mixture.

✳ Activate the Sleep Spell by holding the sachet and speaking your intention aloud. If you need inspiration, consider the following:

• *I sleep deeply, open to the messages of dreams.*
• *I honor my body's natural rhythms and the call of sleep.*
• *I wake rested, rejuvenated, and ready to approach the new day.*

✳ If you like, write your intention on a small piece of paper, roll it up, and slip it inside of the sachet. Keep the sachet under your pillow, use as aromatherapy in your bedroom or pajama drawer, or place on your dream altar. If you have dried herb blend left over (and you use food-grade herbs), steep into a tea to enjoy before bed as part of your nightly ritual.

SECRET OF THE SELKIE

It will take some time for this place to feel like home. There's no sense in rushing things. You've got a lifetime ahead of you.

The misty morning light, stark white with a slice of sun melting through curtains of fog, shimmers through the window. You haven't yet lit the lamps inside the lighthouse keeper's quarters—you're not sure how. That's surely in the instructions left to you. The most important light, the warning light itself, you've had some training on. The rest—the endeavor to make a life here—is all up to you.

But first, you want to situate the precious few belongings you brought to the headland in your new residence. This involves the considered removal of the mountains of material left behind by the previous lighthouse keeper. Heaps and heaps of books and papers: ledgers, daily logs, photograph albums, and other miscellaneous records. They also left behind personal belongings of all sorts: clothing, furnishings, knick-knacks, and kitchen wares.

Some of it you'll undoubtedly decide to keep: the existing furniture is usable, and there are some delightfully strange decorations you wouldn't mind holding onto. A small brass sculpture, for example, of a two-tailed mermaid, an elegant crown upon her head. You can tell that framed photographs once hung on the walls in the modest quarters connected to the lighthouse. The now mostly bare walls give up numerous squares of darkened wallpaper, unbleached by the intruding sunlight. You wonder if the former keeper hung pictures of their family or a long-lost sweetheart across the sea.

Feeling an urge to get some fresh air, your mind swirling with thoughts of the previous keeper's life and romances, you step outside into the cool morning. The surroundings are conducive to such speculation. The lighthouse sits atop the limestone cliffs of the cape, towering over the crashing waves of open sea. Miles from the only town center on the island, itself remote in the region, there's an isolation that's haunting and romantic. The distance from everyday civilization and the closeness to nature—the vastness of nature in cliffs and waves and shorebird migration—is at once solemn and sublime. You think how small your silhouette must appear should an onlooker glimpse you standing on the cliffs. Tiny and overwhelmed by the majesty of it all, the age-old rock and the movements of natural forces that care not for human affairs.

You could get used to this, you think, feeling how the wind tousles your hair and the salt spray air conditions your skin. You close your eyes for a moment, just listening to the sound of the waves crashing below. Distant, and yet incredibly close. Abstract, and yet entirely tangible. You have a sense of lightness, floating. You anchor this sensation in the back of your mind, for the moments of doubt you anticipate—cramped in the tight quarters of the lighthouse trimming the wick or maintaining the clockwork. *Just come back out here*, you think. *Just step outside and feel the limitless expanse of the land, sea, and sky*. It'll set you right.

Your head clear, you return inside to continue the task of organizing the living space. You keep a window slightly open; why endure a stuffy cabin when such invigorating air lies just outside? You set about packing away a mountain of photo albums, though your wistful heart won't let you tuck them in a box without first peaking at them. Inside, you find yellowed images of the island and the townsfolk. There's one picture of a husband and wife in front of a small white building, whom you recognize as younger versions of the couple who still operate the post office. You met them when you arrived, and they made you promise to pay them a visit from time to time, lest you become too cooped up on the cliffside. The memory of their playful ribbing brings a smile to your face. There are more photos of local business owners, some whom you recognize from your brief time in town, and others who look familiar enough that they might still reside in the village—or their descendants might.

The albums are a fascinating documentary history of the island. Your imagination strings together stories that connect the photographs through time. This person must have married into that family, and they opened such-and-such fish market. But they left for the mainland when they came into family money and were never heard from again. This young lady left the island with hopes of becoming a famous actress, but after some time on the stages in London, she returned and never spoke of the intervening years. You enjoy making up such stories, though you imagine you'll learn the true histories of the island in time.

There's a face that pops up here and again in the photos. At first, you didn't pay it much mind, because the person is usually swept to the side of the photographs or stuck in the backgrounds, never the camera's focus. She's a handsome woman with dark hair and features. She wears, always, a somewhat morose expression. Perhaps that's not the right word. There's just something forlorn about her. Lost. You wonder if she still lives on the island. She'd be older now, but you're curious about her story.

After a long morning of sorting and packing, you finally endeavor to move the box of photo albums to a closet in your bedroom. You have to shift a few things around in the closet to make room, teetering some small boxes precariously upon an inner shelf. As you're moving items in the dark—you haven't yet figured out the lamps and there's hardly any natural light in the bedroom—your groping hands fall upon the unexpected texture of worked leather. If you're not mistaken, at the back of the closet, there's a large and heavy chest, its surface leatherbound. You can feel grooves in the leather, indicating some sort of decoration or design.

It takes some exertion on your part, but you manage to heave the chest from the depths of the cupboard and slide it into the living space where you can see better. Indeed, there are intricate designs pounded into the reddish-brown leather. Circles and spirals and discs that remind you, vaguely, of the Pictish symbol stones unearthed on some of the surrounding islands. You wipe away a thick layer of dust from the surface to better observe the patterns.

You're quite overcome with curiosity. What could be hiding within such an elegant piece of craft? The former lighthouse keeper left many curiosities behind, but this chest is surely of high value. You're surprised it wasn't pillaged by the townsfolk after the post was vacated. No one must know about it.

But just as you go to lift the lid, you finally see the rusted lock. Still, you try, hopeful, to open the chest, but it's securely fastened. You sigh. There must be a key somewhere—you were given a ring of keys when you arrived for the living quarters, the lighthouse, and various pieces of equipment. You fetch the keys and try every single one in the lock on the chest. None are the right fit. Somewhat disappointed, but all the more intrigued about the contents of the mysterious chest, you slide it back into the closet and set your mind to the work at hand. You'll find the key, surely. It's a matter of time. For now, it's best the thing stay out of sight.

Your first days as the new lighthouse keeper on the island pass uneventfully. You receive a handful of visits from the townsfolk, bringing homemade food and welcome gifts. A mail carrier comes by most days. He's the son of the couple who own the post office, and he makes sure to remind you—every time he comes—that his mother and father expect a visit from you. He brings you letters, mostly intended for the former lighthouse keeper, but there's the occasional correspondence from your friends and family on the mainland. It's good to hear from them. You throw the letters for the old keeper into a pile, unsure of what to do with them—whether to read them or cast them out to sea. Perhaps they'll come back for the letters one day.

You take to the job rather well. You find you're a natural at keeping up the equipment and maintaining the lighthouse. But there's a certain kind of loneliness that creeps in at the edges. After a fortnight, you decide it's time to take that visit to town. You ride your bicycle to the center of the village, enjoying the downhill breeze on the headland. The post office couple treats you to lunch, and the wife introduces you to several important people. The mayor: an absent-minded old man with white whiskers and thick glasses. The librarian: a sweet, put-upon woman looking after a gaggle of young children. Many others. It's a town of only a few hundred people, and by the end of your outing, you feel you've met at least half of them.

As you prepare to return to the lighthouse, you steal a glance at a handsome residence. There's a movement in the window—a rustle of drapes—as if someone was watching you from behind the curtain and hastily dropped it when your gaze turned their way.

The visit fills up your heart, replenishes your energy in a way. You like solitude (otherwise, why would you have accepted such a posting?), but it feels good to be welcomed into pleasant company. You light a fire in your residence as darkness falls on the cliffside. You sleep well.

The next morning, as you're outside cleaning windows, you notice a human presence ascending the hill toward the cliffs. It's not the right time for the mail carrier to come by, and you wouldn't expect a visit from the townsfolk so soon after your journey. The figure draws closer. She's a willowy woman with wild, long dark hair, black as the ocean at night. She's the woman from the photographs, you're sure of it. Older, certainly, but not by as much as you'd expected. Her features are unmistakable.

But she doesn't come toward you—she doesn't introduce herself. Instead, she breezes past you and the lighthouse, hardly acknowledging your presence, and glides toward the edge of the cliff. For a moment, her head held high and eyes aloft, you fear she may walk right off the edge, and you almost run after her. But she stops before she reaches the end of the cliff. And she stands. And she stares.

You decide not to disturb her, so you go about your tasks for the day. Maintenance. Cleaning. Still organizing the living quarters. Trimming the wick. Cleaning the lens. Every time you look outside, she's there, hair and dress whipping in the wind, gazing out at the sea. Then, at dusk, she turns and goes. Back the way she came.

You fix yourself supper and retrieve one of the old photo albums from storage. You flip through the pages as you eat. The resemblance is too uncanny for it not to be the same woman unless there's a close relation to be accounted for. But given the dates on the pages of the album, if it is indeed the same woman, she's barely aged in the years since the images were captured. It's the sea air, you think. She must come here for the benefits of sun and salt and spray, to keep her looking young.

She comes back a few days later. She still ignores your presence.

And later in the week, she comes again. And stands at the edge of the cliff. And stares out at the sea. For hours.

Finally, you decide, you'll talk to her. You'll introduce yourself. The next time she comes, on a clear September morning, you call out to her as she strides toward the cliffside. For the first time, you see her up close. See how her dark, stormy eyes match the impression of the photographs. How her brow furrows at your intrusion on her private cliffside ritual. But she warms to you quickly enough.

Her name, you discover, is Tess, and she's lived on the island for several years. She came here for love, of all things. She married a man who'd been here all his life. He's gone now, and she stays with a cousin of his. She doesn't say any more than that. You don't press her for the details. You don't ask about the photographs in the lighthouse. Not yet.

Tess comes back more frequently, now that she knows you. Every other day, sometimes on days back-to-back. Most days, you give each other friendly waves, exchange a few words about the weather or the goings-on in town. There's a familiarity growing between you. An understanding. You don't ask her why she comes to stare at the sea or why she looks so sad when she watches the ocean waves. She doesn't ask you why you left your life behind to take up the lighthouse post.

As autumn marches on and the island settles under an ever-present fog and chill, you're surprised to see Tess continue to visit so frequently. She shivers under a knit shawl on an especially chilly day, the fog dampening her dark hair in coils against her skin. There's an electricity in the air, in the particles of fog. A storm is coming—you're sure of it. Twilight comes earlier and earlier now, and you beg Tess to come inside and warm herself by the fire. Finally, she agrees.

As soon as she enters the residence, you sense a change in her. You retrieve a wool blanket from your bedroom and urge her to wrap it around her shoulders; her slight frame is still quivering from the bone chill of the dense fog. You prepare a hearty stew and tear off hunks of rich bread from the village baker. She protests, but you insist that she eat something, to warm her from the inside. You light a cozy fire in the fireplace. Outside, a heavy rain descends upon the cliffs. The oil lamps flicker, lending an exquisite tranquility to the scene.

After supper, the storm continues to rage outside, but the tiny residence—which has survived a hundred years or more in the shadow of the lighthouse—feels sturdy and protective against the elements. You're reminded of a long-forgotten storm from childhood when you cowered in your bed against the breaking of thunder and flashes of lightning, a blanket over your head. That very night, a loving caregiver held you and assured you all would be all right. That in the morning, the sky would be light again, and the storm would be passed.

You describe the memory to Tess. You're not sure why, but you feel compelled to give her this window into your past as an offering—so she might let you into her story in return. Your words seem to cast a spell. Her face, so solemn, so infinitely forlorn from the moment you first beheld it in the old photographs, finally breaks into a smile. She's picturing you, as a child, reaching out for the warmth of a protector. And you feel, in this moment, in the shining light of her smile, that you've become the very dearest of friends. You could so use a friend.

The storm breaks, finally. Night has fallen, but the skies clear. You and Tess step out onto the soggy grass and look out at the ocean, black and tempest-tossed in the suddenly cloudless skies. A silver moon waxes against a backdrop of stars and casts its fluttering reflection on the stormy sea. You're mesmerized by the ocean's subtle disturbances, the push and pull between peace and agitation, stillness and motion on its surface. Wordlessly, Tess departs, her feet quiet on the spongy earth. You don't see her go. You behold her silhouette upon the cliffs long after she's left. You sleep deeply that night, your dreams a vision of wayward ships under heavy skies.

Tess doesn't return soon after. You look for her on the cliffs as you wind the clockwork or polish the lens, but she doesn't come. You fear you became too vulnerable, offered too much of yourself during the storm. That you frightened away the possibility of a true friendship.

You take another bike ride into town, ostensibly to pick up supplies at the market and say hello to your neighbors. You're hoping to see Tess though, to make sure she's all right. You don't find her in the market, or at the post office, or the library.

But she comes to the cliffs again a week later. Your heart exhales when you see her. Somber as ever, dark and brooding as she gazes longingly at the tides. She's brought a picnic basket. You share lunch in the breezy grass on a sunny afternoon.

And now—perhaps emboldened by her return—you decide to ask her about the photographs. The ones now packed into a box, gathering dust in your bedroom closet. There are dozens of images of her, you explain, of the face that's hardly aged in these many years.

Tess is silent for a long time—a silence filled only by the calling of gulls and the crashing of tides. But you sense that something changes, softens, in her. When she speaks again, she asks if you've yet been down to the beaches that lie below the limestone cliffs. You haven't.

She leads you down a steep and treacherous path—one that's been concealed from your view till now. It's all you can do to keep from tumbling down the side of the cliff, but Tess navigates it with striking ease. As you cling to the crags of white limestone, the wind smooth against your skin, every few moments, you meet that sensation again—of floating, weightless.

You're grateful for the feeling of solidity when your feet at last meet the ground. The beach below is more like a narrow strip of pebbles and rock betwixt cliff and sea. Judging by the waterline in the cliffside, this slice of land likely spends much of high tide underwater. You think of the storm a week ago and wonder how high the waves rose that night. Now the waters are quite calm. A serene smile crosses Tess's lips.

The sun emerges from behind clouds to warm the shore, glittering golden on the surface of the water. The light catches something out there in the waves at a distance, something dark and shining and organic. Tess holds a hand to her brow, shielding her eyes from the sun. She's looking straight at whatever's out there. You squint and try to make it out. The forms, for there are a few of them, seem to be drawing closer. Leaping above and below the surface of the water.

Soon you recognize the shapes as the silhouettes of grey seals, playfully jumping in and out of the water. There are three of them, as far as you can tell. They stop before they reach the narrow shore, but they're close enough to see them more clearly. Heads above the waves, they blink their big, watery eyes, observing you with curiosity. You've seen similar eyes before. Haven't you? Dark, inquisitive, knowing eyes?

Tess breaks the silence. She wonders if you've ever heard the legends or folktales of the selkies. Do they tell stories like that where you're from?

At the word *selkie,* your mind fills with many broken images. Glittering tides. Sad maidens. Lovelorn husbands. Seals resting on pebbled beaches. Of course, you've heard the legends. They're told all over this part of the world.

The version you remember clearest, and this you begin to detail to Tess as it comes back to you, was recited by the same beloved caregiver who carried you through that childhood storm. In it, a farmer waited by the sea for the seals to come ashore, where, according to legend, once a year, they'd shed their skins and take human form for one night. He saw one seal shed her skin and take the form of a beautiful woman, and he was struck at once with mad love. He stole her seal coat so she could not return to her true form, and he locked the coat away in a chest, never daring to remove the key from his person. The farmer married the seal woman, who pined still for the sea despite caring for her husband. And, all the while, the chest containing her seal coat remained locked away in the chest. Until one day, the farmer left his key at home when he went to the fields. When he came back, he discovered the chest lying open and empty, and his wife gone, returned to the ocean.

Tess's eyes fill with emotion as you recount the tale. She's heard such a version, too, and many others. But, she wonders, do you believe the legends? Or do you assume they're merely the fancy of old wives and fisherfolk, conjuring up folklore to survive the bleakness of the fog…or explain away the mysteries of nature?

A curious question, but you have to think about your answer. You've never really thought about it enough to believe or disbelieve the local tales. You were just a child when you first encountered them, accustomed to a world of wonder and magic and make-believe. If you really think about such legends—shapeshifting seal maidens and undersea cultures?—you must dismiss them, surely. Still, you suppose there's a part of you that's always longed to believe in the magical and mysterious, the unexplained. And, living here at the edge of the world, you haven't the pride to assume you know all of nature's secrets.

But now you're beginning to see. In Tess's eyes, there's the same dark curiosity of the blinking seals out at sea. Her forlorn wanderings on the cliffside and wistful gazes to the open water. The leather chest languishing in your closet. The missing key.

Finally, Tess tells you everything. She came ashore one night and shed her skin, eager to walk among humans for just one day. She climbed the steep path toward the top of the cliff and collapsed on the moonlit grass, unused to having human legs. The lighthouse keeper found her there, shivering and damp, and he brought her inside. He fed her, clothed her, and let her warm up by the fire. He was kind and lonely, so she decided to stay a little longer than a day.

Within a month, they'd married. The lighthouse keeper had stolen down to the rocky beaches and retrieved her seal coat there, hiding it somewhere. She never knew where. They were married for many years. They never had children, but Tess looked over her husband's cousin's brood most days, becoming a second mother to them. She thought of the sea often and sometimes longed to dive right into the waters and swim away. She loved the island, her husband, and her family, but there were times she felt disconnected. Trapped. She wept for the freedom of her seal days.

As the years went by, though her face had more lines, Tess looked almost as youthful as she had on the day she shed her skin on the beach. But her husband, the lighthouse keeper, grew older. A lifetime of climbing the spiral stairs, maintaining the property, cleaning the lenses, and winding the clockwork had taken its toll. One day, he died. With him went the secret of Tess's lost coat and all hope of returning to the ocean.

But you know the story didn't end there. For a new lighthouse keeper came to the island shortly after Tess's husband's death. And now, you stand beside her on the shore, learning a secret no other living soul has heard.

When she finishes speaking, your heart aches for Tess. In the short time you've known her, you've come to respect her and cherish her company. You couldn't have guessed at the source of her sadness or her endless longing.

You want to show her something. She leads you back up the rocky trail to the lighthouse, grasping your hand tightly when you fear stumbling. You bring her to the closet, and you dust off the heavy chest once more.

Tess runs a hand across the Pictish swirls and spirals in the leather. Her breathing is shallow, and her voice quivers. This must be it. The seal coat must be in here. But you haven't the key.

A sense of anticlimax falls over you and your friend. Tess's freedom lies, presumably, just within reach at the bottom of the box before you. But there's no way of getting inside. You tell her you've tried every key on the ring and you've searched the likely places in the residence. She sighs that the key probably went with her husband to his grave. Perhaps he wore it round his neck when they buried him. Or maybe, all those years ago, he cast it into the ocean so she'd never be able to leave him. Feeling hope dwindle in the silence, you and Tess part ways for the afternoon. She goes back to the village and you go back to work.

Over the next few weeks, you become almost obsessed with finding the key. You search the nooks and crannies of your residence, the corners of the closets, under loose floorboards. You search the lighthouse itself as you work. Between the gears. You come close to digging up the gardens outside. But it seems to be a lost cause. Tess visits every few days, bringing you fresh bread or books from the library. You can see in her eyes the lurking hope, that one day she might come up to the cliffs to find you brandishing the key. You're sorry to disappoint her. But you don't speak about it much.

Time goes by, and you settle naturally into your role. You master the duties of caring for the lighthouse, and you even take to planting native shrubs and plants around the residence, giving the place a more inviting atmosphere. The townspeople all know you by name now, and you're a welcome visitor at local businesses.

But as the air grows colder and the year weakens toward winter, you find yourself withdrawing more and more into your private space, less inclined to hop onto your bicycle and ride into town. Tess visits less, too. Several heavy snows slow down any movement between places.

One afternoon, as you polish the lens, fingers trembling in the unheated tower of the lighthouse, you see a dark silhouette trudging through the snow toward your home. The figure is wrapped so tightly in scarves and coats that you can't make out many details about them. You head down the iron stair to greet the visitor.

It's the mail carrier. You usher him inside the living quarters, and he brushes flurries of snow from his coat as he steps across the threshold. He's brought you a letter from the mainland; it's only a greeting from a cousin who wants you to know of their plans to visit the Americas. Hardly anything so urgent that it needed to be carried through all this hideous weather.

But the mail carrier also brings a verbal invitation to Christmas dinner at his parents' house. You assure him that won't be necessary; you'll have a perfectly fine feast on your own here. But the mail carrier insists that all the townsfolk have fought over who would coax you to dinner for the holiday, that it's no imposition or charity, but a sincere desire to see you and welcome you into their homes. You're touched by the genuine plea. You agree to join them for supper.

Christmas comes a week later, with clear skies and melting snow. You ride your bicycle into town for the first time in over a month. You imagine you won't run into Tess, as all the townsfolk are probably inside, decking their halls with evergreen and preparing supper for their families. But you find a pleasantly bustling market square upon your arrival. Cheerful people greeting each other, buying last-minute finishings for their feasts. You do meet Tess in the square, surrounded by her cousin's children, who beg for sweets and gifts. It's a quick meeting with a friendly hello and little more.

You meet the couple who invited you to their home, presenting a bottle of sherry as a gift. A handful of cousins and their son, of course, are present. They fuss and fight over you, taking your coat, remarking how long your hair has grown, and asking if you ever intend to get married. The evening is warm and pleasant, with drinks and games by the fire, the delighted shouts of children at the hearth, and, at last, a modest but delicious dinner. You count yourself fortunate to live among such people who refuse to let you languish entirely alone at your post.

After supper, you sit by the fire again, enjoying being regaled by one of the cousins with stories from the mainland. Suddenly, the wife from the post office lets out a little gasp, as though she's just remembered something incredibly important. She runs from the room without a word, leaving you and the bewildered family behind. When she returns, she's holding a small box. The contents rattle as she walks. It's not wrapped like a Christmas present, but rather made of forged metal. A safety deposit box, you recognize.

The wife gives you the box with an air of significance. You give her a puzzled look. You haven't opened a safe deposit box on the island. "It belonged to your predecessor," she explains. You blink. Still, you wonder, why on earth would it be given to you? And not the widow? "There were special instructions," she says, "that it be given only to the next person to take up the posting." She's simply forgotten up until now—she'd lose her head if it wasn't screwed on. She gives you the key to the box. You don't open it. Not yet. Your head is spinning. Could it be that what you've been searching for has fallen into your lap?

The weather holds, and you ride back to the lighthouse that night under a brilliant moon, wrapped in layers of warm clothing. Once home, you light a fire and brew some tea. You sit down and take a deep breath as you retrieve the safe deposit box and its key. You open the box.

Inside is a surprising assortment of small objects, none of apparent value. You smirk that someone should take out a secure space for such innocuous things. A fossilized seashell with a pleasant weight in your hand. A brass ring, tarnished and discolored with age. A deck of cards. A faded yellow photograph of the lighthouse. And in the corner of the box, a small, silver key.

You hold the thing in your hands. You have no doubt. You think of Tess, probably having dinner with her family. Of the icy foam on the seawater. Of a warm, stormy night by the fire. Of picnics on the cliffside. Of staggering down the steep paths to the rocky beaches. Of the truest friend you've made in many years and the only person on this island with whom you feel truly comfortable and unguarded. What would you do to hold on to such a friendship? For the first time, you can understand the previous lighthouse keeper's impulse to hide the mechanism of her escape. You can understand why he tried to keep her here. You think about holding onto the key for a little while. Maybe Tess will realize she prefers living on land. Maybe she'll stay.

But then you remember the longing in her eyes when she looks at the sea. You remember her sea-swept hair and stormy sadness. You think what a gift her freedom would be. And you ride back to town.

Tess accompanies you to the lighthouse under the milky moon. Much lies unspoken, but she knows what you possess. Together, you unearth the leather. You let her turn the key in the lock. She has to force it, crackling through years of rust. You help her open the lid, which is tight from the expanding leather and years of sealing.

A soft luminescence from inside the chest. A glow like moonlight on snow and the ocean's surface. A folded, amorphous thing. Tess's eyes reflect the luminosity. She reaches inside. You feel a tender hand touch your cheek, leaving an imprint of warmth there.

You seem to behold her—eyes shining as she reaches into the chest— for a long time after she's gone. You don't see her go. She's just gone.

When you finally have the courage to move, you follow footsteps in the melting snow over the clifftop. At the edge, you gaze out over the blackness of the ocean. You think you see dark, organic shapes moving playfully, swiftly, across the horizon.

What must such freedom taste like? you wonder. *To have the whole ocean at your disposal and no obligations on the shore?* You return to your residence, extinguish the fire, and retire to your bedroom, feeling a tingling warmth over your body.

The skies remain clear. On your next visit to town, the village folk remark on the sudden lifting of the island's ever-present fog. There hasn't been even a slight mist since Christmas day.

You become one of the townsfolk. You visit frequently, learning every name, celebrating every birth, and welcoming every newcomer. You learn the peculiar local variations of folk legends, and you tell wild stories to all the town's children. They look forward to your visits and your exaggerated reports of magnificent sea creatures visiting your shores. You look forward to it, too.

Once a year, at low tide, a bob of seals arrive on the beaches below the cliffs. Sometimes, they shed their skins and walk among you for a day. And then they return to the ocean.

EXERCISE: RITUAL BATH TO SHED THE SKIN

We are shapeshifters, all.

Use this ritual soak or the accompanying meditation to reveal yourself *to* yourself. Slough off the layers you wear to unveil what's underneath.

SUGGESTED MATERIALS:

Dried herbs or flower petals
Bath salts
Essential oils (be sure they're safe for use in the bathtub)
Candles
Body scrub or exfoliating cleanser

* Begin by drawing a bath. Add herbs, bath salts, or safe essential oils to encourage deep thought and connection. I like to use rose, petals from my gardenia, or a few drops of lavender essential oil. Enrich the atmosphere by dimming the lights, lighting candles, or playing music. If you draw your bath at night and have a window that faces the moon, pull the curtain aside to allow moonlight to fall on the water.

* As you step into the bath, take keen notice of the sensations—the heat of the water, the smoothness of the tile, the way the steam opens up your breath, and the difference in temperature between your submerged and unsubmerged body.

* As you soak in the tub, mentally recount your day. Think about all the different spaces you occupy throughout a typical day. Your home, perhaps your job, school, hobbies, or activities… Consider how your identity may shift throughout your day, how you might adapt, like a chameleon, to the changing environments. How do you conform to—or depart from—established societal conventions?

* Now take it one step further by considering your relationships and your roles within them. You might be a parent, a sibling, a child, a spouse or partner, a colleague, a friend, a boss, or any number of other things in your daily life. How do these roles

inform your image of yourself? Try to consider this from a neutral lens, without judgment.

* Lastly, think about the deepest, most essential part of your identity. The "real" you. Who you are when you are alone with yourself. Beyond your roles in society, your work, your relationships, your likes and dislikes, who are you?

* While you contemplate this, scrub the body from head to toe with an exfoliating cleanser or body scrub. Imagine you are removing layer after layer to reveal inner authenticity. Pay respect to the different needs you serve, the different hats you wear, and appreciate the deepest version of you that sustains within.

Repeat the following phrase out loud or in your head as you go:

> *I am a shapeshifter. I move through many worlds.*
> *I take on many roles. I am ever-changing,*
> *but I am connected to an abiding inner self.*

* Soak in the tub for as long as you like, embracing the benefits of the hot water and your chosen accoutrements. Acknowledge all that you carry, enjoy a few moments of freedom, and close the ritual when you are ready.

THE GREEN
KNIGHT'S GAME

Your eyes drink full of the vibrant green hue, so lively against the white winter snow. One last look at the Green Chapel before you depart; the deep emerald of it, the overgrown ivy that marks its threshold. Such a strange name for a place like this: a chapel. It's more like a rending in the earth, a gap of stone and tree roots that form a natural chamber, all moss-covered and dappled with vines and leaves. A recess that somehow staves off the winter cold, the kiss of snow and ice; so green it's like eternal summer.

This place makes you think of those practitioners of the old religions, those Druids who held their worship in no structure made by man, but only under open skies and in ancient groves, in the sacred spaces of nature's creations. Perhaps that explains this year you've had and all these strange encounters. Perhaps you've had a brush with something of the old world—the ancient, wild magic once lost.

As you turn your eyes from the Chapel a final time, letting your gaze fall upon the purity of untouched white snow, you blink hard against its brilliance. Yet a haze of green still seems to creep, uninvited, at the corners of your eyes. Will it ever go, you wonder? Or will you always sense its presence, the creeping green, like slowly gathering moss? You wonder if it will be more nuisance or comfort.

You tighten a small satchel through the loops of the saddle upon Gringolet, your beloved horse. If only he could speak; what a conversation you'd have on the ride back to Camelot—what marvelous laughter and puzzled merriment you'd share as you look upon all that's happened to you this year. And now, adjusting the green girdle round your waist, your touch lingering on the texture of gold thread woven into it, with a heaving groan, you hoist yourself atop the saddle. You gently kick the horse's sides and he's off, disturbing with his hooves the immaculate snow.

Could it all have been a dream? you find yourself thinking as Gringolet marches through the drifts. Every turn and twist of this winding journey seems so; the way remarkable things come to occur with such little ceremony, and the way details (faces, objects, fancies) from the waking life become untangled and repositioned in the dreamworld. In whatever country you have walked this year past—be it the world of dreams, the realm of man, or of faery—you never thought you'd see such wonders and such wildness cross your gaze.

It began at Christmastide, when King Arthur lay at his court in Camelot a great feast and celebration. All his knights—seven score—returned from their scattered quests and wanderings, from their castles and families, from the forests of adventure. All was jubilant and jovial with great greenery hung all about his halls, tables laden with ripe oranges and apples, puddings and pies. Oh, never let it be said that the good King Arthur did not know how to host fine festivities. But all the dazzling decorations, the delicacies, even the torches and the candles in their brightness could not compete with the glow of the king's magnanimity. He shone like the brightest of stars at his elegant seat, next to his fair Queen Guinevere, lovelier than ever. You wonder, briefly, if your memory—and the ordeal that followed—has added a rosy tint to the scene in your mind. Can it really have been so bright? So peerless?

Perhaps most clear in your recollection—and most cherished among all your memories—is the fondness with which Arthur looked upon you, his kin, as he welcomed you to your seat at the Round Table. The tenderness with which he kissed your cheeks and said your name. Maybe this reverence with which he greeted you played a part in your actions to come. You only know for sure that you were seized by the desire to prove yourself—to live up to the admiration in Arthur's face. To become the knight he already believed you were.

And oh, the feast was divine. The food was rich and succulent, the mead flowed plentiful in your goblets. All the guests sat sated and sleepy, slumped back in their seats. You, at the right hand of the king. Full and happy, you surveyed the faces about the table: the Round Table, at which no one—not even the king—sat higher than any other. There was Sir Lancelot, matchlessly handsome, even if somewhat sorrowful. And there was Sir Kay, lovable grump and foster brother to the king. And dear Percival sat nearby, hardly more than a boy but brave and willing, full of innocent longing for adventure.

It is among the greatest pleasures of a knight, you think, *to rest in good company.* Surely, the tournaments, the battles, the adventuring—these are the deeds the bards will sing of one day. These are the things for which you'll be remembered. But they do not make a knight. *No, what makes a knight,* you think, *is fellowship.* The strong bond between kin and companion, forged in fighting and at the feast table. The feeling of warm and hearty welcome, stories and humor shared between friends—that is the reward. You'd trade all the glory in the world for it. At least, you would now.

But on that Christmas Day, though you basked in the warmth and contentment of your company, glory and honor were still at the forefront of your mind. How single-minded you were then. And when, at last, the feast was done, bellies full and eyes glazing over, the king addressed his many companions with a Yuletide toast and a curious plea.

On Christmas Day, he said, he should not leave this table till he heard some tale of great adventure or witnessed some marvel or miracle. You can remember the smirks and the murmurs and whispers round the table; your eyes, and many others, fell upon Sir Lancelot, who always had great adventures to tell of, but he did not so much as open his mouth to speak. So, in the absence of a knightly volunteer, someone to impress the king with a song of peril or jubilation, as if on cue, there came a great groan and creak at the door to the hall.

The door swung open, heavy and thundering, and all eyes were fast upon it. You wondered if it was some knight of Arthur's who'd ridden day and night to join the feast and sadly missed it. Pellenore, perhaps, whose face you do not see today; maybe he comes at last to brag at the slaying of the dragon in his kingdom.

But it was not a familiar face that the light of lanterns fell slowly upon. There was silence around the table, a cavernous silence against which the sound of hooves upon the flagstone floor beat all the sharper. Into the light he rode, monstrously large and imposing—so huge and hulking he might have been a giant—and he sat upon a horse sturdy enough to hold his height and girth. Bushy was his beard and hair and broad was his neck. With each step the horse took into the hall, each hoofbeat, came the sound of shivering bells, though from where they rang, you could not see.

Most marvelous of all, he was—though you thought your eyes played tricks—head to toe, ink-green. Green was his hue, top to bottom, his hair and beard, his face and neck. He was green as grass, as overgrowth. Green were his garments, too; his boots and tunic, richly green. He had neither helm nor hauberk, no armor girding his awesome stature, no shield upon his arm. In one hand he held a sprig of holly, and so looked like one attending to the festivities. But at his waist, he had a weapon—indeed, a prodigious one. An axe of such size and length befits half a giant; it too was green and also gold, brightly burnished steel that seemed to soak up the flickering light of the lamps all about. Its handle, finely carved and wound with iron, engraved with symbols indecipherable—and green.

Even now, as you recall the moment of his arrival, you feel a shiver penetrate the warmth of your garments. You spur on Gringolet through the thinning snow; whether to hasten toward Camelot or away from the Green Chapel, you do not know. The wood lies ahead, now no more a mystery as it was on the journey hence, but a comforting place where the thick vegetation and dense canopy will provide cover from the cold wind.

Upon the Green Knight's entry to the king's hall, Arthur himself was obliged to stand and welcome the uninvited guest. Never before had the king appeared small to you, rather he was always a monumental figure, but now the Green Knight towered over him. The greatest king was only a mortal, facing whatever he would—god or devil? Even now, you do not know.

But the Green Knight laughed and spurned the king's welcome, held in contempt his courtesy. He chided you all for children playing at knighthood. Such an insult to the king—and to the Round Table, this greatest fellowship of knights ever assembled—could not be tolerated. You felt the heat rising in your cheeks, your blood ran hot.

But the Green Knight's laughter persisted—booming and flagrant in the echoing chamber. A Christmas game, he proposed, as he dismounted. Still, he stood head and shoulders over any knight without the additional height from his horse. He wrested the axe from his hip; in his strong hands, it looked light as a feather, though the steel was thick.

With the weapon in one hand and the holly in the other, he smiled, the apples of his cheeks green instead of rosy. "By this holly branch," he explained, "you all must know I come in peace to pass the hour." He went on to say that far and wide, word spread of the chivalry of this court, of the games and tourneys held here. He thought there might be, among you, a worthy opponent. But now he sees that only children tarry here, and none befit to face him. Unless someone round this table, king or knight or cupbearer, should agree to his Christmas game.

Stroke-for-stroke is what he proposed, the axe gleaming green in his hand. Blow-for-blow. If anyone be warrior enough to face him and deal the first blow, the Green Knight would give as a gift the glorious weapon. Then, with a respite of twelve months and one day, the winning warrior must agree to receive a blow in return.

Such a curious proposition—and though the axe was covetable indeed, it seemed hardly a task worth volunteering for. Silence again hung like a mist over the feasting hall; the Green Knight's grin split wider by the moment. In a moment of impulse, feeling fierce loyalty and desperate desire to avenge the insult to your king and kinsman, before a logical thought could calm your rushing mind, you sprang from your seat. Begging leave of King Arthur to take the task in defense of his grace and the honor of his court, you leapt lightly to it. Knowing in your heart it was folly, you fought all the more heartily to claim the privilege.

You were so foolish then, and so prideful. How humbly and falsely you proclaimed to the king that your life would be the least loss at the table should you fall before the Green Knight. How thickly you lay on the self-criticism. How much, though you did not admit it to yourself then, you imagined Lancelot would envy you as the king's champion.

With some reluctance but ultimately resigned, the king blessed your blade and bade you give the Green Knight a blow. An agreement was struck between the man in green and yourself, that after you deal your blow today, you should seek him out one year and one day hence. Then he knelt and bowed his head and held out his axe to you. The green steel caught the lantern light and glimmered; a gleam in your eye. You took the axe, which had a pleasant heft in your hands; a substantial weapon, solid and strong. It seemed you grew in size and stature holding it, became more capacious, more poised. The Green Knight bared the flesh of his neck and bade you make your attempt. Gladly, you gripped the axe and gathered it up high, then lay the blade down sharply, dealing your end of the bargain. The steel was so sharp that it met no resistance, and in an instant, your spoils lay upon the floor, silent and ever green.

How can it be that what happened next was not a dream? Such things are the domain of fairy stories. Now, atop Gringolet, the wintry sun cascading through the forest canopy like sheets of gold on white, you touch your own neck, feeling the supple flesh there. Even now, you feel relief and release a sigh. But on that Christmas day, the Green Knight, cloven in two though he was, reached nevertheless for his head and stood once more before the Round Table. He was still taller than you by far, taller even than the king. You might not have believed your eyes but for the gasps of a hundred and fifty other knights, all aghast and marveling at the sight.

And under his arm, the Green Knight's head was cheerful as ever, laughing still. The good queen Guinevere looked likely to swoon, and soon Sir Lancelot was at her side; her ladies too, to catch her fall.

Presently, the green man chuckled gaily and gave you again your instructions; this time he gave you the name of the place where you should seek him one year hence. "The Green Chapel," was all he said. And with his laughter booming, he climbed again atop his horse and rode forth from the hall as if it were only a nick on the neck he'd suffered, leaving you all stunned and silent at the Christmas table.

You pass now by a glade, through which you came first before this morning's dawn. How different it looks now, with mid-day sun above it, thawing the snow, beneath which branches creak and crackle. How bright and new it seems.

You carried with you, all the year, the Green Knight's axe, and his promise. You trudged through deepest winter, cold and quaking. In your dreams, you saw the knight, heard his laughter, and knew he'd greet you at year's end. But when spring came, you fought in tourneys, spirits lifted, and looked on your encounter as a distant memory. A Christmas myth to be told again at Yuletide when the king requests a marvel. At times, with the fields aflower and friends about, he even slipped from your mind, the knight all clad in green. Until again, seeing how green were the groves, he'd cross your thoughts, and you'd grasp again the axe.

At Pentecost, the king called for his knights, as every year, to renew their oaths of chivalry. At this great gathering, it was upon the axe blade, not your sword, that you were sworn anew. And on the swearing—to the virtues of friendship, generosity, purity, courtesy, and piety—you thought again of the Green Knight and your baleful bargain.

But summer was long, and the days were long, and you had many adventures with your companions. Soft winds sprinkled seeds across the fields and forests. Rarely, then, did you think of him, or of the hastening harvest on your heels, for the summer lingered so languidly.

Then came the time of reaping, when the scythe and sickle struck the stalks; then you clung to the axe at your side, for the time of your reaping would soon be upon you.

How swiftly the year yielded and leaves from lindens loosely fell, the frost forthwith. All the grass that was once green was now gray; all that was ripe now rotted. The axe weighed heavy at your side and your oath upon your heart.

At last, when winter nipped at your fingers, you begged the king, your lord, for leave to seek the Green Knight and receive your blow. You would not balk at your side of the bargain. You would not swerve from your strange destiny.

Mournfully, the king granted your request and summoned all the best of his knights to counsel you. On the morn, you were made ready. In the finest garments they dressed you, with soft linen and knots of gold thread. In shining mail, hauberk, and helm. A silken sash and rich gold spurs. They brought you your shield, upon it the pentangle painted in pure gold. The five-pointed, five-sided star gleamed bright on your arm, symbolic of your virtue (you chuckle to think of it now). Of the five virtues of chivalry. Of your five faultless senses, five wits, and five fingers. How fair you looked with the shield and the axe, your armor aglow. Gringolet, too, splendid with a saddle fringed with gold, a steed fit for the greatest of knights—which, you had no doubt, on that solemn day, you were.

That shield is at your side no more. Nor the axe.

You set forth from the court of Camelot before the first snow fell, though it came quickly behind you. You kept no company but Gringolet and rode far northward through the woods of North Wales into the mountainous midlands. In every village to which you came and at every hermit's door on which you knocked, you asked about the knight in green. None could tell you a tale of such a man, though they often offered you food and hospitality.

Quivering cold settled soon about the country, but on you rode, even as icicles clung to the sides of your helm. Through your difficult journey, as all went white and gray around you, still the leaves of holly and fir were green. Greener than ever, and even more emerald for the contrast with the snow. Into this same forest, you ventured, the one through which Gringolet now bears you. And it struck you as a most wonderfully wild wood; the hazel and hawthorn were all twined together and covered with moss, the trees tangled and mired. You soldiered on, praying for a path or to stumble unto some hermit's hearth where you might be shielded from the night's cold.

Then, as if the prayer of your heart had fallen upon some eager ear, through the briar and brambles you beheld a light, aloft upon a hill, shining in the night's cold and darkness. You wondered if it was a mirage, a trick played upon you in this state, but there, though you blinked, it remained. A castle, not so elegant or extravagant as the one at Camelot, but most welcome to your weary gaze. Gringolet's step, too, was springier as you directed him toward its light, hoping the hosts had some hospitality.

Now you pass beneath the castle again in the light of day, where not hours ago you slept fitfully. Where for three days and nights, you feasted in the company of its lord and lady. In the wintry daylight, it seems to quietly smirk from its hilltop, wily and coquettish. Nothing in the world would bring you back through its doors, you think, spurring Gringolet on, away from its shadow.

In that castle, you were offered food and drink and lodging for as long as you needed. You were pleased to accept, but Christmas was drawing near again, and on St. Stephen's Day, you were expected at the Green Chapel, you explained. At this, the Lord laughed, his laughter booming to the high ceilings of his hall; why, the Green Chapel was not half a day's ride from the gate. He knew the Green Knight of whom you spoke. So, here you'd stay, in the comfort of your own chambers, and you'd be welcomed by all the guests of the castle, who longed to hear tales of adventure in the elegant speech of a knight of the Round Table. Indeed, your name was well known in this region already, and you were lauded as chief among Arthur's knights; the most virtuous and most gallant.

It was in that castle that you struck another bargain, this one with its jovial lord, knowing not how tangled the threads of your promises would soon become. But this bargain seemed so simple to uphold: while each day of your stay, the Lord would go to the hunt, you would remain here within the walls, enjoying the warmth and comfort of his hospitality. At the end of each day, the Lord promised to present to you, as a gift, the spoils of his hunt. And, at the end of each day, in return, you would present to the Lord any gifts you received while within the castle. Of what gifts he might speak, you could not conceive. But you shook on the bargain, bemused as ever, while the web spun about you unseen. The spinner, though you did not know it so then, sat silent beside the Lady: an old woman, nameless, who looked upon you with curiosity and care.

You held up the bargain, and so did the Lord, still with pleasure and laughter as he laid his quarry before you each evening. And you presented your winnings, too, though holding your tongue as to where each was won. On the first day, a kiss you exchanged for a deer. On the second, two kisses for a boar. And on the third...

On the third day, you gave three kisses to the Lord, but you withheld your true winning. For while the Lord was out on the hunt, his Lady had come to your chamber and offered you something more precious than gold. A ring, first, bright as the sun with a crimson gem set in it. This, though tempting, you refused. But then she offered you a girdle of green—green as the knight you would come to face—all embroidered with shining gold thread and soft as the finest silk. A remarkable thing, but all the more wondrous for the power it held.

For the Lady said, whomsoever wears this sash of green wears a charm of protection to keep him safe from worldly harm.

That this might fall into your lap on the very eve of your encounter struck you as most miraculous, and although the Lord's bargain gnawed at your thoughts, you accepted the Lady's gift, and tied the sash tight round your waist, concealed beneath your tunic. The Lady bade you swear to keep the girdle secret, and you kept your word that night at the exchange of winnings.

To say it did not tear at you, this secret betrayal, would be a lie. But on that day, you weighed your life against your honor and made a choice. Three kisses to the Lord in exchange for a fox. The Christmas feast commenced in good humor.

When Christmas Day had come and gone and the red crest of sunrise slipped over the horizon, you donned your charmed green girdle, your shield, and the glorious axe, mounted Gringolet, and rode to meet your strange destiny. Your pace was slow but determined, and you held high your head: the sash seemed to keep you warm, though it also set your thoughts to stir.

It was only a short ride to the place described by the Lord of yonder castle, where dwelt, he claimed, the knight in green. And as it came into your sight, you had no question that you had found the Green Chapel indeed. It was not a chapel in the style with which you were familiar, nor would you have called it such had you come upon it unknowingly. It was more like a great fault in the earth, as if the Green Knight, large as a titan, had brought his axe down heavily upon the ground and, from the rending of the earth, had poured luscious greenery in untamed spirals. You steeled yourself to slip between the rocks into the natural opening, where lay the dealer of your destined blow.

And he was there, of course, green as ever and yet not so brilliant as before; for now, in his chapel, he seemed to blend with the natural tones of the grass and moss and vines about him. It was as if he himself were a growth, which, having one day set himself to it, had pulled up his roots from this very ground and become a man. There was laughter in his eyes, just as there was fear in yours. But the green girdle warmed you still, calmed your beating heart. The shield on your arm and the axe in your hand, you bowed your head and presented the weapon to its master.

You'd come at last, upon the destined day, to complete the Christmas game.

Even now, as you emerge from the wood, you wince to remember it. You tenderly touch your neck once more, as if to ensure it's still there. It is. Oh, without a doubt, it is. For the Green Knight missed his blow, after all this time, though you did not but flinch.

It's only hours ago, and yet the details seem to slip away, again making you question whether all of this was but a dream. Still, the sash adorns your waist.

The Green Knight's laughter echoes within the chamber of your memory, the persistent and familiar laughter. How could it have taken you so long to notice? How could you have failed to hear the ringing echo of the knight in the laughter of the Lord of the castle? The curious coincidence of the Lord's knowledge of the chapel? Or the predilection they shared for games and tricks at Christmas time?

The Green Knight dropped his axe and laughed, and in so doing, his green hue reddened and his face ruddied till his cheeks were shining like ripe, red apples. His hair turned brown as the hair of a boar, and his stature was suddenly not so imposing. An artful disguise, the Lord admitted, spun up by none other than Morgan le Fay, King Arthur's half-sister. The Green Knight was no devil, no ancient god, but a man like any other. And he'd be glad to bring you back to his castle, raise a cup to you, and drink to your honor. She was there, after all—Queen Morgan, in the guise of an old woman, and she'd be curious to know the outcome of her play.

It was all a game, you deduced—a wicked game. A web in which you were spun, unknowing, and stitched into an impossible knot. Then the Lord gestured to the slip of green silk that slid from beneath your tunic. Though you concealed it and dishonored the terms of your latest bargain, he forgave you—after all, you only valued your life, and what man could think less of you for that?

Dazed and daunted, you politely refused the offer of return to the Lord's castle. The thought of showing your face there after such an encounter—and facing the woman who designed your delirious destiny—was unappealing, even thinking of the warmth of the Lord's fire. You thought only of Camelot; leaving your shield and the axe in the Green Chapel, where the Lord's ceaseless laughter pealed like Christmas bells, you dashed off to start toward home.

Around your waist, the green girdle is bound still and will be bound henceforth. You've set yourself steadfastly to it. After such an ordeal and such a failure of your renowned chivalry and courtesy, you'll wear it as a mark of your disgrace. You tie it outside your tunic, over your shirt of mail, so it might be seen, in its greenest hue, by all.

The ride to Camelot takes several days, but it passes lighter and swifter than before; for though your heart is heavy with humility and the winter's chill sets deep into your bones, the end of the journey is home. You've left the chapel of the Green Knight in one piece, and you are grateful for each glimpse of green holly on the boughs, and even for shivering birds on bare, icy branches. It's a return you never thought you'd make, and you bless the goodness and beauty of the natural world for guiding you forth.

You seek shelter each night in the homes of humble folk, weary of the games and tricks in noble houses. At each, you're welcomed and praised for your renowned virtue; and to each, you tell the story of your strange encounter with the Green Knight, your honor besmirched, and your mark of shame in the green girdle. Your pleas of ignominy fall unheard by the glowing admirers that surround you.

At last, when you and Gringolet are most in need of it, the towers of Camelot crest over the horizon. Already you can taste the flowing mead and fresh bread that await you in the king's hall. You wonder if word has yet reached the court of your survival, or if your return upon the New Year will be a welcome surprise.

You ride through the castle gates and find lodging and food for your hungry horse in the stables. You stroke Gringolet's mane and neck; what a good friend he's been to you throughout your ordeal. How grateful you are that you'll see more adventures together.

Then through the heavy oaken doors in the company of the king's guard, you pass into the familiar halls of the castle. Never before has it seemed so welcoming, so warm, and so cherished as it does now. You thought you'd never see these halls again, and you treasure every inch—from the gray, polished stone to the cavernous ceilings. And now to the feasting hall you go, where already you can hear the sound of a joyous gathering; so they haven't all departed yet, your companions. Some have stayed to ring in the New Year alongside their king and queen. And perhaps, to remember you in solemn mourning.

The guard swings open the doors, and for a flash, you feel taller than yourself, greater in stature, and swelling with pride. You feel supernaturally strong, a being of powerful magic. But as the hall erupts in cheers and shouts of welcome and the faces of your friends come into focus before you, you diminish once more to your own size and state. A hundred hands are clasping yours. Your name on the lips of the greatest knights at court. Lancelot is beaming with pride as he congratulates you. And there is Percival—oh, heartily you embrace him, so much more a man than he was at your last parting. The king and queen are there, and in Arthur's eye, you see such sparkling admiration that you can hardly bear it.

Indeed, you can hardly bear any of it. For none of them will hear your plea that it is no honor to return unscathed. None of them will accept the green sash as a symbol of your failure. Instead, each and every one pledge to adopt the girdle as the newest fashion in honor of your great quest and well-matched victory over the Green Knight.

You can no longer protest their praise, and so, after courses and courses of fine, rich foods, you retire to the guest chamber made for you.

Tenderly, you untie the green sash round your waist, and you feel a great exhale rush forth when you've removed its constraints. It really is a work of wondrous craft. You wonder whether, in fact, there is a charm woven into it or if you merely believed it so out of longing and hope. Did Morgan, the king's own half-sister and well-known sorceress, sew it with spells the way she made Arthur's scabbard? That gift, too, protects its wearer from harm, even more so than the sword it sheaths. The silk slips across your fingers, and the threads sparkle in the light of the dying fire. You hang it by the hearth, admiring the craft. Even if it reminds you of your failure, you can admire it.

On the morrow, it will be a new year. A new start. All the perils and marvels of this time may pass away into memory or myth. You'll tell this tale again at the king's Christmas table, to be sure. You'll try not to change the details too much or make yourself seem braver, nobler, stronger.

It is a pity, you think, to close out a year feeling as though you're a step back from where you started. But perhaps that's all right. Perhaps it's the nature of things to crest and fall; to win and lose; to struggle and to triumph. You might not mark the years, or yourself, so sharply if that were the case. You might look upon yourself as you look upon your friends, and they upon you. With recognition, support, and esteem.

There will be time to contemplate it all. For now, you are thankful to have found respite in Camelot, among friends and cherished kinsfolk.

A garland of greenery hangs above the modest fireplace. Brought in from the outside, pulled down from the trees that never lose their hue as a reminder of the promise of new life and new growth. Was it only some trick, some cruel test you've endured? Or have you had a brush with that old magic...the realm of fairy? You think of the Green Chapel far away, which, even in bleak midwinter snow, flushes full with ferns and green growth, erupting in the magnificence of life. You can see him there now, the knight, with his axe. A figment, an illusion, a trick...no. Not to you.

You'll sleep tonight in gratitude—for your life and your breath and your companions. You'll wake tomorrow in the light of a new year. And when the sun rises and you dress for court, you'll make the choice of whether to don the sash or not. You'll choose anew each day.

Sleep comes over you in a haze of gold and green.

EXERCISE: INVOCATION FOR THE NEW YEAR

The New Year is a time when many make resolutions. While admirable, the culture of New Year's Resolutions can set us up for unrealistic expectations and disappointment. Instead of—or in addition to—resolving to make a significant change this year, this simple invocation is intended to cultivate sustainable change and inspire self-forgiveness when we fall short.

SUGGESTED MATERIALS:

Candle or incense and flame
Pen and paper

* Designate your chosen space as sacred by lighting a candle, incense, calling in the four directions, or in any manner meaningful to you.

* Take three deep, cleansing breaths and close your eyes.
* Bring your awareness to your chest. Feel warmth and radiant love in your heart, visualizing the color green and the element of air.

* Visualize a pentangle: a five-pointed, five-sided star.
  Allow your inner eye to travel across its lines and angles.
  Consider how the lines overlap, creating a continuous, unbroken design.
  Visualize that star at the center of your heart.
  Spend a few minutes breathing with this visualization.
* When it feels right, write down, or simply speak aloud the following invocation:

I am capacious and capable of change
In the New Year, I make peace with who and where I am
I am in progress, I am continuous
Like the unbroken lines of the pentangle
I have infinite capacity for
Love, kindness, understanding, harmony,
peace, forgiveness, and bliss.

* Close your sacred space with gratitude.

You can store the written invocation in your journal, burn it safely in a burn bowl as an offering, or post it somewhere you can see it regularly.

The Song of Persephone

I. Demeter

How far down do roots grow? you wonder as you sow the seeds of cypress in the ground. Perhaps, if rightly placed and carefully nourished, the roots might burrow so deep into the earth that they burst through the very roof of Hades' palace and tickle the face of the unhappy queen. But it's been so long since anything grew, and the behavior of roots below ground is outside your domain. You are still reacquainting yourself with the patterns of plants. For many long months, all seeds were watered only by your tears, shaded by the gathering clouds of your grief. Soil turned to ash on your approach, and whole cities hungered for fruit and grain.

After the maiden was taken, your once-abundant fields receded. No more did the wind whisper through stalks of wheat, and a frightful frost blanketed the dying grasses. As the flora withered, so did you. Forswearing the nectar and ambrosia of the gods, your once-bright hair grew brittle, your skin dry, your eyes red with weeping. You bent as a wilting tree, assuming the face of the crone, and all radiance you once boasted grew dim. You shunned the company of your brothers and sisters who dwell in Olympus, and you cursed the name of Zeus, the thunderer on high, for his part in your suffering. In all your divine authority, the entrance to the unseen kingdom remained a mystery to you. Gods and mortals heard your weeping and wept themselves at the dying of the crop and lessening of the yield. You turned away from them all and chose to wander barefoot over the wide, cold world in search of the child who was stolen from you. You imagined her tracing similar patterns below ground, calling your name from the shadows.

Thus, you came to the city at the end of the earth: Eleusis, fragrant with incense. There, the king and queen took you in; and their people, thinking you of humble origin, treated you with pity and charity. You blessed them in return, raising the infant sons of the noble house of Eleusis.

When he saw the destruction wrought by his indifference, Zeus, commander of oaths, at last relented to your plea. Sweet Kore, the maiden stolen by the god of the dead, would be returned to you. But the victory was bittersweet; in her innocence or hunger, the maiden had taken the food of the Underworld, and thus would be compelled to remain there for a part of the year. Condemned by six pomegranate seeds.

This is the fate of all parents and caregivers, you remind yourself. To move from one being to two, and to drift further from that part of yourself with each passing year.

Little by little, in preparing the way for Kore's return, your spark reignited. The guise of the elder fell away, and soon, the people of Eleusis witnessed the full splendor of your divinity. They built a temple in your honor; this became your refuge from unfeeling Olympus and a place of renewal for your grieving spirit.

You taught yourself the ways of tenderness again, and you turned to the children of Eleusis to impart the teachings of plants and agriculture. You taught them to sow seeds in the ground and the alchemy by which plants transform the rays of golden Helios into nourishment. The children watched magic trickle from your fingertips into the soil. By witnessing your work, they cultivated a kind of theurgy: a reenactment of your devotion to the toil and harvest. Like the plants, they flourished by your efforts. This is a gift only you can give: the wisdom of your hands and the cycles of the earth which bring forth the miracle of grain. It need not rest only on your shoulders but in the care of the collective.

These cypress seeds, now resting in their earthen cavities, waiting to break open, are a testament to the darkness through which you've crawled. At last, beyond Eleusis, you've discovered the frontier of the Underworld; here you plant the foundations of a sacred grove, more holy than any monument of stone. Your true temple can be found in any such grove of trees, field of grain, threshing floor, or abundant hearth. You are honored in every humble act of reciprocity with the green earth.

You tend to the cypress as seeds, then as seedlings and saplings. They grow swiftly in your divine presence, as though they too are eager to look upon the maiden's face when she returns. Indeed, all the land, though hesitant, begins to bud and flower in anticipation. One morning, you awake to the sweet perfume of hyacinths. You step through a patch of demure primroses on the way to the grove. Each day, as dawn skates across the sky, her fingers blooming, you smile upon new surprises, new heralds of her ensuing arrival. Blankets of aconite adorn the forest floor, and golden daffodils spring up in the cities. The whole world quivers with the excitement of oncoming spring. You rediscover the delight you once had in flowers—they, like the cereal grains that feed the people of the earth, bring richness to the soil and peace to the heart. There's a joy in their stewardship that's just as profound as the cultivation of crop.

The blessed day comes at last, and you tremble with anticipation. You want to be there to greet her, to catch her if she stumbles in the overwhelming light of the sun. You keep your hands busy—and steady—with the upkeep of the saplings.

How strange, and yet inevitable, to find yourself here, at the ends of the earth. How uncanny to stand upon the precipice of renewed motherhood, as if time is running backward and forward all at once. Maybe motherhood is present in every aspect, you reflect, as you watch the water trickle into the pockets of air in the soil, seeping deeply down into the earth. (*Might the water travel far enough down to fall in droplets upon the face of the lost daughter, the sunken queen?*) Motherhood is a wound, a great rending which never quite closes. It is the breaking of oneself, and the ensuing grief; the constant longing for the maiden's return (*she who you bore, or she who you once were?*). But motherhood is also the space the grief creates, in the aching heart and in the open fields of the wide earth: the space for new, surprising growth. It is the seed, breaking apart, and striving the find the light.

You take a full breath of snowdrop-scented breeze. Something has changed. A cloud scuds dreamily across the sun, casting the meadows in pale, momentary shadow. The wind rises, making your skin prickle. The ground beneath you seems to hum and vibrate softly, tuning to an unknown frequency. Around you, the cypresses are twisting and stretching toward the open sky; it's like they're breathing in, swelling upward, growing a year's worth in an instant.

Now, the most miraculous thing: a few paces away, the earth yawns open with a mighty grumble and groan. Where before was only hillside, here gapes the mouth of an unfathomable cave. Within, only darkness. As the first bulbs of spring, after sheltering so long underground, send their first green stems as emissaries—out steps a single, tentative bare foot upon the dewy grass. Where it falls, a cluster of crocus blooms. Then *she* emerges.

She was an iris, fragile and full of grace when she was taken from your side. Now, she is something new. Nightshade, perhaps, with deep roots. Datura, twining and twisting through the crevices between worlds. A vespertine creature, poised on the threshold between creation and destruction. She is Kore no longer, but Persephone: wise and beautiful and terrible. An uneasy thought swims across your mind—what if she no longer needs you?

Oh, but the maiden flickers in and out of sight with the shifting light of the sun through streaks of cloud. She is here in many aspects at once—as are you. Together, you are a winding ouroboros of identities. You flow like rivulets in and out of innocence and experience. Maiden into Mother into Crone and back again, like the ever-shifting face of the moon. She needs you. You need her.

Time slips to the rhythm of the wind, and the cypress grove becomes a quiet chorus of witnesses to your reunion. The trees are your first initiates.

All the world is peaceful, every seed and sprout poised to spring forth. You open your arms to receive the queen of the underworld, the goddess of spring, ready to hear her tale.

II. Persephone

A coin for the ferryman. Even you, even now, owe him that if you expect to be borne across the river. For months, you've yearned for the start of this return journey; now that it's at hand, it feels strange somehow, as if it's being undertaken by someone else as you look on in distant curiosity.

You pay the good boatman, and he bows deeply as his wrinkled hands close around the coin. There's a contract between you now, a bond formed by the silent ritual of the exchange. He knows you, and he shows you the proper reverence but he makes no extravagant supplication, for his is a power outside the reach of gods and sovereigns. You step into the boat, which rocks beneath your feet on the black river. *How many souls have traveled thus in his vessel?* you wonder. But then, of course, most souls can only travel one way.

There was one, you recall, who made the long journey to this world and then returned to the other—he traveled deep and overcame many perils in search of a lost love. It was not long after you came here that he first knelt before the throne and begged—in song and poetry—for an impossible boon. He made his plea to the king of the dead for the restoration of his wife, unfairly taken by serpent's venom on the very day of their wedding. How you seethed, at first, at the presumption. Why should a common nymph be released from the covenant of death, when you, one of the immortal few, should remain captive against your will? Who would lament for you? Who would sing for Kore?

But oh, such tender, sweet songs he made on his harp! And his voice, like honeyed silk, sang of a consuming grief. There is rarely music in the underworld. The melodies, though mournful, were like medicine, nourishing and enfolding you. Here and there, the doleful strains would ascend, the voice briefly harmonizing with its own echo, turning the minor key momentarily to major—by turns haunting and triumphant. It was a song of the surface world, like those you once sang with your mother. You remember the shivers of wakefulness that climbed your spine as the song climbed the air; a part of you, dormant as flowers in winter, was revived.

His suffering stirred your heart, awakening an empathy you thought was lost. Such a request should have been dismissed without ceremony, but you, just learning what powers you possessed, championed the poor bard's cause.

"Let her go with him," you entreated Hades, king of the underworld, knowing him at least capable of reason. "Will she not, as everyone who walks upon the earth, return to you in time?"

And so you persuaded him to release the poor nymph, not as a gift to the poet, but as a promise. Both souls, after all, would return to the subterranean kingdom in the end.

You went with your attendants to have the maid robed in fine white silk, pure and bright as moonbeams. She was ghostly pale as she was brought to the gates, where her husband waited in the company of the gods' gracious herald. She was not much more than a shadow, it seemed.

The king's sole condition of her release was simple: she must walk behind her husband till they reach the surface, and until then, he must not turn back to look upon her. Only when both were met by sunlight should he turn and see his love's face. The messenger god, guardian of the gates, would accompany them to ensure the poet kept his word.

Watching the trio depart together in solemn procession (the husband at the lead, his wife a few paces behind, and Hermes, the messenger, abreast), you felt a twinge of bittersweet triumph. You'd won over the cold heart of the underworld god. Because of your compassion and wisdom, a young couple, unjustly parted, would be reconciled. But who would bargain for your freedom? Who in the world would entreat for Kore?

It was not until some time later that you learned of the second tragedy to befall the young lovers. The moon-clad nymph was spirited back to the underworld on the wings of swift Hermes. Not long after, her husband arrived at the gates once more to make his final journey across the river. The bard, it seems, could not resist the temptation to turn his head. He could not overcome the creeping doubt that whispered over the silence of his wife's footsteps.

After so many months below ground, you have also learned to listen to doubt's whispers. She sneaks into all quiet moments. When water drips from the tips of stalactites in the cavernous realm of Hades' palace, doubt is there in the smallest pause between the plink of the water on the pool beneath and its echo on the ceiling above to utter a melancholy phrase. When a conversation loses steam and yawns into uneasy pauses, doubt murmurs sleepily.

Even now, as the boat glides across the river, the ferryman's paddle driving and listing in the calm backwater, you can hear doubt's purr. But the journey is underway, and all conditions of the compact already in motion. Hard as it is to believe, there is no guile or trick to trap you now as there was for poor Orpheus.

Your time here has not been marked only by despair. After the early days, when your tears were shed and you were guided by curiosity, you endeavored to explore the reaches of your new home. As you wandered, you imagined your mother tracing similar paths overhead, calling your name as she blessed the crops whose roots delve into your domain. It was a gift you never sought, but one you quickly grew to cherish: the ability to move across the thresholds of unseen worlds. The borders no mortal is permitted to cross are yours to traverse at will.

You did not know such power, nor such independence, in your life on the surface. Your mother was your home, she was the bountiful harvest that fed you, and she was the hearth at which you warmed yourself. She planted you like a seed, nourished your roots, and watched you blossom. You understand now that her love, though essential to your growth, was also a kind of shade. In the shelter of her devotion, you had no need to seek sunlight or food or water for yourself, but you could not grow beyond her.

Yes, you're wistful for the time before. Sometimes you yearn for it. But there is peace here, too. There is comfort in knowing yourself and your power; there is solace in living among the dead. Every soul, every shade has a story. Each has a longing to tell his tale and a dearth of listeners to sit and hear. To hearken to the dead—this is a kindness only you can bestow.

With an open heart and gentle hand, you've led such souls to the banks of the river Lethe, where they drink full of the waters of forgetting. As the cool liquid touches their lips, you've seen shoulders drop and muscles relax, furrowed faces settle into serene euphoria. Relieved of earthly memories and cares, they are reborn to childlike innocence. You, the repository of their last testament, have looked on in poignant praise. You harvest stories like the fields of waving wheat over which your mother presides on earth before the waters wash clean the minds of men. Onward travels the mighty, swift-footed Achilles, all memory of his deeds surrendered to blissful oblivion. And so passes Heracles, at last absolved of his earthly torment. You have, of course, considered tasting the waters yourself—the sweet kiss of release from painful memories, within reach—but something always stays your hand.

You've wandered the meadows and coasts of this misty realm with unending inquisition. A network of tributaries connects and divides the kingdom, stewarded by the old ferryman, collector of coins and souls. In the deepest recesses of the underworld lies the dreaded Tartarus, where you've looked on in sympathy at the tormented: Sisyphus and his rock, Tantalus and his eternal thirst. Beyond the waters of Lethe lie the sprawling Asphodel Meadows, where wander countless souls through fields of pale and ghostly flowers. There, the air is filled with the sweet scent of things that blossom, though it's different than in the world above—it smells of artifice. That was the hardest thing to accept when you were brought here: the absence of the fragrance of life.

And then there is Elysium. In that undying place, a rosy, gilded dawn is always blooming over calm waters. It is forever suspended in that hazy glow to which the living long to cling, about which they compose poetry and song. Lapping waves lightly kiss the fine sands of the Islands of the Blest. You like the feeling of your toes in sand and the ever-gentle caress of morning light. The taste of citrus and salt on the breeze that rises so delicately from the ocean. It's easy to get used to those peach-tinted lands; that's the purpose, you suppose, of paradise. To cradle the virtuous and valorous souls, to heal them of their wounds, and hold them forever in tender, golden reward.

But it's not the true sun, after all. Not the true dawn. No chariot waits to trace its path across the mist-swept sky. You've caught yourself wandering that oasis once or twice, longing for the light to slice through the wisps of cloud and bring real heat. You've ached for the sizzle of sunlight on your skin; for a sensation beyond what even paradise can conjure.

This world belongs to you, as much as it belongs to the melancholy god. The rivers, the sparkling shores, the labyrinth of caves, and the restless souls: all are yours to honor and sustain. It was not by your will that you first came here or that you were made to sit on the throne of the unseen kingdom. But you have transformed your grief and helplessness into profound wisdom, self-knowledge, and power. You've reclaimed your agency. You've stroked the heads of the monstrous hound Cerberus and made him to lie curled up at your feet. In a land of unfeeling law, presided over by a cold-hearted king, you've affirmed the value of compassion and flexibility. You have stood upon the threshold of life and death, acknowledging the connections between them. The never-ending cycle of growth and decay, of forgetting and resetting. You are loved, revered, and venerated by the earthbound and the dead. You've shed your former name and grown into a new kind of creature: a chthonic sovereign, nourished by darkness, pomegranate seeds, and stories.

And so it is strange to stand now in the boat, poised on the river of woe, en route to sunlit shores.

After so much time below ground, will you scorch and diminish in the light? Will your mother recognize you? Will the earth welcome you back? Doubt whispers in the lapping current of the river.

But this is the covenant. Half a year below, roots seeking shelter and moisture in the unseen kingdom. Half a year above to blossom, bear fruit, and give thanks.

Not far ahead: the suggestive glimmer of light on rippling water, white on swirling black.

The ferryman digs his paddle into the shallows and the boat slows to the banks. He can go no further; it is a short walk to the surface.

Your robes trail over the rocks. Your footfalls are soft and noiseless. You approach the opening, from which spills a dazzling splash of daylight. It has been so long since you looked upon such rays that as your eyes fixate, the white light seems to split into shining fragments of infinite hues—rich blues and greens and yellows and scarlets, all reaching to caress the hidden corners of the cavern. A hard blink and the spectrum resets.

For just a moment, as you stand at the mouth of the cave, halfway between darkness and light, you feel the tremendous power of your twofold nature. Creator and destroyer, bringer of flowers and harbinger of decay; a lesser person might be rent apart by such contradictions. But you, who thrive upon thresholds, recognize your dual aspects now as fluid and self-sustaining. Kore in the light and

Persephone in the shadow: they feed each other and are strengthened by the duality.

Who will lament for the maiden? Who will sing for Kore? *You will, Persephone.* You will sing for and unto yourself.

And then you emerge. Your eyes sting with the sunlight till they brim with tears. Your skin prickles, little hairs standing on end in the sizzle of true morning. It is all too much at first: heat and light and breeze. Tender grass under your bare feet. Where your steps fall, there spring violets, crocuses, and narcissi. You breathe deeply, inhaling their perfume; the fragrance of life and abundance is all around.

As your eyes adjust, you become aware of your surroundings. The gates of the underworld are girded by a semi-circle of cypress saplings. The trees are young but hearty—surely planted less than a year ago and in such elegant design that they must be intended for ceremony. This, you can see, is a burgeoning sacred grove.

A woman, richly robed, tends to one of the trees, kneeling to pour water at its roots. She looks younger than you remember—but perhaps it's just the way the light plays on her gleaming hair.

The woman turns to you, her face like the sun itself, shining with tears. You have so much to tell her. Your story and the stories of so many others in your care. She will be proud of who you've become, you're sure of it. As flowers spring from the earth, you fall into your mother's embrace. She bends to you like an ancient willow, and she stands just as true.

EXERCISE: MAIDEN, MOTHER, CRONE MEDITATION

There is wisdom and magic in every season of life. The archetype of the Triple Goddess (Maiden, Mother, and Crone) is one model that encourages us to find the magic in these seasons—and to recognize the fluidity between them. This meditation, inspired by the Triple Goddess archetype and the lessons of the preceding story, can be a relaxation tool as part of your nightly ritual or a psychic exploration of how these archetypes are present within you at every moment.

Practice this exercise as you are preparing to fall asleep or any time you wish to find peace in your body and path.

EXERCISE:

* Dim the lights in your room.
* Sit comfortably in a chair with your feet flat on the floor or lie down on a flat surface. Take as much time as you need to become as comfortable as possible here. You might roll your neck, wrists, elbows, or ankles to loosen up your joints. Once you've found a comfortable position you think you can remain in for a few minutes, come to stillness.
* Close your eyes. Deepen your breath, filling the belly up like a balloon with each inhale, and feel yourself relax more and more with each exhale.

Bring awareness to the sensation of your body in space. Beginning with the soles of your feet, let your awareness travel upward like a wave, allowing each part of your body to relax. As you soften against your chair or surface, imagine your body filling with a warm, white light. Fill your body with this radiant white light, from the soles of your feet to the legs, the pelvis, the belly, the back, the chest, the arms, the neck, and the head. Feel your forehead and the crown of your head radiating with this warm, white light. Now feel the whole body, radiant with white light.

Imagine you are in a meadow, seated or lying in the tall grass as clouds move slowly overhead. It is just before morning, and beads of dew already cling to the blades of grass. Around you is a semicircle of cypress saplings. Feel the energy of this place. Feel the care with which the saplings were planted. Feel held and cradled by the solid earth beneath you.

Now, take a deep, focused breath with the archetype of the Maiden: innocence, wonder, and limitless potential.

As you exhale, visualize your breath wakening a blanket of flowers from the softening earth. What kinds of flowers do you see in your mind's eye? What are their colors? What feelings do they stir in you?

Turn your attention to the silvery crescent moon in the sky. Feel how the waxing moon's energy tugs on your spirit and energizes the landscape.

Return your awareness to the physical body. Starting again with the soles of the feet, soften, and visualize your body filling with a soft, red energy. Let this red light or energy travel up the body, from the soles of the feet to the crown of the head. Let the whole body radiate with this resonant crimson energy.

Now return, in your mind's eye, to the meadow. The sky is illuminated by a glorious full moon, splendid and scarlet.

The cypress trees are growing strong and mighty in a semicircle. Notice how they bend, ever so slightly, toward you—as if in reverence. Know that you are a bestower of gifts, which may never be fully repaid.

Take a deep, focused breath in with the archetype of the Mother: creativity, generosity, and resilience.

As you exhale, visualize your breath as a gentle rain over the meadow, nourishing the seeds and roots that grow there.

Return your awareness again to the physical body. Once more, starting with the soles of your feet, slowly move your awareness throughout the body. This time, as your awareness travels, let your body sink into a sensation of cool, dark purple peace, as though you're sinking down a level of consciousness toward a deep violet veil. Bit by bit, let your body sink deeper and deeper into this invisible energy.

Find yourself once more within the meadow. The moon overhead is only a wisp of ghostly, waning light, but the stars shine bright enough to recognize the grove of cypress. The trees, now mature and monumental, bend toward you with unspoken admiration. Know that though they tower over you, they walk in your shadow.

Take a deep breath in with the energy of the Crone: wisdom, experience, and perspective.

As you exhale, imagine your breath as a wind that shakes the trees, tousles the grasses, ripples pools, and undulates across fields of wheat.

Remain in the meadow, breathing in and out with the energies of the Maiden, Mother, and

Crone. Feel how your breath moves through each archetype, fluidly, until the borders between them fall away. Feel the potential, power, and peace in all three.

You can stay here in the meadow for as long as you like, until it feels right to depart, or you drift to sleep.

Wishing you meaningful rest and connection in this season and all the seasons to come.

Blessed be.

ENDNOTES

i   Segments of "The Road Not Taken" (1915), a poem by Robert
    Frost featured in the collected work *Mountain Interval* (published
    by Henry Holt, 1916), were selected for use in the short story
    "Fairies of the Forest Floor."

ii Segments of the poem *"Cad Goddeu* (The Battle of the Trees)"
    by Taliesin, from the fourteenth-century *Book of Taliesin,* were
    selected for use in the short story "Cauldron of Cerridwen."